Florian Ade

Local public choice:
five essays on fiscal policy,
interest rates, and elections

 Nomos

Die Deutsche Nationalbibliothek verzeichnet diese Publikation in
der Deutschen Nationalbibliografie; detaillierte bibliografische
Daten sind im Internet über http://dnb.d-nb.de abrufbar.

Die Deutsche Nationalbibliothek lists this publication in the Deutsche
Nationalbibliografie; detailed bibliographic data is available
in the Internet at http://dnb.d-nb.de .

Zugl.: Berlin, Humboldt-Univ., Diss., 2012

ISBN 978-3-8487-0226-8

1. Auflage 2013
© Nomos Verlagsgesellschaft, Baden-Baden 2013. Printed in Germany. Alle Rechte,
auch die des Nachdrucks von Auszügen, der fotomechanischen Wiedergabe und der
Übersetzung, vorbehalten. Gedruckt auf alterungsbeständigem Papier.

Acknowledgements

Writing this thesis seemed a huge challenge at the beginning and has proven to be a rewarding experience from which I have learned and profited a lot. I am therefore happy to thank all those who have supported me along the way.

First of all I would like to thank my thesis supervisor, Charles B. Blankart, for backing my academic projects ever since we got to know each other well in 2004. At that time he encouraged me to present a paper at his research seminar (and later at several conferences) that I had written while a visiting student at the University of Colorado at Boulder. Concurrently, I followed his inspiring lecture on public finances and Public Choice. He then supervised my Diploma thesis and, fortunately, agreed to do the same for my doctoral work. Not just his plentiful suggestions and comments, but also his guidance and feeling for topics have been a great influence on my work.

Furthermore, I am highly indebted to Viktor Steiner, my second supervisor, for continuous valuable support throughout the whole dissertation project. Following some good discussions in his economic policy seminar he invited me to work at the DIW Berlin Department of Public Economics. In particular I profited from his important advice regarding the empirical strategies of the different papers.

I want to stress the positive and collaborative atmosphere at DIW's Public Economics Department with its open doors, frequent discussions, and seminars. Especially, I would like to thank Peter Haan for inviting me to stay at the Department until the end of the dissertation, as well as my co-authors Ronny Freier and Christian Odendahl for the perpetual enlightening exchange of ideas.

Finally I would like to thank my family, in particular my wife Maren, my daughter Charlotta, my parents, my brother and my in-laws. You have created a loving and supporting environment for me. This work is dedicated to you.

Contents

General introduction   13

1 Do constitutions matter?   21

  1.1 Introduction   21

  1.2 Literature review   23

    1.2.1 Horizontal separation of powers   24

    1.2.2 Local constitutional economics for Germany   26

  1.3 Institutional background   29

    1.3.1 Levels of local government in Germany   29

    1.3.2 Responsibilities, autonomy, and taxing power   30

    1.3.3 Local constitutions   31

    1.3.4 Reforms in the 1990s as a natural experiment   32

  1.4 Empirical strategy   35

    1.4.1 Single constitution dummy   35

    1.4.2 Adjustment effects   36

    1.4.3 Hypotheses   37

  1.5 Data   38

  1.6 Results   41

    1.6.1 Single constitution dummy   41

    1.6.2 Adjustment effects   43

    1.6.3 Sensitivity analysis   44

  1.7 Summary and conclusions   46

2 Divided government versus incumbency externality   55

  2.1 Introduction   55

  2.2 Institutional background: voting rules and local government 61

    2.2.1 Voting system and rules   62

    2.2.2 Local government   63

	2.3	Data and descriptive statistics	64
	2.4	Empirical model and methodology	67
	2.5	Results	69
		2.5.1 Effect of the mayor's political identity on subsequent town council elections	70
		2.5.2 Effect of the mayor's political identity on elections for higher levels of government	75
		2.5.3 Effect of town council elections on run-off mayoral elections	76
		2.5.4 RDD validity and robustness tests	78
	2.6	Conclusions	80
3	**Incumbency, party identity and governmental lead**		**89**
	3.1	Introduction	89
	3.2	Theoretical and institutional background	92
		3.2.1 Theoretical considerations	92
		3.2.2 Electoral system	94
	3.3	Empirical strategy	95
	3.4	Data	98
	3.5	Results	99
		3.5.1 Main results	99
		3.5.2 Discussion	103
		3.5.3 Robustness and Validity	108
	3.6	Conclusion	110
4	**When can we trust population thresholds?**		**123**
	4.1	Introduction	123
	4.2	Empirical model and methodology	126
		4.2.1 Basic model	126
		4.2.2 Identifying assumptions	127
	4.3	Institutional setting	129

	4.4	Results		132
		4.4.1	Importance of simultaneous exogenous co-treatment	132
		4.4.2	Simultaneous endogenous decision making	135
		4.4.3	Manipulation of the population numbers around the thresholds	138
	4.5	Conclusions		139

5 Do creditors discipline local governments?   149

	5.1	Introduction		149
	5.2	Literature review		150
	5.3	Institutional background		153
	5.4	Data and descriptive statistics		155
	5.5	Empirical strategy		157
	5.6	Results		159
		5.6.1	Main analysis	159
		5.6.2	Sensitivity	163
	5.7	Conclusion		163

Bibliography   173

List of Figures

2.1 Design 1   71

2.2 Design 2   73

2.3 RDD validity check – predetermined variables   86

2.4 RDD validity check – vote share in last town council   87

2.5 RDD validity check – frequencies around the threshold   88

3.1 Incumbency effect for the CDU – CDU *not* in government   102

3.2 Incumbency effect for the CDU – CDU in government   103

3.3 Probability of winning vs. vote share as an outcome variable, SPD in 2009 104

3.4 Incumbency effect – from party C's standpoint   111

3.5 Incumbency effect – again from party C's standpoint   112

3.6 Vote share for the direct candidate of the Left party   115

3.7 RDD validity – frequency histograms   120

3.8 RDD validity – predetermined variables   121

4.1 RDD validity – frequency check   139

4.2 Share of full-time mayors over the population distribution (in 1984)   141

4.3 Distribution of full-time mayors around thresholds   142

4.4 RDD validity – frequency check   143

List of Tables

1.1	Average municipality revenues by source, 1998–2007	31
1.2	First mayor elections	39
1.3	Descriptive statistics of key variables	40
1.4	Time trends for key dependent variables, 1992–2007	41
1.5	Effect on tax rates	49
1.6	Effect on expenditures	50
1.7	Effect on tax rates	51
1.8	Effect on expenditures	52
1.9	Effect on tax rates (extended sample)	53
1.10	Effect on tax rates (extended sample)	54
2.1	Data set – number of observations and elections	62
2.2	Data set – defining different samples	66
2.3	Interdependency between mayor's office and town council elections	70
2.4	Interdependency between mayor's office and higher level elections	75
2.5	Run-off mayor elections	77
2.6	Data set – higher level elections	84
2.7	Design 1 – strongest party	84
2.8	Design 1 – effects by party	85
2.9	Design 1 – placebo test (-5 percent, +5 percent)	85
3.1	Descriptives – federal elections	99
3.2	Federal elections – party incumbency and government participation	101
3.3	Federal elections – probability of winning	105
3.4	Descriptives – state elections	112
3.5	Effects by region: incumbency in the former East and West	113
3.6	Effect on the left party	114

3.7 Federal elections – party incumbency and government participation in the proportional vote 116

3.8 State elections – party incumbency and government participation 117

3.9 Winners of close races by governmental lead 118

3.10 Placebo tests – majoritarian vote of center-right party in federal elections 119

4.1 Changes at council size population thresholds 130

4.2 Replication of the results by Egger and Koethenbuerger (2010) 133

4.3 The results of council size on state grants and municipality fees 134

4.4 The results of council size on predetermined mayor status 136

4.5 Main results – council size effect with controlling for mayor status 137

4.6 Defining the budget: population thresholds in Bavarian law 144

4.7 Defining local institutions: population thresholds in Bavarian law 145

4.8 Communal budgeting – shares of expenditure and revenues 146

4.9 The results on expenditure categories controlling for mayor status 147

4.10 The results on revenues controlling for mayor status 147

5.1 Descriptive statistics 158

5.2 Effect of debt per capita on interest rates 166

5.3 Effect of per capita debt increase and the debt and interest to budget ratios on interest rates 167

5.4 Effect of debt repay help and and cash credit ratio on interest rates 168

5.5 Joint effects on interest rates 169

5.6 Spline regressions 171

General introduction

Public Choice is defined as "the application of of economics to political science" (Mueller 2003, p.1). Thus the field deals with analyzing different institutional settings and details of political systems while keeping in mind that political actors are not benevolent but rather maximize their own utility. Therefore, Public Choice is concerned with some of the most important decisions in society – how to design the rules of decision-making in order to achieve the best for all. This dissertation aims to add some evidence to this research program by empirically investigating both economic/fiscal policy and political effects of electoral systems and their rules (chapters 1, 2, 3, 4) and rules and yields in the local credit markets (chapter 5).

Empirical work in Public Choice and political economy has profited from exploiting country data (be it cross-sectional or panel) for a long time. There are two advantages for using this approach: first, easy availability of relevant data, and, second, the appeal of talking about international questions for a broad readership. However, there is criticism of this approach (e.g. Voigt 2011; Acemoglu 2005). Countries differ in many dimensions and it is challenging to isolate the effects of individual rules or institutions. In particular, events happening simultaneously, reverse causality and omitted variable bias are of significant concern. One possible solution to this problem, which is increasing in popularity, is to investigate the very same question using local level data. While this data is more challenging to acquire and requires a thorough understanding of the institution (as chapter 4 illustrates), there are three key advantages: (1) the municipalities within a country are at a comparable stage of development and operate in a similar institutional setting; (2) reforms can often be clearly identified; and (3) the large number of observations creates a powerful basis for statistical inference. Using a new data set with municipality level and election district data from Germany, this thesis aims to broaden the empirical evidence on fiscal policy, elections, and interest rates within the field of Public Choice.

Beyond empirics, there are numerous advantages for studying local level governance in Germany. On the one hand, German municipalities are in charge of important tasks (such as local infrastructure and administration of social services). On the other hand, municipalities are governed by institutional structures that often differ across time, states, and municipalities. In Germany there are a total of roughly 12,500 municipalities governed by locally elected municipality councils and mayors. In addition to deciding how money is spent in the municipality, these institutions are also responsible for financing part of the budget themselves through several taxes, debt issuance, and the charging of fees.

Beyond the broad joint substance of the papers and the joint subject, there is a third common element of the papers: a focus on robust identification. As pointed out above, one of the advantages of local data is that identification can often be more easily achieved. Chapter 1 makes use of a natural experiment brought about with the introduction of the direct mayoral elections in municipalities. Chapters 2, 3, and 4 rely on regression discontinuity designs, a method that makes use of random variation just around a threshold that is deterministic for a political or financial event. Finally, chapter 5 uses an instrumental variable strategy to estimate the effect of municipal indebtedness on interest rates.

In the following I give an overview of each of the five papers.

Chapter 1: Do constitutions matter?

This paper explores a change in the underlying rules regarding German municipality governance. These rules can be considered *constitutional* as they deal with some of the topics a constitution at the national level deals with too (division of power, election system, etc.).[1] In particular the paper investigates whether it makes a difference for spending and taxes if mayors are elected by the voting public or by city council members. The theoretical underpinning is the discussion about parliamentary versus presidential systems, which can be directly applied to local case in Germany where, with some simplification, municipalities with directly elected mayors resemble a presidential system and those with council-elected mayors a parliamentary one. In theory one would expect lower taxes and less government spending in a presidential system compared to a parliamentary style system. This is because the checks and balances should work better in a presidential system, which leads to lower rents and, hence, taxes. Furthermore, in a parliamentary system a stable majority in parliament is required, which makes it easy for the coalition to claim additional revenue and spend it in a way that benefits the majority's supporters.

The empirical analysis partly supports these predictions and partly rejects them. Municipalities with directly elected mayors have a property tax rate that is about two points lower than municipalities with council-elected mayors. This is in line with the prediction of lower taxes in a presidential system. However, from the analysis that follows, municipalities with directly elected mayors are associated with about five euro per capita higher spending on personnel, which can be more easily influenced by the mayor than other spending categories, although there is no significant effect on total spending. This contradicts the prediction of lower spending in presidential systems.

---

1   The laws that establish these rules for the municipal level in Germany are often referred to as *Kommunalverfassung* – municipal constitution.

These results may, however, be caused by vote-maximizing mayors who know that they need motivated staff present in order to execute their decisions and represent their policy to the voters on a daily basis.

The paper further explores whether municipalities change spending and taxes before the first direct mayoral election and if it takes time for the mechanisms to become effective after the first election. There is evidence that increased personnel spending and property tax cuts took time, although municipalities reduced its trade tax prior to the first direct mayoral election.

In a sensitivity analysis, the data set is extended with 2,256 (compared to a total of 686 municipalities so far) small municipalities in the state of Rhineland-Palatinate. These are not in the main data set as these all have their first mayoral election on the same day, whereas the first mayoral elections occurred on different days over a period of several years for the municipalities in the main analysis. Overall the results of the sensitivity check support the main results and even report at statistically significant levels that directly elected mayors lead to lower rates for trade tax and tax on agricultural land.

The identification of the paper relies on the unique natural experiment of the introduction of the direct election of the mayor. State parliaments decided that mayors should be directly elected by the people and determined that the first mayoral election would be when the term of the then in-office municipality head ended. As these dates differed in each municipality for historical reasons, and could neither be influenced by the state nor by the municipality, the actual date of the first mayoral election was exogenous.

This paper is presented first because it deals with an explicit change in the rules governing municipalities. It shows that rules matter for economic and political outcomes. The following chapters 2 and 3 explore this general idea further by exploring the effects of stable voting rules on political variables.

Chapter 2: Divided governments versus incumbency externality

The second paper investigates interdependencies between voting decisions for different political bodies at the local level. In particular, we determine whether the party affiliation of the mayor exerts an effect on the party's vote share in the subsequent council election and on higher level elections. We also ask the question the other way around by estimating the effect of the result of the council election on the subsequent run-off mayor election. While initially these issues may seem technical, these are important for the composition of the representative organs and policy outcomes.

The key results of our analysis are that the party of the mayor receives a bonus of 4 to 6 percentage points in the following council election a couple of years later, if the elections for the two bodies are held simultaneously. In the case of sequential election, i.e. when the two elections are on different dates, there is no such positive effect. Also, there is no effect of the partisanship of the mayor on higher level election, either federal or European.

From these results we follow that the timing of elections is crucial for determining voter behaviour and thus for the council composition and the outcome of the mayoral race. In designing electoral institutions, policy makers should be aware of the consequences of such seemingly minor differences in the rules regarding the timing of elections.

Furthermore, we estimate how council election results affect subsequent mayoral run-off elections. We find that for every additional 10 percentage points in vote share that a party receives in the council election, its candidate loses 2.5 percentage points in the run-off mayoral election.

We relate our empirical results to two main theories regarding voter behaviour, which may help explain the observed differences. The first is an incumbency externality effect from the mayor's office that suggests that a party will profit in the council election if the party also holds the mayor's office (see also chapter 3 for detailed discussion of incumbency). Second, the theory of divided government assumes that a voter preference for a government that is not dominated by any single party. Put simply, we argue that that the incumbency externality effect is evident in joint local elections, while the divided government effect can be observed through mayoral run-off elections and that both effects are present when the mayoral election is before the council election. To get to this conclusion we work through the theoretical implications of the timing of elections and the information available to the voters in the different cases.

Methodologically, this paper relies on a regression discontinuity design using tight mayor elections. The key assumption is that there is a random component in the aggregate electoral decision that turns races that were won by a slight majority and those that were similarly barely lost into good counter factual observations. The paper also uses a second design that exploits the institutional details of the mayoral run-off race for identification.

This paper is closely linked to the third paper in this dissertation, which studies heterogeneous incumbency effects for federal and state elections while using a similar methodology.

Chapter 3: Incumbency, party identity and governmental lead

Even for people not familiar with research on elections it is not a huge surprise that incumbents have an advantage when running for re-election. This paper seeks to add greater detail to the understanding of incumbency advantage by studying a new aspect of this effect – namely whether the advantage differs depending on whether the incumbents party is part of the government or not.

We use data from both federal and state elections in Germany to estimate the party incumbency effect for district representatives. We find overall incumbency effects but can also identify that the effects are heterogeneous with respect to whether the party of the district representative is part of the government or not: both district representatives from the center-right Christian Democrats (CDU) and the center-left Social Democrats (SPD) profit from an incumbency effect but only when the SPD is in government.

In the next step we explore what might drive the heterogeneity of the effect. We observe that when we split the sample there only is a significant effect after German reunification and that the effect is stronger in eastern states. We furthermore find that when a district has a SPD representative and the SPD is in the government, then the far left party, The Left[2], loses votes. Based on these results we assume that the increased competition from The Left, that is much stronger in the East than in the West, is responsible for the heterogeneity. Given the data, we cannot fully prove this hypothesis but check for alternative explanations for the heterogeneity of the effect, such as share of women in parliament, tenure and qualification and local ties but do not find indications that those could matter for the heterogeneity.

The identification of the observed effects is based on a regression discontinuity design that relies on close election outcomes for the district candidate in one period (similar to chapter 2 where the mayor election was the decisive vote). The incumbency effect is then determined in the next period when comparing close district winners with close district losers.

We underpin our empirical analysis with some theory that explores how the incumbency advantage might be related to whether a party is in government and what this means in a two party system. We find that the interpretation of an interaction effect of government participation and district incumbency is difficult: it cannot cover the full

---

2   The Left or in German *Die Linke* is the current name of the party that once ruled socialist East Germany and was then called SED. After the fall of the wall the party changed its name to PDS which then later merged with a spin-off of the SPD and is called *Die Linke* since. We use the name The Left as umbrella term for this party after the introduction of democracy in East Germany.

government participation effect on the incumbency advantage. The reason is that the interaction effect of one party is just the opposite of the effect for the other party.

This paper directly relates to chapter 2 by studying another aspect of electoral advantage and shares the basic methodology with chapter 2. The following chapter, chapter 4, which deals with population thresholds (instead of close elections) in regression discontinuity designs, also shares the same basic methodology.

Chapter 4: When can we trust population thresholds in regression discontinuity designs?

In the search for empirical designs that create causal inference the use of population thresholds in regression discontinuity designs is increasing in popularity. The approach is to study rules that differ by size classes of municipalities (e.g. either above 10,000 inhabitants, or below). This paper develops suggestions on how work using populations thresholds can be further improved. The suggestions are based on three observations: (1) more rules than the single rule under consideration can change at the same population thresholds (simultaneous exogenous co-treatment), (2) at the point in time when changing population figures trigger a change in rules municipalities often decide endogenously on other issues as well (simultaneous endogenous co-treatment) and (3) population figures may be subject to manipulation.

The paper builds on recent work by Egger and Koethenbuerger (2010) in the American Economic Journal: Applied Economics. These authors estimate the effect of several population thresholds applying to Bavarian municipalities on government spending. The authors observe sizable increases in spending at the thresholds, which they relate to increases in council size that are legally set to happen at these thresholds.

Looking at the population thresholds in Bavarian legislation we found 16 different legal rules that determine local institutions and the financial endowment of a municipality and differ by population size class. Except for one threshold (200,000 inhabitants, which only applies to a handful of municipalities) all thresholds that are decisive for council size also matter for at least one other legislative rule.

We further show that simultaneous endogenous co-treatment may matter for estimation. Before each election the councils of small and medium sized municipalities in Bavaria must decide whether they want their mayor to work full- or part-time during the next term. At the same time, the council knows whether the municipality has reached a population threshold that requires additional council members and/or other rule changes. If the mayor's status changes at the same time as other threshold induced policies, which we show, this puts identification in jeopardy.

Finally, we demonstrate that municipalities in Bavaria do manipulate population counts around the thresholds. Considering that the regression discontinuity design depends upon the assumption of random assignment around the threshold, this is a problem for causal inference.

While chapters 2 and 3 use regression discontinuity designs to draw causal inference, this chapter discusses how the practical application of such designs can be further improved. We conclude that to use regression discontinuity designs based population thresholds, researchers should understand the underlying legislation and carefully check the underlying assumptions.

Chapter 5: Do creditors discipline local governments?

This paper investigates the credit market for German municipalities by asking what role the financial situation of a municipality plays in determining the yield of municipal debt. Typically creditors demand higher returns when an asset is riskier or less liquid and one might expect the same behaviour in the market for municipal debt. However, German municipalities operate in a special institutional setting that may cause the market to behave differently than for "normal" creditors, such as companies, individuals or even nation states.

There are two key norms important for the market for municipal debt: the autonomy of the municipalities is guaranteed by the German Constitution and insolvency-proceedings are forbidden by law. In this setting bailout funds have been repeatedly established by the states. Another feature that makes the market for municipal credit special is that most creditors are banks that are owned by federal, state and local governments. From a research point of view it is now interesting to study whether these institutions distort the normal functioning of the credit market.

Using data for West German municipalities, the paper finds that there is no robust positive relationship between a poor financial situation (measured by an array of financial soundness indicators) and the interest rates paid by the municipalities. This means that creditors ignore the municipal financial situation when loaning money, thus supporting the view that the special institutions governing the market for municipal credit cancels the normal higher debt, higher yield relationship.

A sensitivity analysis, using spline regressions, checks whether this is due to inlinearities in the risk assessment. It might well be that it does not matter for banks whether a municipality has a low or medium debt burden, as long as it is considered sustainable. Once it reaches a critical threshold banks might only be willing to hand out money with increased interest rates. An overall estimate of the effect could thus hide a positive relationship for the highly indebted municipalities. Yet, the results of the spline regression do not indicate that the market deals differently with the higher indebted municipalities.

Methodologically this paper relies on a panel instrumental variable estimation. This is necessary as the debt variables on the right hand side of the estimation equation are likely to be endogenous with the interest rate on the left hand side: not only might a high debt burden lead to a higher interest rate, but a low interest rate might also foster incurring more debt.

This paper contributes to the dissertation by broadening the discussion of local institutions and determinants of local finances. If municipalities do not have to pay premia for more debt this is likely to influence decisions on spending and taxes, and, hence, budget deficits. For example, the policy outcomes of the direct mayoral election (discussed in chapter 1), higher personnel spending and lower property taxes, lead, ceteris paribus, to budget deficits, which can be more easily maintained if the credit market does not discipline municipalities.

Chapter 1: Do constitutions matter?

Evidence from a natural experiment at the municipality level[1]

Abstract:

Economists often wonder what impact constitutions have on economic outcomes. While this is frequently investigated empirically at the country level, evidence is mixed due to endogeneity and identification issues. This paper uses a new panel data set of the 686 municipalities in three German states and finds that presidential-type government (as opposed to a parliamentary-type) reduces tax rates and increases spending on government personnel. These effects are identified based on a reform of the municipal constitutions that was exogenous from the point of view of the municipalities in content and timing. The reform forced a quasi-randomly selected groups of municipalities to introduce the constitution in a particular year.

1.1 Introduction

Traditional economic theory deals with decisions taken by different stakeholders in the market place. In this, fundamental rules are assumed. Constitutional economics goes one step further by putting these fundamental rules (often called constitutional rules) at the center of analysis (e.g. Buchanan 1989, 1990). Two key questions directly emerge form the basic idea of constitutional economics: How do constitutional rules emerge? What consequences do the rules have?

This paper paper deals with the latter question by using a new and unique data set of 686 constitutional reforms at the municipality level in Germany. The features of these reforms facilitate a causal analysis of the effects of presidential vs. parliamentary types of government. In particular, I investigate the economic effects of the direct election of the mayor on spending and tax rates.

Estimating the economic effects of constitutions is gaining the attention of empirical economists. Notably, Persson's and Tabellini's book *The Economic Effects of Con-*

---

1   I would like to thank Charles B. Blankart, Viktor Steiner, Ronny Freier, Alasdair Rutherford, the seminar participants at DIW Berlin, Humboldt University Berlin, EEA Congress 2011 in Oslo, EPCS Meeting 2011 in Rennes and at SMYE 2010 in Luxembourg for helpful comments and suggestions. The DIW Berlin Public Economics Department helped with obtaining most of the data for which I am particularly grateful. Furthermore I am indebted to Helke Seitz who provided excellent research assistance with organizing the data.

stitutions (2002) received prominent praise (e.g. Acemoglu 2005; Mueller 2007) and stimulated research. So far the scientific discussion almost exclusively analyzes constitutional rules at the country level (see e.g. Voigt (2011) for an overview). At this governmental level, however, there are a multitude of problems both from econometric and conceptional points of view. Some even question the reliability of the results generated so far. For example, Voigt (2011, p. 247) writes:

> Recently, cross-country studies as such have come under attack. The main methodological concerns seem to be simultaneity, reverse causality, and omitted variable bias. But behind these technical concerns hides the implicit—and problematic—assumption that one model is sufficient to "explain" various developments in vastly different environments and development stages.

Furthermore, the statistic validity of these results is also limited as there are only a few countries for which data is available. Voigt concludes that due to these issues many of the constitutional effects presented in the literature are not robust to thorough verification.

Most of these issues can be resolved using municipality level data. This is because municipalities in a country are at a very similar stage of development and are subject to an almost identical institutional framework. Furthermore, reforms of constitutional rules occur more often, and typically there is a large number of cases that can be used for analysis. Nonetheless, only few scholars have analyzed constitutions at the subnational or local levels.[2]

In investigating sub-national level governments one does however not automatically resolve potential reverse causality. The latter appears when we cannot assume that constitutional rules are exogenous but rather must presume that these rules could be determined by e.g. the level of wealth (which is typically considered exogenous in the analysis). This problem is closely connected to the issue of endogeneity that can arise if third factors influence both the rules of the constitution and the variables treated as endogenous, such as the level of wealth. Furthermore, a causal interpretation is often problematic as the observed correlations could be due to unobserved factors.

In this study I overcome the issues by taking advantage of changes in local constitutions in several German states during the 1990s. The advantage of these reforms is that the changes were implemented at municipality-individual dates. Neither the state

---

2 For example Funk and Gathmann (2008, 2009) analyze the influence of direct democracy and proportional representation on fiscal policy at the municipality and canton level in Switzerland. Blume (2009) investigates – based on a small sample – constitutional change at the municipal level in Germany. (Egger, Koethenbuerger, and Smart, 2008, 2010b) explore the effects of the direct election of the mayor in Lower Saxony on government spending and on the trade tax.

government nor the municipality's local government could set the date at which the changes came into effect in the particular municipality – resulting in a natural experiment. The key change in the reforms of the 1990s is the direct election of the mayor by the citizens – before the reform the voters only directly elected the city council, which then elected the mayor. This changed drastically the horizontal separation of powers – going from a parliamentary system to a presidential system. Using this constitutional switch, I find that the direct election of the mayor reduced the property tax on non-agricultural land and increased spending on government personnel.

The paper is structured as follows: Section 1.2 presents the current state of the economic discussion of the economic effects of constitutions. Section 1.3 presents the special features of the local constitutions in Germany and briefly presents the reform process. Section 1.4 presents the econometric model and the key hypothesis. Section 1.5 highlights key features of the underlying data and section 1.6 presents the results, section 1.7 concludes.

1.2 Literature review

> It is the institutions that govern the performance of an economy.
> Coase (1998, p. 73)

The area of constitutional economics shares the basic assumption with (new) institutional economics that institutions/fundamental rules are important. Being the broader of the two research areas, (new) institutional economics extends the ideas of neoclassical economics by introducing a broad range of institutions such as legal rules, customs, and traditions and by understanding their implications like transaction costs.[3] Constitutional economics mainly focuses on legal constitutions and key rules of the political decision making process. In doing this, constitutional economics is mainly concerned with "how rules affect economic performance, and how the choice of the rules govern the political sector" Tollison (2007, p. 3). Brennan and Hamlin (1998, p. 401) describe the field as the analysis of the "basic rules under which social orders may operate"[4].

Beyond the work on normative questions of constitutional economics (e.g. Buchanan 1989, 1990), there is also a focus on the positive aspects of the field (Besley and Case 2003; Persson and Tabellini 2002; Voigt 2011, 1997). The results of this positive research provides input to the normative recommendations for constitutional design, which are undoubtedly a key part of the public choice discipline (Blankart and Koester 2006).

---

3   For a brief overview of the field see Williamson (2000).
4   One should note that constitutional economics and public choice are part of the same research program (Blankart and Koester, 2006; Rowley, 1997). In this text I primarily refer to constitutional economics as its narrower definition more precisely describes the research objective of this paper.

Within the field of positive constitutional economics, Voigt (1997) identifies four key areas, with most attention paid to the analysis of *the economic effects of constitutional rules*[5]. The constitutional rules investigated in this field of research can be summarized in five categories: (1) voting rules and systems, (2) horizontal separation of power (presidential vs. parliamentary system, bicameralism, judiciary), (3) vertical separation of power (federalism), (4) Representative vs. direct democracy, (5) Other, e.g. Democracy vs. autocracy.

This paper contributes to the discussion on the effects of the horizontal separation of power for which I present a summary of literature below.

1.2.1 Horizontal separation of powers

When speaking about horizontal separation of powers one generally thinks about the executive, legislative, and judicial branches. The relationship of the first two is of particular interest to the analysis of local constitutions as both institutions are subject to local decision making. The analogies to government and parliament at the national level and head of municipality and municipality council at the local level are palpable. However, in Germany local judiciary is administered by the state or national bureaucracy.

When considering different forms of separation of government and legislature in democracies there are two dominate options: presidential and parliamentary democracy. To classify any given system one determines whether: (1) power is factually divided between the government and the different branches of the legislature, which is typically the case in presidential democracies; or (2) if government depends upon the confidence of the parliament, which is typically the case in parliamentary democracies (Persson and Tabellini, 2002). One may conclude from this classification that a typical parliamentary democracy is actually designed to prevent separation of powers by forming a strong tie between the majority in the parliament and the executive while a presidential democracy is set up to generate this separation (compare e.g. Lienert 2005).

The literature investigates the effects that these different setups may have on economic outcomes. The theoretical reasoning regarding economic outcomes assumes that in

---

5   The other three areas are: *(1) Procedures leading to constitutional rules.* This stream examines how different procedures of the process of the creation of the constitution determine the contents of the constitutional rules. *(2) Preferences influencing constitutional rules.* This area asks what influence individual preferences exert on the rules in the constitution and to what extent shifts in values and norms have on constitutional change. *(3) The constitutional rules and constitutional change.* This area deals with the causes of different types of constitutional changes and what role constitutional rules, like the separation of powers, play.

a presidential democracy that the checks and balances between the government and the parliament work better than in a parliamentary democracy, thus resulting in lower rents to politicians and, subsequently, lower taxes. Also, it is easier for the electorate to hold politicians accountable for rent-seeking behavior. Persson, Roland, and Tabellini 2000. Furthermore, the confidence requirement in parliamentary democracies forces a stable majority in the parliament (both within a party and within a coalition) - the same legislators vote together on any proposal (e.g. Diermeier and Feddersen 1998; Heller 2001; Huber 1996). This effect – as opposed to a presidential system where changing majorities in the parliament are common – makes it attractive for the majority to claim any additional revenue and spend the money to benefit the majority. This is also true for higher taxes where part of the cost is imposed on the minority. Hence parliamentary regimes lean towards higher taxes and government spending (Persson, Roland, and Tabellini 2000). Roubini and Sachs (1989) present another argument in the same direction, stating that in coalition governments (which typically occur in parliamentary systems) it is very difficult to reach agreement among the partners to reduce budget deficits.

Although these theoretical predictions about the fiscal effects of presidential vs. parliamentary systems are tested empirically in the literature, using country panel data, none can, however, be considered to be validated or refuted by the available evidence. On the one hand, Persson and Tabellini (2002) confirm their predictions using a cross section of 60–80 countries in the 1990s based on ordinary least squares (OLS), instrumental variables (IV), and matching estimates. They find that countries with presidential systems spend about 5–6 percent less of GDP than parliamentary democracies. They also compare presidential systems with plurality rule to proportional parliamentary systems and find that the former spend even 10 percent less of GDP than the latter. They also find a hint that presidentialism reduces welfare spending. With regards to budget deficits they cannot present significant results. Persson and Tabellini (2002) also investigate the effects of presidential systems on corruption (negative), government efficiency (insignificant), and productivity (negative).

On the other hand, Blume, Mueller, and Voigt (2009) claim that the results are not robust to the size of the data set. In particular, they find that the dummy for presidential regimes is insignificant for government spending when the number of observations is increased from 80 to 92. The same occurs when they slightly adjust the definition of the presidential system dummy and when they use total instead of central government expenditure. They also get different results for corruption and productivity. Acemoglu (2005) criticizes Persson and Tabellini's (2003) empirical methodology, concluding that "there are reasons to question whether this research has successfully uncovered causal effects". Rockey (2010) takes up part of Acemoglu's critique in his estimations. Although he confirms the results of Persson and Tabellini (2002) with regard to government spending in presidential vs parliamentarian systems, Rockey also finds that extending the data set with countries that become democracies in the 1990s – as Blume, Mueller, and Voigt (2009) do – removes significance. He argues that this may be expected "if the consequences of constitutions take time to emerge".

From a political science point of view, Gerring, Thacker, and Moreno (2009) ask: "are parliamentary systems better?" They use data on more than 100 countries over several years and find that parliamentary systems increase GDP, bureaucratic quality, life expectancy and reduce corruption, thus contradicting Persson and Tabellini (2002)) with the latter point. However they do not investigate government spending or general tax level. Using country panel data from 1820 to 2000, Knutsen (2009) finds no effects of presidentialism on growth.

To summarize, the literature mainly relies on country data (with three exceptions that are important to this paper which I present in the following subsection) with its imminent limitations (see section 1.1) and has not yielded a consistent picture of the economic effects of presidentialism versus parliamentarism.

1.2.2 Local constitutional economics for Germany

As this paper focuses on German municipal data, in this subsection I present the relevant empirical work within constitutional economics at the local level for Germany, in particular on the local division of powers.

Political scientists and researchers in law were the first to delve into the analysis of local constitutions Germany. For example Borchmann and Vesper (1976) give an overview of the discussion to reform the local constitutions in the early 1970s. More recently the discussion focused on the distribution of power at the local level (e.g. Buss 2002) and hence the question of the horizontal separation of powers. Economists, too, are analyzing the economic effects of constitutional rules at the local level. However, the literature is still not very extensive and empirical studies are often limited to the analysis of a single state or are constrained to relatively coarse country data.

One group of papers deals with the vertical separation of powers in the sense of competition between local authorities. The key topics of these studies are tax and expenditure competition and the effect of fiscal equalization schemes (e.g. Buettner 2000, 2005; Borck, Caliendo, and Steiner 2007; Egger, Koethenbuerger, and Smart 2010a). They find that the competition induced by federalism leads to lower taxes and interaction in spending behavior while fiscal equalization schemes cause higher taxes.

Egger and Koethenbuerger (2010) take a different look at local constitutions by studying the effect of the size of the municipal council on overall expenditure for which they find a positive relationship. Another strand of research analyzes the efficiency of the local public sector (e.g. Geys, Heinemann, and Kalb 2009). These authors find that fiscal autonomy, voter turnout, and the size of the municipality increase efficiency. Ade and Freier (2011) show that voters behave differently depending on whether the town council and the mayoral election are held jointly or not.

For this paper there are three studies of particular relevance: Blume (2009)[6] investigates the interdependency between key feature of the local constitutions (horizontal separation of power, electoral system, direct democracy) and economic policy outcome variables. Egger, Koethenbuerger, and Smart (2008) investigate the effect of the introduction of the direct election of the mayor in Lower Saxony on local government expenditures and the same authors (2010b) investigate the joint effect of the direct election together with a change in the fiscal equalization system[7].

Blume (2009) finds, with regards to the horizontal separation of power, that the introduction of the election of mayors by general election (instead of election by the municipal council) in the state of Schleswig-Holstein correlates with falling expenditures and revenues when compared to the state of Baden-Württemberg where mayors have been elected by the public for long. Using time series data, breakpoint tests indicate that overall expenditures fall significantly from an average of 99% of Baden-Württemberg's value to 97%, revenues from 102% to 99 %, and tax revenue from 91% to 89%. In another specification the author uses a panel of the states of Bavaria, Baden-Württemberg, Hesse, and Schleswig-Holstein. Here they find that the direct election of the mayor reduced the growth in per capita spending by 22 euros. Another OLS regression yields that the local expenditures fell in Schleswig-Holstein by 21.5% relative to Baden-Württemberg.

These are a important and relevant results as they support the hypothesis deducted from theory that presidential systems foster austerity However, when looking at the methodology and the data used suggestions for further research can be derived. On the one hand Blume works with a very limited data set as he uses aggregate data at the state level[8]. On the other hand a causal interpretation of the observed correlations is not possible as the effects of the evaluated reform cannot be separated from state-specific effects that occur at the same time. This is particularly important as only a small part of municipal spending is subject to the discretion of local government. For

---

6   The part of Blume's book (2009) that is relevant to this research was also published as a paper (Blume, Doering, and Voigt, 2008).

7   These papers are not yet published.

8   The number of observations is between 29 and 112 depending on the regression.

example, the measured effects could be due to changes in other state policies affecting municipal spending (e.g. through transfers). Another plausible cause for the reduced spending in Schleswig-Holstein relative to Baden-Württemberg may be a generally worsened economic condition, which is plausible when we consider the falling relative total and tax revenues reported by the authors (local authorities can only influence tax revenue to a limited extent and are highly dependent on transfers from higher levels of government).

Egger, Koethenbuerger, and Smart (2008) investigate the direct election of the mayor in Lower Saxony in the 1990s. This reform is similar to the reforms I consider in this paper. Both in Lower Saxony and in the states in my analysis, the new rules were phased in over a period of several years and in both cases the reform mandated the direct election of the mayor. The reform differ however in the quality of the changes that occurred. While in the states I analyze the powers of the mayors remained unchanged by the reform there was a huge reform-based increase in competencies of the mayor in Lower-Saxony. This included agenda setting power and voting rights in the council[9].

Egger, Koethenbuerger, and Smart (2008, 2010b) take a different approach to motivating their investigation than I do. While I bring forward the argument that the introduction of the direct election of the mayor constitutes a change in the degree of presidentialism, these authors argue that the reform rather describes a switch from a proportional electoral system to a majority system. Which of these two approaches is true cannot be shown in the data[10]. In the end it depends on whether one believes that the central characteristic of the direct election of the mayor – with respect to policy effects - is the fact that (a) she is elected using a majority rule or that (b) she possesses increased accountability and independence of the council after the reform.

The study of Egger, Koethenbuerger, and Smart (2008) is of great relevance to this paper as the authors analyze the effect of the direct mayor election on spending using the phase in of the new rules for identification. The study finds that the direct mayor election increases total government spending by about 1.2 percent (significant at the ten percent level). The authors also investigate the effect on different spending categories and discuss interaction affects with party affiliation of the mayor and council fragmentation. They find that if the mayor is affiliated with a major party total spending increases by 1.9 percent (significant at the one percent level). There is no significant

---

9   Lower Saxony started with the North German Council constitution and switched to the South German Council Constitution (see Appendix for a detailed description of these constitutional types).

10   However, it should be noted that the key decisive body of the municipality, the council, is still elected using a proportional system and that a direct mayor election can only be carried out as majority election. Also taking into account that the power of the mayor increases through the reform in Lower-Saxony, I believe that the authors rather measure the effect of increased power of the mayor combined with higher accountability and independence than the effect of its majority election.

effect for independent mayors. Looking at different spending categories they find that the reform increases social security spending when a party mayor was in place and reduced social, administrative, and cultural spending when an independent mayor was in place.

In their second study, the same authors (2010b) interact the change of the local constitution with a reform in the fiscal equalization mechanism for municipalities. They use a subsample of all municipalities in Lower Saxony to create two groups: one that had already switched the local constitution when the equalization reform came into place and one that did not switch the constitution for some years after the reform. The question the authors aim to answer is whether different electoral rules at the local level impact the degree to which municipalities react to a reform in the fiscal equalization mechanism. When comparing the two groups they find that the business tax rates adjust more in municipalities that have already switched to the direct election of the mayor. Depending on the specification and estimation method the authors find that municipalities with directly elected mayors adjust about 30 to 100 percent more than municipalities without. The effects are rather small in magnitude and range from -0.4 to -1.2 points for municipalities without directly elected mayors and -0.8 and -1.6 points respectively. Hence municipalities with directly elected mayor adjusted about 0.4 points more.

1.3 Institutional background

German federalism is complex, particularly at the sub-state level. However, the state governments possess the power to set the key rules of local government, a rule that insures that the same institutions are in place within one state. This section presents the design of the sub-state federal system in Germany, the decision power of the municipalities, the different constitutional types at the local level, and the layout of the reforms in the 1990s.

1.3.1 Levels of local government in Germany

The German federal systems comprises three main levels: the federal government, the states (or *Länder*), and the local level. The local level is itself divided in two main sub-levels for which representatives are democratically elected: the municipality and the counties.

Furthermore, in bigger municipalities (usually those denoted as "cities") representations can also be elected for subsets of the municipality. In addition, smaller municipalities are often grouped into administrative unites below the county level for which representations are elected (e.g. the *Verbandsgemeinde* in Rhineland-Palatinate and the *Samtgemeinde* in Lower-Saxony). Between the county level and the state there may be yet another entity that has a democratically elected representative body. In Bavaria for example counties are grouped into districts (*Bezirke*) and in other states bodies are elected for certain agglomerations around bigger cities (e.g. the region around Stuttgart in Baden-Württemberg). These government entities typically have only limited decision power. Counting together, one voter may have to elect representatives for up to four local government levels.

Beyond the elected bodies there is also a further purely administrative level run by the state government that groups a certain number of counties into administrative regions (*Regierungsbezirk*).

1.3.2 Responsibilities, autonomy, and taxing power

Communities in Germany are in charge of most local decisions and the right to self-government is guaranteed by the German constitution (Art. 28, 2). From a public choice point of view the tasks executed by the municipalities may be grouped into three buckets: (1) Mandated spending (*Auftragsangelegenheiten*). This group comprises services that the higher level governments have handed over the local administration for execution. Communities have to follow the norms set by the higher authorities. These tasks include the social assistance, the registrar's office, statistics, passport administration. (2) Limited autonomy spending (*Pflichtige Selbstverwaltungsangelegenheiten*). This category comprises services the municipalities have to provide but the quality of the services is subject to local decision. These services comprise e.g. school buildings, fire departments, and sewerage. (3) Discretionary spending (*Freiwillige Selbstverwaltungsangelegenheiten*). This category comprises areas that are under the full discretion of the local government (e.g. public recreation, culture).

To finance the expenditures related to their multiple responsibilities, municipalities rely on a relatively complex scheme of taxes, transfers from higher government levels, redistribution to poorer municipalities, and fees charged for services. Taxes are of particular interest as municipalities decide on the tax rates (but not on the base) for some of the duties. The municipality's key duties are the business tax, the property tax, the VAT, and the income tax. While the municipalities have no discretion over the tax levels for VAT and income tax, they set the rates for the trade tax and the property taxes A and B, which represent a total of 16.7 percent of all local government revenues (see table 1.1, unfortunately the budget statistics do not provide information on how much money is spend along the different levels of autonomy, see section 1.5).

Table 1.1: Average municipality revenues by source, 1998–2007

Revenue category	EUR per capita	Percent
Total revenues	1,410	100
Non-tax revenues (e.g. transfers)	846	60.0
Tax revenues	564	40.0
Trade tax (net)	159	11.3
Property tax A (agricultural)	5	0.4
Property tax B (non- agricultural)	71	5.0
VAT	20	1.4
Income tax	301	21.3
Other (e.g. dog tax, pleasure tax)	8	0.6

Note: Average of all 686 municipalities in the data set, years prior to 1998 not included as VAT data for Hesse not available for this period.

1.3.3 Local constitutions

The literature on local constitutions in democratic post-war Germany (e.g Kost and Wehling 2003; Schrameyer 2006) typically refers to four types of constitutions: the North German Council Constitution, the Magistrate Constitution, the Mayor Constitution, and the South German Council Constitution. This classification is derived from two key features of the constitutions: how much power the mayor has, as defined by the constitution, and how independent the mayor is from other players in the local arena (council, committees). However, these constitutions differ also in other rules such as the role of direct democracy and the ballot structure. The characteristics of the four types of the local constitutions are presented in the Appendix.

The rules of the local constitutions are set by the states and not by the municipalities themselves – a fact that assures a unity of rules within the state and makes the rules set in the local constitutions exogenous in our analysis. However, there may be different rules at work within one state at the same time based on size restrictions for different constitutional rules to apply or constitutional changes that do not come into effect at the same time in all municipalities of a certain state.[11].

---

11 The local constitution are also worth while analyzing from a theoretical perspective: As they are determined by a higher government authority the local constitutions cannot be regarded as a social contract among the citizens or as a device managing a principal-agent relationship between the constituency and the state (see e.g. Voigt 1997, pp. 27–30). Rather, the local constitutions must be seen as a mere commitment device of the state-wide constituency. It is a set of rules aiming at organizing the authority granted to the municipalities and could hence in a narrow sense not be viewed as a constitution. Also legally the local constitutions in Germany do not have the rank of a constitution. They are normal laws set by the states legislature and subject to frequent modifications.

1.3.4 Reforms in the 1990s as a natural experiment

In the 1990s most German states reformed their local constitutions. Starting off from the four different constitutional regimes described above, all states reformed their rules in a similar way: they reformed their constitutions to be similar to the South German Council Constitution. The latter is characterized by a directly elected strong mayor and was already in place in the states of Bavaria and Baden-Württemberg. These reforms and their their implementation schedule in particular provide the basis for my identification strategy.

Having decided on the rules of the new constitutions the state legislators had two options for implementation. They could either set a single date by which the new rules would come in place in all municipalities. This procedure was sensible whenever the term of the predecessor[12] of the first mayor elected by the people ended at the same time in all municipalities. When this was not the case, it was easier to set the effective date of the new constitution to the time when the term of the last not publicly elected head of the administration was previously scheduled to end. This phasing in provides for a natural experiment as neither the municipalities nor the state governments influenced the particular date at which a municipality switched to the new constitution. Or, to put it differently, the particular date of introduction of the new constitution was exogenous to both the state and the local government. This fulfills the requirement of "good natural experiments" as defined by Meyer (1995, p. 151) according to whom they "are studies in which there is a transparent exogenous source of variation in the explanatory variables that determine the treatment assignment"[13]. To make the exogenous source of variation that this paper uses clear there is a detailed description of the reforms used below.

Of the eight west German non-city states, two did not change their constitution with respect to the mayor's position (Bavaria and Baden-Württemberg already had directly elected mayors), five states used the phase in mechanism (Hesse, Rhineland-Palatinate, Saarland, Lower-Saxony, and Schleswig-Holstein) and one state (North-Rhine Westphalia) switched at a single date. In Hesse, for example, the new constitution became effective in the municipalities over a time period of 6 years with 45 to 86 municipalities switching constitutions each year. See Table 1.2 for an overview of Hesse, Rhineland-Palatinate, and Saarland, the states covered in this analysis.

---

12 This could be either the mayor elected by the council or the city manager, depending on the state.

13 Meyer (1995) points out that the research design understood by economists as "natural experiment" should rather be called "quasi-experiment" as in psychology to stress that the underlying data was not generated in a real experiment. This paper sticks to the term "natural experiment" as it is more common in economics.

Reform in Hesse

In the state of Hesse, municipalities are led by a small board (the magistrate) over which the mayor presides. Pre-reform, the members of the magistrate, including the mayor, were elected by the council and could be recalled with a 2/3 majority in the council. In municipalities bigger than 50,000 inhabitants full time mayors and magistrate members could be recalled with a single majority but only within six months after the election of the council[14]. The magistrate decides by majority – with the mayor's vote being pivotal in a tie (both pre- and post reform). The mayor decides on the individual topic portfolios of the members of the magistrate and executes its decisions. Furthermore the members of the magistrate must not be members of the council. In the bigger cities, some of the members are full-time while in smaller municipalities all members except the mayor are unsalaried. Typically the full-time members are in charge of the more important departments while the nonsalaried members take care of less time-consuming areas. The term of full time mayors and the other full time members of the magistrates was six years before the reform, the term of non-salaried mayors and magistrate member was 4 years. The term length of the council was four years too, and in municipalities with non-salaried mayors the terms of council and magistrate were aligned.

In 1991 the constitution of the state of Hesse was changed in a referendum, now providing for the direct election of the mayor. The according laws were changed as of May 1992. Staring in 1993 Hesse then gradually phased in the new rules over a 6 year period (see table 1.2). The first general mayor election in a municipality was held when the term of the previous (council elected) mayor ended. The reform kept the powers of the mayor constant while only changing its elections scheme. The mayor is now completely independent of the majority in council and can only be recalled in a referendum, while the other members of the magistrate can be recalled with a 2/3 majority in the council. In cities with more than 50,000 inhabitants magistrate members (excluding the mayor) can be recalled with a single majority in the first six months following a council election. The terms of the mayor and the full time members of the magistrate are now six years, the term of the council is four years (five since 2001). The non-salaried members of the magistrate have the same term length of the council and are elected of the beginning of the council's term. (Dressler 2003; Dressler and Adrian 2005; Repp 1989; Schefold and Neumann 1996).

Reform in Rhineland-Palatinate

As opposed to Hesse, Rhineland-Palatinate did not install a magistrate, rather it grants all rights of leading the administration to the mayor. She presides over the council, in which she has a vote. She heads the administration, prepares the decisions of the

---

14   In 1998 there were 12 municipalities with more than 50,000 inhabitants

council for which she also sets the agenda. Pre-reform the mayor was elected by the council for a period of ten to twelve years in the case of full-time mayors. The term of non-salaried mayors was aligned with the term of the council which was five years. Mayors could be recalled by the council since 1973.

In October 1993 the parliament of Rhineland-Westphalia decided to introduce the direct election of the mayor. The updated rules were enacted in June 1994 and were then phased in over a period of eight years (see table 1.2). Full-time mayors can now be recalled by the voting public but not by the council. The legal powers provided to the mayor were not affected through the change in rules.

Historically, the municipalities in Rhineland-Palatinate are rather small (many below 1000 inhabitants). To increase administrative efficiency smaller municipalities were grouped into joined municipalities in the 1970s, which took over an important part of the task of their member municipalities. They are in charge of key tasks such as high schools, regional social infrastructure (retirement homes, etc), and water services. They are, however, not able to set the local tax levels, which are still determined by the member municipalities. These joint municipalities are governed - as all other municipalities – by a mayor and a council, and were also affected by the constitutional reform. Mayors are full time in the bigger municipalities (term 8 years) and nonsalaried in the member municipalities of joint municipalities (term 4 years equivalent to council). The member municipalities of the joint municipalities all elected their first directly elected mayor in 1994 (Ipsen 2007; Oster 2003; Priebe 1997; Schefold and Neumann 1996).

Reform in Saarland

The local constitution in Saarland is very similar to the one in Rhineland-Palatinate: the mayor heads the municipality and its administration, presides the council, sets its agenda and prepares its decisions. As opposed to Rhineland-Palatinate, she does not have a vote in the council. Prior to the reform mayors were appointed for a period of 10 years by the council. From 1973 onwards the council could recall the mayor.

The reform – decided by the parliament in May 1994 – introduced the direct election of the mayor and set the term to eight years. The powers of the mayor and the horizontal separation of powers remained unchanged. The first mayors were elected by the citizens in 1994 and the new rules gradually became effective over a period of 11 years (see table 1.2). The mayors can be recalled by the voting public. The term of the council is five years. (Ipsen 2007; Priebe 1997; Schefold and Neumann 1996).

Common elements of the reforms in the three states

All three states switched from a mayor elected through the council to a directly elected mayor. Other significant parts of the local codes with respect to the horizontal separation of power between the mayor and the council were not changed in any of the three states. The mayor's direct election and the fact that she can only be recalled through a referendum provide her with independence from the council. She no longer requires the support of a majority in the council for her reelection and for staying in office. Hence, following the definition of Persson and Tabellini (2003), the local constitutional systems may after the reform be roughly categorized as "presidential" as (1) the power is divided between the mayor and the council to a huge extent and (2) the mayor does not depend on the confidence of the council. Before the reform the constitutional systems can be classified as "parliamentary" as the mayor was elected by the council and required its approval for staying in power.

1.4 Empirical strategy

1.4.1 Single constitution dummy

In order to best use the properties of the reform in the three considered states, I use a difference-in-difference approach to estimate the causal effects of constitutional reform on a set of spending and tax variables. More specifically, I estimate models of the following form for municipality i in year t:

$$y_{it} = \alpha_i + \delta_t + \beta d_{it} + \sum_k \gamma_k x_{kit} + e_{it} \qquad (1.1)$$

where y_{it} is either a component or total government spending or one of the tax rates, α_i are municipality dummies, and δ_t are year dummies. d_{it} is a dummy variable indicating that the new constitution is effective. It is equal to one in years after the first mayor election and equal to zero in all previous years. β is the parameter of interest. x_{kit} are additional explanatory variables, and γ_k the according parameters. All expenditure variables are measured as per capita values.

Given the properties of the data, both time and municipality dummies are key for producing consistent estimates: On the one hand, the time dummies absorb common shocks as economic crisis and inflation that could distort the estimates of the constitutional dummy – particularly if they occur in years where not many or a huge majority of municipalities have switched to the new constitution. On the other hand, the municipality fixed effects capture huge persistent differences in municipalities, including differences between the states. These may stem from e.g. historical differences in tax levels or varying spending preferences.

I include additional covariates to control for differences along other key time-varying dimensions x_{kit}. These are population density, to cover for different spending and taxing patterns in rural and urban areas, the share of population over 65 and under 15, to account for potential special needs and preferences of these age groups. Furthermore, a measure to capture the economic strength as compared to the other municipalities is included. This is important as municipalities with a stronger economic base may generally spend more and may have different incentives in setting taxes and allocating spending than less strong municipalities. I will explain in detail in section 1.5 how this measure is constructed. Moreover, I control for second order effects in population density and economic strength.

To control for potential correlation within a municipality I use a clustered variance-covariance matrix estimator in order to prevent a too high confidence in the estimate of the constitutional effect. This estimator is equivalent to the Huber/White/Sandwich estimator of the covariance matrix. For an introduction to the problem see Angrist and Pischke (2009), for the technical implementation of the estimator see StataCorp (2009).

1.4.2 Adjustment effects

When thinking about a change in fundamental rules such as the direct election of the mayor one may argue that the effects are time-varying for two reasons: (1) changes may take some time to take effect, (2) political actors might anticipate the reform and pre-adjust. Regarding the latter one could think of either a council wishing to hand over solid finances to the first directly elected mayor or a council majority trying to assure that their candidate wins the race. Another form of council pre-adjustment would be (along the lines of public choice reasoning) a council that tries to push through a maximum number of projects before a directly elected mayor may make this more difficult. To capture for these possible effects, I estimate a second specifications that explores whether there are pre- and post-adjustment effects. To do this I add dummies identifying the first three years after the first election and the dummies for the year of the first election and the two preceding years to equation 1.1. This then becomes:

$$y_{it} = \alpha_i + \delta_t + \beta d_{it} + \sum_{l=1}^{6} \lambda_l h_{itl} + \sum_k \gamma_k x_{kit} + e_{it} \tag{1.2}$$

Here, as before, d_{it} is the dummy indicating that the mayor in the municipality is elected by the people (equal to 1 in the years following the first election). h_{itl} are six dummies ($l = 1...6$) identifying the distance to the first election of the mayor for each year t in municipality i (three years after the first election, the year of the first election and two years before), and λ_l are the corresponding coefficients. In the first three years following the first direct election both d_{it} and one of the h_{itl} are equal to one.

1.4.3 Hypotheses

Based on the existing literature presented in section 1.2, I can test two key hypothesis with respect to the constitutional change. However, the particular properties of the reform and the institutional setting suggest modifications of the ones suggested by the literature. I first depict the hypothesis derived from the literature and then present the extensions.

The first hypothesis derived from the literature is that local government expenditure is lower if the constitutional system in a municipality is close to a presidential system compared to municipalities where the constitutional system resembles more a parliamentary system, i.e. that government spending is lower when the mayor is elected by the people instead of by the council. This hypothesis stems from the considerations about presidential and parliamentary systems. For example, according to these theories, it is easier for the electorate to punish politicians for rent seeking behavior in presidential systems and the checks and balances are working better. This should lead to lower taxes and government expenditures.

The second hypothesis derived from the literature is that the tax rates are lower in systems with a higher degree of presidentialism, i.e. when the mayor is elected by the people. This is due to bigger accountability in presidential-style systems on the one hand and lower expected expenditure on the other hand.

Taking into account the institutional setting at the local level in Germany warrants some extensions to the two hypothesis just presented. As described in subsection 1.3.2 municipalities in Germany only have limited autonomy regarding their total spending. A huge part of their expenditures are mandated (such as social assistance) and can only be influenced to a limited extent by the municipalities. For this reason I only expect a small effect on total spending. Unfortunately, the official statistics do not show how much money is spent on discretionary items but is rather organized along a traditional structure. However the available data contains also information on spending on government personnel. While the municipalities have to provide sufficient personnel to execute the mandated tasks they are free to decide how much staff they need. That is why I use personnel spending as an additional dependent variable. There is a second reason why spending on personnel is a promising variable: the mayor is in charge of the administration and its staff; he needs the support of the people working for him to make his policy choices happen and to represent the administration (and hence her) in positive way when interacting with the inhabitants of the municipality. This is of particular importance as the German local administration is based on a merit system as opposed to a patronage system. A mayor will therefore always try to create a positive spirit among his staff – e.g. through wages, actual working hours, promotions and additions employees. [15] Moreover, due to the high share of transfers from higher government levels voters may not perceive that they actually have to pay for additional staff.

When considering the key taxes set at the local level (property tax, trade tax), I expect strong effects particularly in areas where the mayors can use tax cuts for gaining votes. This is particularly the case for the property tax B (on non-agricultural land) as it is borne by all voters. The trade tax is charged to companies which also employ many out-of-municipality staff and may be owned by out-of-municipality investors so tax cuts do not profit voters to their full extent. The property tax A is relatively unimportant (see table 1.1) and concerns only a small fraction of the voters so I only expect a small effect here.

1.5 Data

For this paper I have compiled a new data set covering key political, fiscal, and socioeconomic variables at the municipal level in Germany. I obtained data for the states of Hesse, Saarland, and Rhineland-Palatinate[16]. The data originates from the statistical offices of the respective states and the state election supervisors, and is available upon request. It comprises data for the 686 municipalities in the three states, of which 426 are in Hesse, 209 in Rhineland-Palatinate and 51 in Saarland. In Rhineland-Palatinate member municipalities of the joint municipalities are not included in the main data set, as in these municipalities mayors are elected on joint dates with the council and hence all held their first general mayor election at the same date[17]. Table 1.2 gives an overview over the years of the first mayoral election[18].

The data is on annual basis for the years 1990 to 2007 for Hesse (expenditures variables are only available from 1992 onwards) and is available for all municipalities in all these years. For both Saarland and Rhineland-Palatinate, data is available for the years

---

15 Furthermore, the staff of her administration represent an important group of voters.
16 Data on the first mayoral elections could not be obtained for the states of Lower-Saxony and Schleswig-Holstein which also use a phase in of the direct election of the mayor.
17 An extended version of that data set also included the data for the 2256 member municipalities of joint municipalities and is analyzed as sensitivity check.
18 In Rhineland-Palatinate the member municipalities of the joint municipalities are in charge of setting the tax rates. For this reason, the joint municipalities are excluded from the tax analysis. This leaves us with 49 municipalities in Rhineland-Palatinate that can be used for the tax analysis. Within this group the first mayor elections are also distributed over the years 1994 to 2001.

Table 1.2: First mayor elections

Year	Communities with first mayor elections			
	Total	Hesse	Saarland	Rhineland-Palatinate
1993	86	86	0	0
1994	111	85	4	24
1995	105	79	4	22
1996	108	85	5	18
1997	65	45	3	17
1998	70	46	5	19
1999	27	0	5	22
2000	26	0	7	19
2001	73	0	5	68
2002	4	0	4	0
2003	7	0	7	0
2004	2	0	2	0
Total	686	426	51	209

1992 to 2007 for all municipalities (expenditure variables are only available from 1995 onwards).

As dependent variables I use the per capita values of total expenditures of the municipality and personnel expenditures. The values are in euros and were not corrected for inflation as I use year fixed effects. On the revenue side I investigate the tax levels for the trade tax, the property tax for agricultural land "A", and the the property tax rate for all other land "B". The tax rates are multipliers of the tax base and are noted in points[19].

The explanatory variables in the data set include the dummy indicating that the new constitution is effective. I set the dummy to one for all years following the year of the first election and to zero for all previous years. The share of population over 65 and below 15 are also included. The variable relative economic strength covers differences in economic activity. It is constructed based on the tax base of the trade tax. Obviously the tax base of the trade tax and the tax rate of the same tax are interdependent. With

---

19 The tax amount due by the owner of e.g. a house is calculated based on the value of the house as defined by tax law (for the sum of ground and buildings). This value is then multiplied by a low number to identify the tax base (e.g. in the western part of Germany today either 0.0026 or 0.0035 depending on the value). This tax base is then multiplied with the tax rates (in "points") that the municipalities set. The tax amount for the trade tax is calculated equivalently but on the base of the trade tax which is mainly determined by the profit of the enterprise.

a higher tax rate one would expect a lower tax base. Hence, including the economic strength variable in the regressions that have the trade tax rate as dependent variable might lead to misspecification. For this reason I also estimate equations without the economic strength variable when estimating the constitutional effect on the the trade tax rate. To compute the economic strength variable, first, the tax base per capita is computed to measure the economic ability per capita in a certain year. Then, to account for the fact that the tax base is highly sensitive to the business cycle as it depends to a huge extent on the profits of the enterprises, the relative position of the municipality as compared to all municipalities is computed. This value is then denoted relative economic strength. The value can be negative as companies that have negative profit also count into the tax base. When analyzing tax levels joint municipalities in Rhineland-Palatinate were excluded from the analysis as they are not in charge of setting the tax rates for which their member municipalities are responsible. Table 1.3 gives an overview of summary statistics.

Table 1.3: Descriptive statistics of key variables

Variable	unit	mean	median	std. dev.	min	max	# obs.
Expenditure sample (including joint municipalities in Rhineland-Palatinate)							
Total exp. p.c.	EUR/cap.	1436.1	1342.3	455.6	16.9	10768.3	10246
Personnel exp. p.c.	EUR/cap.	310.8	295.6	96.6	2.17	1454.1	10246
Dummy new constitut.	yes/no	0.71	1	0.45	0	1	10246
Population density	inhab/km2	336.8	204.8	363.3	21.9	2672.8	10246
Share over 65	percent	17.5	17.4	2.9	8.4	31.2	10246
Share below 15	percent	16.0	16.0	1.6	10.0	2267	10246
Relative econ. strength	–	1.01	0.68	1.40	−2.10	52.96	10246
Tax sample (excluding joint municipalities in Rhineland-Palatinate)							
Rate trade tax	points	329.0	320	38.5	200	515	9266
Rate prop. tax A	points	260.7	260	43.7	0	450	9266
Rate prop. tax B	points	253.8	250	49.3	108	570	9266
Dummy new constitut.	yes/no	0.64	1	0.48	0	1	9266
Population density	inhab/km2	376.1	226.7	392.7	21.9	2672.8	9266
Share over 65	percent	17.2	17.0	3.0	8.1	31.2	9266
Share below 15	percent	15.9	15.9	1.7	9.9	22.7	9266
Relative econ. strength	–	1.06	0.70	1.49	−2.10	52.96	9266

All dependent variables increase over the time period when taking the population average. Table 1.4 summarizes this time trend. Both expenditure variables grow by about one and a half percent per year. There is also a clear trend to higher tax rates in the observed period. While the tax rate of the property tax on non-agricultural land increases by an average of 2.47 points per year, the rates for the trade tax and the tax on agricultural land only increase by 1.01 and 1.29 points respectively.

Table 1.4: Time trends for key dependent variables, 1992–2007

Variable	Average value (4 year intervals)				Growth 92–07
	92–95	96–99	00–03	04–07	
Total exp. p.c.	1366*	1371	1468	1560	1.70% p.a.**
Personnel exp. p.c.	285*	297	322	342	1.51% p.a.**
Rate trade tax	324	330	332	336	1.01 points p.a.
Rate prop. tax A	255	260	263	268	1.09 points p.a.
Rate prop. tax B	242	253	260	272	2.47 points p.a.

Note: Values for the tax rates do not include the joint municipalities in Rhineland-Palatinate as they are not in charge of setting the tax rates.
* 1995 value, as earlier data for Rhineland-Palatinate and Saarland not available
** Growth 1995–2007, as earlier data for Rhineland-Palatinate and Saarland not available

1.6 Results

In this section I highlight the empirical findings. First, I present the estimates based on the simple constitution dummy. Then, I discuss the results from the adjustment effects analysis and finally I turn to the sensitivity analysis.

1.6.1 Single constitution dummy

Table 1.5 presents the effects of the direct election of the mayor on the three key local tax rates, the trade tax, the property tax A (on agricultural land), and the property tax B (on non-agricultural land). For each of these taxes two specifications demonstrate the effects: the first includes only the dummy indicating the new constitution as well as year and municipality fixed effects. The second includes a set of further covariates.

The introduction of the new constitution reduced the tax rate on non-agricultural land by 1.91 points in the basic and by 2.06 points in the specification including additional covariates. Both estimates are significant at the five percent level. Compared to the median tax rate of 250 this is a reduction of about .8 percent – a relatively small effect. Regarding the trade tax and the property tax on non-agricultural land, I observe the expected negative signs. However, the point estimates are not significant[20].

---

20 I also estimated specification (6) excluding the economic strength variables for the trade tax to cover for potential endogeneity of the economic strength variable. There was only a small change in the other parameters estimated. I did the same for specification (6) in table 1.7 and could also only detect a marginal change.

The additional covariates have the expected signs. Population density increases the property tax on non-agricultural land by 0.41 points and decreases the tax on agricultural land by 0.18 points (at the five and ten percent significance level respectively), hence more densely populated municipalities tax non-agricultural land higher while rural areas tax agricultural land higher. There is no significant effect of the population density on the trade tax rate. Communities that have a stronger trade tax base, measured by the variable economic strength, have lower tax rates. The coefficient is -2.95 for the property tax B (significant at the 1 percent level). That means that a municipality that has a tax base that is twice as high as the average municipality has a tax rate that is 2.95 points lower. There also are negative effects (at the one percent level) on both property tax A and the trade tax. The share of the population above 65 significantly (at the one percent level) increases the tax on non-agricultural land. A one percentage points increase in the share of this age group increases this tax by 3.13 points. This hints that the municipalities try to cover income tax revenues lost when people retire by an increase in the property tax. There are no significant effects of the share of population over 65 on the property tax on agricultural land and the trade tax. The share of population under 15 years does not have any significant influence on the tax rates.

The hypothesis tested is that taxes are lower in presidential-type systems. In particular, I expected a strong effect on the property tax on non agricultural land, as cutting this tax profits all inhabitants and hence voters. For the same reason I expect a smaller effect for the tax rate for agricultural land and the trade tax as they only benefit small parts of the population. The estimates provide support for the hypothesis.

Table 1.6 depicts the constitutional effects on total expenditures per capita and personnel expenditures per capita. Regarding the latter, I find that in the simple regression that the new constitution increased spending by 4.80 euros and in the extended specification by 5.24 euros (both significant at the one percent level). The additional covariates are only partly significant. At the ten percent level, a one percentage point increase in the share of the older population increases personnel spending by 2.52 euros per capita while a one percentage point higher younger population reduces this spending by 2.97 euros. One might argue that the increased per capita spending under the new constitution is due to higher costs caused by a directly elected mayor. This is unlikely to be true as the post filled by the directly elected mayor existed before the reform too, only its way of appointment changed.

The results with respect to total government spending do not show a significant influence of the direct election of the mayor. The additional covariates, however, are highly significant and relatively large. Population density decreases total spending per capita, hence total spending in urban areas is lower. Communities with a higher tax base spend significantly more. The share of population under 15 has a strong positive effect on total spending. A one percentage point increase in this age group increases total spending by 24.76 euros. The share of the population over 65 does not have a significant influence.

These findings on the effect on spending confirm my expectations. While the literature predicts lower government spending in presidential systems in general I only expect small effects on total government spending in the case of the German municipalities as they only have limited discretion on this aggregate level. The results show no significant effects at all. When it comes to spending on personnel, municipalities have higher influence. As the literature predicts lower government spending one might expect lower personnel spending too. In the special case of the institutions governing municipal spending, I expect higher spending as the mayor is interested in motivating his staff through promotions, additional officers, etc. as she urgently needs them to make her policies happen and to convey a positive image of the administration among the voters. Furthermore, due to the high share of transfers voters may not perceive that they have to pay for additional staff. The estimates support this hypothesis.

1.6.2 Adjustment effects

Starting off from the results on the single constitution dummy I now present results describing pre- and post-adjustment effects using additional dummies for the two years before, the year of, and three years after the first mayoral election, compare equation 1.2.

The regressions with the tax levels as dependent variables are in table 1.7. After including the six additional dummies the effect on the new constitution is now -5.37 points in the simple model (significant at the five percent level) for the property tax B. The additional constitution dummies are not significant. After adding the set of additional covariates, the estimate for the constitution dummy is -4.82 points (now only significant at the ten percent level). Here, the dummies for the three years after the first election are positive and significant (at the ten percent level) and thus indicate that it took some time to adjust policy after the constitutional change. In the estimates of the trade tax I observe a different pattern. Here the dummies indicating the two years before the first election and the year of the first election are negative and significant at the five and one percent level (compare columns 5 and 6). This is interesting as the councils of the municipalities that switched the constitution lowered the trade tax knowing that a mayor would be elected soon. Looking at the constitution dummy in these specifications, I find that the magnitude of the dummy is higher than in the single dummy specification and now significant at the ten percent level in the simple specification (column (5)).

The estimations examining pre- and post-adjustment effects for the expenditures are presented in table 1.8. The dummy on the new constitution is now 10.47 in the simple specification and 11.43 when including the additional covariates (significant at the five percent level), about twice as high as in the single dummy specifications. When looking at the six additional dummies I find significant negative effects for the first three years after the first election. In the case of the full set of control variables these dummies are −4.51, −3.64, and −3.64 and are significant at the ten/five/one percent level. Together with the increased estimate on the the new constitution dummy these estimates indicate that policy takes time to adjust to the new rules – as in the case of the property tax on non-agricultural land discussed above. Regarding total spending there are, again, no significant effects of the constitutional switch.

1.6.3 Sensitivity analysis

With the aim to maintain the structure of the natural experiment characterized by the phasing in of the new constitutions in the three states I excluded the member municipalities of the joint municipalities in Rhineland-Palatinate so far. In these municipalities the term of the mayor is aligned with the term of the council and both elections are held at the same time. Hence, in all these municipalities, the first general mayor election occurred in the same year – 1994 (no phasing-in)[21]. Now, I include these municipalities in the analysis. The reasoning is that the fact and the date of the introduction of the direct mayor election was exogenous to these municipalities too – as it was to all other municipalities. From an econometric point of view the sheer number of these municipalities (2256, as compared to all other municipalities in the sample, 686) will add a lot of information and thus may help to improve results. Beyond the phasing in argument there is another reasoning why I present the results of this extended data set in the sensitivity analysis only: the control group for the member municipalities of joint municipalities is rather small as all of them change their constitution on the same date. As the data on expenditures for Rhineland-Palatinate only dates back to 1995 and the first mayoral election in the member municipalities of the joint municipalities occurred already in 1994 I cannot use these municipalities for drawing robust inference. Hence I only conduct the analysis including these municipalities for the tax rates.

Table 1.9 presents the effects of the single constitution dummy on the three tax rates. The estimated specifications are the same as in the main analysis presented above. The effect of the new constitution on the property tax B on non-agricultural land is −2.25 points in the basic specification and −2.19 in the specification including further covariates. Both coefficients are significant at the one percent level. The magnitude

---

21 In municipalities in where no candidate seeks the position of the mayor in the public election the mayor is elected by the council.

of these estimates is comparable to the estimates based on the smaller sample that are −1.91 and −2.06, respectively (significant at the 5 percent level). The estimates of the extended sample hence confirm the smaller sample estimates. Regarding the property tax A on agricultural land the estimated effects are now −1.63 and −1.68 and are significant at the five percent level. Compared to the estimates of the smaller sample significance is higher and the estimates are bigger in magnitude (the estimates of the smaller sample are −0.13 and −0.33 and are not significant). When it comes to the effect on the trade tax rate I find an effect of −2.56 and −2.54 in the extended sample (significant at the one percent level, compared to −0.99 and −1.04, not significant, in the smaller sample). As in the case of the property tax A, both magnitudes are higher in the extended sample[22].

The estimates for the other covariates in the larger sample are also similar the estimates in the smaller sample. Population density still increases the tax on non-agricultural land significantly and the economic strength of the municipalities exert a negative highly significant influence on the tax rate, the magnitude of the point estimates is with −0.77/−0.55/−0.38 on property tax A, B, and trade tax respectively, lower than in the smaller sample (−2.95/−1.89/−1.56). The share of the population over 65 is not significant for the property tax B (as it is in the smaller sample) but there is now a hint of a negative influence on the trade tax rate. The share of the population under 15 is now slightly significantly negative on the property tax B.

In the second specification that uses six additional dummies to gauge pre- and early post-adjustment effects (see table 1.10) the dummies indicating the new constitution are all significant and negative at the one percent level in the extended sample. In the smaller sample only the dummies for the property tax B and for the trade tax in the simple regression are significant at lower levels. The signs of the coefficients are negative in both samples while the magnitude is higher in the extended sample. They are now about 17/13/18 for property tax B, A, and trade tax respectively. The dummies indicating two and one years before and the year of the reform are all highly significant and negative and thus show a clear pre-adjustment effect before the reform. The councils cut tax rates ahead of the first direct mayoral election. This finding is in line with the smaller sample estimates regarding the trade tax, in the case of the property taxes these dummies are not significant in the smaller sample. When looking at the dummies indicating the first three years after the reform the estimates are now all positive and significant. The magnitudes decrease with every year and hence indicate that policy takes time to adjust to the new rules. In the limited sample these estimates are

---

22 As for the smaller sample I also estimated specification (6) excluding the economic strength variables for the trade tax to cover for potential endogeneity of the economic strength variable. There was only a small change in the other parameters estimated. I did the same for specification (6) in table 1.10 and could also only detect a marginal change.

not significant except for the case of the property tax B that shows the same pattern yet at a lower magnitude and significance.

Overall the findings of the sensitivity analysis support the results from the smaller sample. They confirm the negative influence and the magnitude of the direct election of the mayor on the property tax on non-agricultural land. They also give a clear indication that direct election of the mayor also reduces the trade tax and the property tax A, a view not backed by the analysis of the smaller sample. There is also strong support of the hypothesis that municipalities pre-adjust prior to the first election of the mayor by already cutting taxes and that the new rules take some time to reduce taxes to the full extent.

As a further robustness check adding to the specification that controls for pre- and post-adjustment effects (see equation 1.2) I explored the effects of a set of dummies each indicating a particular year after the reform. I use one dummy for every year after the constitutional switch[23]. The coefficients of these regressions are difficult to interpret[24]. Nonetheless, the estimates show no contradicting evidence to the results presented above. The tables are available upon request.

1.7 Summary and conclusions

In this paper I examine the effects of a change in the constitutional rules in the 686 municipalities in the German states of Hesse, Saarland, and Rhineland-Palatinate on the local tax rates and on expenditures. The aim is to estimate causal effects for the constitutional change that introduced the direct election of the mayor and can be regarded as a switch from a parliamentary to a presidential system. I drew causal inference based on the design of the constitutional switch in the selected states in the 1990s, which gradually phased in the new rules over a period of several years and was exogenous to the municipalities concerned.

To estimate the effects I use data at the municipality level for the period from 1990 to 2007 for Hesse and for 1992 to 2007 for Saarland and Rhineland-Palatinate. I find that presidentialism (when the mayor is elected by general election) compared to a parliamentary regime (when the mayor is elected by the municipality council) reduces the property tax on non-agricultural land by 2.06 points, a decrease of about .8 percent. I

---

23 Hence, equation 1.1 becomes:

$y_{it} = \alpha_i + \delta_t + \sum_l \beta_l d_{itl} + \sum_k \gamma_k x_{kit} + e_{it}$

where d_{itl} is a dummy indicating that in municipality i the first mayor election occurred l years ago from the point of view of year t.

24 E.g. a dummy indicating six years after the first election captures the effect of this sixth year compared to all other years – also including e.g. year five and seven in which the constitution was also effective.

do not find consistently significant effects of the direct election the trade tax and the property tax on agricultural land while there is evidence that the effect is negative too. These findings are in line with the theoretical predictions of the effects of presidentialism on taxes and the expectation that a mayor will rather try to reduce a tax that directly concerns all voters (property tax on non-agricultural land) than taxes that only concern some voters (property tax on agricultural land, trade tax).

Looking at spending I find that the direct election of the mayor increases spending on government personnel by 5.24 euros per capita, an increase of about 1.7 percent. Regarding total spending I do not find consistently significant estimates however there are is support in favor of higher spending. These results contradict the predictions of the literature that expects lower government spending in presidential systems but are in line with my expectations and a study on government spending in Lower Saxony. First, German municipalities only have limited decision power when it comes to spending as most expenditures are mandated by higher authorities. Second, the mayor in the German merit-based public administration needs the support of his staff for her policy and to create a good view of his administration among the voters.

In summary, I conclude that the introduction of the direct election of the mayor – albeit a small change in rules as her powers remained unaffected – significantly affects tax levels and government spending. Hence, the results confirm that constitutions matter economically at the local level. As the magnitude of the effects are rather small the implication for policy and normative public choice is that introducing a direct election of the (local) head of government should not be motivated by sympathy for lower taxes and lower or higher government spending.

Appendix

Characteristics of the local constitutions

South German Council Constitution. The South German Council Constitution (SGC), which has been in place in Bavaria and Baden-Württemberg since 1952, arranges for a strong and independent mayor while keeping the council relatively weak (März 2003, Wehling 2003). The mayor's power stems from a multitude of rights allocated to her by the constitution, which can be grouped in three categories. First of all, she presides the council and all its committees in which she has active voting rights. Secondly, she heads the municipality's monocratic administration. Finally, she represents the municipality both externally and internally. Hence, many functions are bundled in the hands of the mayor – a fact that also assures clear responsibilities. The mayor's independence is based on the rules of her designation: she is elected directly by the constituency and typically for a period that is longer than the election period of the council (e.g. in Baden-Württemberg eight years vs. five years for the council) (Wehling, 2003).

The council is referred to as the central body, the *Hauptorgan*, of the municipality in the local constitutions of both Baden-Württemberg and Bavaria (§24 I BWGO, Art. 29 BayGO). It is in charge of all administrative decisions of the municipality provided the mayor is not authorized to do so by law. The powers of the simple members of the council are limited through the mayor's right to set the agenda in both the council and the committees. The council members are elected by the local constituency based on a single election district. Voters have several votes equaling the number of seats in the council. The can allocate up to three votes on one candidate (cumulative) and spread their votes over different lists (vote-splitting).

In Baden-Württemberg elements of direct democracy have been in place all the time while they were only introduced in Bavaria in 1995 (Wehling, 2003) and can thus not be considered as a constituent element of the SGC.

Mayor Constitution.   Closest to the SGC is the Mayor Constitution (MAY) which used to be in place in Rhineland-Palatinate, Saarland, and in the rural municipalities in Schleswig-Holstein. It grants similar powers to the mayor as the SGC but provides less independence: she is elected by the council. The literature uses the term *True* Mayor constitution if the mayor has a vote in the council (formerly in Rhineland-Palatinate) and *False* Mayor constitution if the mayor does not have a vote in the council (formerly in Saarland)(Schrameyer 2006). The council used to be elected via party lists for which the voters could cast one vote. Elements of direct democracy were not in place.

North German Council Constitution.   The North German Council Constitution (NGC) is often described as the model providing the mayor with the least power of all constitutions. It was applied in Lower Saxony and North Rhine-Westphalia. In the NGC the mayor is elected by the council and must be one of its members. She is rather a chairperson than an independent political institution. The chairpersons of the committees were not identical with the mayor and were also elected by the council. While the mayor was in charge of the political leadership and the representation of the municipality, she did not lead the administration which was headed by the city director *(Stadtdirektor)* instead. The latter was merely in charge of executing the council's decisions. He was also elected by the council and could be recalled any time (Schrameyer 2006). When voting the council voters typically had a single vote while later more votes were introduced in Lower Saxony.

Magistrate Constitution. As opposed to the first three constitutional types that focus on individuals heading the municipality, the Magistrate Constitution (MAG) allocates the leadership of the municipality to a board (the magistrate) which is presided over by the mayor. The MAG is still effective in Hesse in an updated version and used to be the rule in the bigger municipalities in Schleswig-Holstein. The members of the magistrate, including the mayor, are elected by the council. The magistrate decides by majority and the mayor executes its decision. Furthermore the members of the magistrate must not be members of the council. Some of the members are full-time while others are nonsalaried. Typically the full-time members are in charge of the more important departments while the nonsalaried members take care of less time-consuming areas. In 1993 Hesse reformed its MAG by introducing direct election of the mayor while keeping her powers constant. When casting the ballot for the council voters typically had one vote. However Hesse introduced more votes and allowed for accumulating and splitting votes. (Schrameyer 2006).

Tables

Table 1.5: Effect on tax rates

	(1)	(2)	(3)	(4)	(5)	(6)
	prop. tax B rate		prop. tax A rate		trade tax rate	
new constitution	−1.91**	−2.06**	−0.13	−0.33	−0.99	−1.04
	(0.84)	(0.84)	(1.06)	(1.03)	(0.66)	(0.66)
pop. density		0.41***		−0.18*		0.07
		(0.09)		(0.10)		(0.05)
pop. density sq.		−0.00**		0.00		−0.00*
		(0.00)		(0.00)		(0.00)
econ. strength		−2.95***		−1.89***		−1.56***
		(0.93)		(0.54)		(0.40)
econ. strength sq.		0.03		0.02		0.02***
		(0.02)		(0.01)		(0.01)
share pop o. 65		3.13***		0.96		−0.13
		(0.69)		(0.97)		(0.50)
share pop u. 15		0.39		0.66		−0.82
		(0.79)		(0.79)		(0.53)
N	9266	9266	9266	9266	9266	9266
r2	0.39	0.43	0.09	0.11	0.23	0.25

* $p<0.10$, ** $p<0.05$, *** $p<0.01$, robust standard errors

Table 1.6: Effect on expenditures

| | (1) | (2) | (3) | (4) |
	total expenditure per capita		personnel expenditure per capita	
new constitution	4.86	6.89	4.80***	5.24***
	(14.47)	(13.80)	(1.66)	(1.61)
pop. density		−7.03***		−0.33
		(1.53)		(0.23)
pop. density sq.		0.00***		0.00
		(0.00)		(0.00)
econ. strength		90.19***		3.93
		(22.79)		(2.44)
econ strength sq.		−1.34**		−0.08
		(0.54)		(0.06)
share pop o. 65		−7.74		2.52*
		(9.30)		(1.53)
share pop u. 15		24.76***		−2.97*
		(9.20)		(1.63)
N	10246	10246	10246	10246
r2	0.12	0.17	0.36	0.37

* p<0.10, ** p<0.05, *** p<0.01, robust standard errors in parenthesis

Table 1.7: Effect on tax rates

	(1)	(2)	(3)	(4)	(5)	(6)
	prop. tax B rate		prop. tax A rate		trade tax rate	
new constitution	−5.37**	−4.82*	−0.38	−0.77	−2.98*	−2.91
	(2.69)	(2.63)	(3.32)	(3.24)	(1.75)	(1.77)
2 yr. bef. 1st elect	−1.30	−0.49	0.10	0.00	−1.74**	−1.66**
	(1.13)	(1.09)	(1.08)	(1.06)	(0.73)	(0.74)
1 yr. bef. 1st elect	−1.32	−0.38	0.42	0.25	−2.32**	−2.21**
	(1.44)	(1.39)	(1.44)	(1.42)	(0.95)	(0.96)
year of 1st elect.	−2.81	−1.88	0.15	−0.08	−3.29***	−3.20***
	(1.74)	(1.68)	(1.76)	(1.72)	(1.13)	(1.14)
1 yr. aft. 1st elect	1.68	1.88*	0.27	0.29	−0.88	−0.90
	(1.11)	(1.12)	(1.39)	(1.37)	(0.87)	(0.87)
2 yr. aft. 1st elect	1.38	1.57*	0.76	0.75	−0.46	−0.50
	(0.87)	(0.89)	(1.06)	(1.06)	(0.66)	(0.66)
3 yr. aft. 1st elect	0.98	1.25*	0.44	0.47	−0.51	−0.50
	(0.65)	(0.67)	(0.77)	(0.78)	(0.46)	(0.47)
pop. density		0.41***		−0.18*		0.07
		(0.09)		(0.10)		(0.05)
pop. density sq.		−0.00**		0.00		−0.00
		(0.00)		(0.00)		(0.00)
econ. strength		−2.95***		−1.89***		−1.56***
		(0.93)		(0.54)		(0.40)
econ strength sq.		0.03		0.02		0.02***
		(0.03)		(0.01)		(0.01)
share pop o. 65		3.14***		0.96		−0.17
		(0.69)		(0.97)		(0.50)
share pop u. 15		0.42		0.66		−0.79
		(0.79)		(0.79)		(0.53)
Constant	279.43***	90.17***	269.70***	294.10***	339.07***	341.16***
	(2.99)	(29.40)	(3.82)	(42.49)	(1.83)	(18.96)
N	9266	9266	9266	9266	9266	9266
r2	0.39	0.43	0.09	0.11	0.24	0.25

* p<0.10, ** p<0.05, *** p<0.01, robust standard errors in parenthesis

Table 1.8: Effect on expenditures

	(1)	(2)	(3)	(4)
	total expenditure p.c		personnel expenditure p.c.	
new constitution	23.34	20.59	10.47**	11.43**
	(39.49)	(37.58)	(4.84)	(4.69)
2 yr. bef. 1st elect	9.58	3.60	1.44	1.53
	(14.04)	(13.80)	(1.75)	(1.74)
1 yr. bef. 1st elect	4.78	−1.96	1.69	2.04
	(17.68)	(17.06)	(2.30)	(2.29)
year of 1st elect.	−0.22	−6.32	2.04	2.55
	(21.72)	(20.79)	(2.86)	(2.83)
1 yr. aft. 1st elect	−22.46	−23.35	−4.27*	−4.51*
	(18.57)	(17.80)	(2.48)	(2.42)
2 yr. aft. 1st elect	−11.29	−12.00	−3.54**	−3.64**
	(16.82)	(16.29)	(1.80)	(1.77)
3 yr. aft. 1st elect	−5.54	−6.86	−3.51**	−3.64***
	(11.99)	(12.14)	(1.38)	(1.37)
pop. density		−7.05***		−0.33
		(1.54)		(0.23)
pop. density sq.		0.00***		0.00
		(0.00)		(0.00)
econ. strength		90.19***		3.93
		(22.79)		(2.44)
econ strength sq.		−1.35**		−0.08
		(0.54)		(0.06)
share pop o. 65		−7.82		2.59*
		(9.30)		(1.54)
share pop u. 15		24.99***		−2.93*
		(9.23)		(1.62)
N	10246	10246	10246	10246
r2	0.12	0.17	0.36	0.37

* p<0.10, ** p<0.05, *** p<0.01, robust standard errors

Table 1.9: Effect on tax rates (extended sample)

	(1)	(2)	(3)	(4)	(5)	(6)
	prop. tax B rate		prop. tax A rate		trade tax rate	
new constitution	−2.25***	−2.19***	−1.63**	−1.68**	−2.56***	−2.54***
	(0.66)	(0.66)	(0.73)	(0.73)	(0.55)	(0.55)
pop. density		0.15***		−0.06		−0.03
		(0.04)		(0.04)		(0.03)
pop. density sq.		−0.00		0.00		−0.00
		(0.00)		(0.00)		(0.00)
econ. strength		−0.77***		−0.55***		−0.38***
		(0.18)		(0.12)		(0.10)
econ strength sq.		0.01**		0.01***		0.00**
		(0.00)		(0.00)		(0.00)
share pop o. 65		0.20		−0.03		−0.17*
		(0.17)		(0.11)		(0.10)
share pop u. 15		−0.28*		−0.06		−0.09
		(0.16)		(0.10)		(0.13)
N	45345	45343	45344	45342	45345	45343
r2	0.55	0.55	0.35	0.35	0.40	0.41

* $p<0.10$, ** $p<0.05$, *** $p<0.01$, robust standard errors in parenthesis

Table 1.10: Effect on tax rates (extended sample)

	(1)	(2)	(3)	(4)	(5)	(6)
	prop. tax B rate		prop. tax A rate		trade tax rate	
new constitution	−16.73***	−16.82***	−13.44***	−13.38***	−17.91***	−17.63***
	(2.29)	(2.28)	(2.28)	(2.25)	(1.59)	(1.59)
2 yr. bef. 1st elect	−9.13***	−9.40***	−7.90***	−7.72***	−8.72***	−8.50***
	(1.03)	(1.03)	(0.92)	(0.90)	(0.71)	(0.71)
1 yr. bef. 1st elect	−9.45***	−9.69***	−8.50***	−8.40***	−10.53***	−10.34***
	(1.28)	(1.27)	(1.15)	(1.13)	(0.88)	(0.89)
year of 1st elect.	−10.74***	−10.96***	−9.77***	−9.65***	−13.22***	−12.98***
	(1.49)	(1.49)	(1.41)	(1.38)	(1.04)	(1.04)
1 yr. aft. 1st elect	5.49***	5.36***	3.30***	3.32***	4.37***	4.31***
	(0.93)	(0.92)	(0.81)	(0.80)	(0.72)	(0.72)
2 yr. aft. 1st elect	3.11***	3.02***	1.99***	2.01***	2.99***	2.95***
	(0.72)	(0.72)	(0.64)	(0.64)	(0.54)	(0.54)
3 yr. aft. 1st elect	1.87***	1.81***	1.11**	1.11**	1.66***	1.62***
	(0.53)	(0.52)	(0.46)	(0.46)	(0.38)	(0.38)
pop. density		0.15***		−0.06		−0.02
		(0.04)		(0.04)		(0.03)
pop. density sq.		−0.00		0.00		−0.00
		(0.00)		(0.00)		(0.00)
econ. strength		−0.76***		−0.54***		−0.37***
		(0.17)		(0.11)		(0.10)
econ strength sq.		0.01**		0.01***		0.00**
		(0.00)		(0.00)		(0.00)
share pop o. 65		0.28		0.03		−0.09
		(0.17)		(0.11)		(0.10)
share pop u. 15		−0.25		−0.03		−0.05
		(0.17)		(0.10)		(0.13)
N	45345	45343	45344	45342	45345	45343
r2	0.55	0.56	0.35	0.35	0.41	0.41

* p<0.10, ** p<0.05, *** p<0.01 robust standard errors in parenthesis

Chapter 2: Divided government versus incumbency externality effect

Quasi-experimental evidence on multiple voting decisions[1]

Abstract:

This paper explores the interdependency of political institutions from the voter's perspective. Specifically, we are interested in: (1) Does the partisan identity of the mayor influence the voter's decision in the subsequent town council election?; (2) Does this partisan identity influence the vote in ensuing higher level elections?; and (3) Do voters condition their vote for the mayor on the result of the last council election? We rely on a regression discontinuity design focusing on close election outcomes based on municipal level data for Germany. We find (1) that the party of the mayor can receive a bonus of 4–6 percentage points in vote share in the next town council election (depending on the timing of the local elections). (2) The mayor partisan identity does not affect federal or European election outcomes within the same municipality. And (3), we show that voters punish mayor candidates of parties that performed strongly in earlier council elections. Throughout the paper, we explore how the findings can be related to an incumbency externality effect and to the theory of voter preferences for divided government.

2.1 Introduction

In modern democracies political power is divided in two different ways: between tiers of government (supranational, federal, state, and municipal levels) as well as between

---

1   This chapter is joint work with Ronny Freier. Acknowledgments: We would like to thank Charles B. Blankart, Tore Ellingsen, Mikael Elinder, Olle Folke, Frank Fossen, Benny Geys, Jens Hainmueller, Magnus Johannesson, Juanna Joensen, Henrik Jordahl, Holger Kern, Erik Lindqvist, Christian Odendahl, Yaniv Reingewertz, Carsten Schröder, David Strömberg, Marvin Süsse as well as participants at the Annual Meeting of the EPCS in Izmir and the seminars at IIES (Stockholm) and DIW (Berlin). Comments of colleagues at DIW Berlin and Princeton University are also gratefully acknowledged. Our particular gratitude goes to Viktor Steiner and Peter Haan who invited us to work at their Department for Public Economics at the DIW Berlin and gave valuable comments and advice. Furthermore, we would like to thank Helke Seitz, Jenny Freier and Heike Hauswald who provided excellent research assistance to help us organize the data. Ronny Freier would like to thank the Hedelius foundation for funding the research visit to Princeton University and the Jan Wallander and Tom Hedelius Foundation for generous financial support. We are further grateful for editorial support from Adam Lederer. The usual disclaimer applies.

several institutions within a given tier (e.g. president and parliament, mayor and town council). As the policy outcomes depend on the complex interactions between these tiers of government and their institutions, we expect voters to be concerned with making the best decision within this system of political integration.

This paper studies voting behavior in the presence of interdependencies between political institutions. We focus on how voters react to the realization of the outcome in the election of one institution when they decide on another political body. Specifically, we investigate three questions: (1) Does the partisanship of the mayor influence the vote outcome of her party in the subsequent town council election?; (2) Is the party identity of the mayor relevant to the election results in subsequent higher level elections?; and (3) Do voters condition their votes in the mayoral election on the result in the town council election that was just previously held?

For elections at the local level, we find (1) that the partisanship of the mayor can matter for the election outcome of her party in the next town council election. Crucially, the results depend on the timing of the two elections. If the elections are held jointly (meaning that the next town council election is held at the same day as the next mayoral election), the party of the incumbent mayor receives a significant and sizable bonus of around 4–6 percentage points in vote share. If elections do *not* run simultaneously, however, the party of the mayor does *not* profit from holding the office. (2) From the analysis for German federal and European elections, we conclude that the partisan identity of the mayor exerts *no* effect on elections at those levels.

Finally, we show (3) that a party's outcome in a council election also affects the next mayoral election. For an additional 10 percentage points in the vote share for the town council election, the party's candidate a the run-off mayor election will see her vote share be reduced by 2.5 percentage points.

We consider two key theories that apply to our analysis: an incumbency externality effect from the mayor's office and the theory of voter preferences for divided government. For the case of council elections, the first is expected to increase votes for the mayor's party while the second would decrease the voters' support for her party. The empirical evidence suggests that under specific circumstances both the incumbency externality effect as well as an effect of the preference for divided government are of importance. Under some simplification, we argue that the incumbency externality effect is evident in the analysis of joint local elections, while the divided government effect can be observed in the mayoral run-off elections, and that both effects are present when the mayoral election precedes the council election.

The main conjecture of the incumbency externality effect is that the position of the mayor provides access to resources that determine the election outcomes for other institutions. Such resources can be both direct financial resources[2] as well as non-monetary aspects, such as media presence for the party and time spent with the electorate during the election period.[3] For example Hainmueller and Kern (2008) find that in mixed electoral systems a party can increase its vote share in the proportional vote when it provides the direct representative of the electoral district, thus identifying an incumbency externality effect of about 1.5 percent. Folke (2010) presents evidence for a spillover effect from government personnel nominated by the patronage system to their party. In spirit, the incumbency externality effect is similar to the well-documented electoral advantage that incumbent office holders receive (see Lee (2008) for US house representatives, Ferreira and Gyourko (2009) for US mayors, Freier (2011) for German mayors).

The theory of preferences for a divided government prescribes a strategic rational to vote for different parties in elections for distinct institutions to establish a political balance. This effect works in the opposite direction as the incumbency externality effect (see Alesina and Rosenthal (1996), Kern and Hainmueller (2006)). The voter is presented with two distinct opportunities (mayor and council election) to make a decision on the political actors governing the community. A rational median voter might prefer to hedge against extreme policy positions in local government by splitting the vote in the two elections and dividing the governmental power between different parties. By electing, for example, a conservative mayor yet a social democratic council the median voter can assure that policy outcomes will be balanced within the ideological spectrum.

At the Federal level in the United States, it is well established that there is a preference for divided government (or electoral balancing). The president's party typically loses seats during Congressional midterm elections (see e.g. Erikson (1988)). The same pattern can also be observed for other countries and at other levels of government (e.g. Norris and Feigert (1989), Folke and Snyder (2010)). While it is straightforward that divided government can occur in a presidential democracy (when the president and the majority in parliament are not from the same party), divided government can also exist in parliamentary systems. Here, divided government can occur via a second chamber

---

2   In local German politics it is, for example, very common that elected officials contribute part of their wages/compensation directly to the account of their party. As funding of political campaigns is not very lavish in German politics, particularly for local politics, the funds offered by elected officials often make for a major share of the campaign budgets in the local elections.

3   Apart from managing the administration of the community and framing public policy, the schedule of German mayors is packed with many social events in the community. At openings of kindergartens, elderly homes, and bowling alleys, the mayors not only promote themselves but is also expected to advertise their party.

of parliament. Kern and Hainmueller (2006) present evidence for electoral balancing in the German parliamentary system at the federal level.

Given the two theories of incumbency externality and divided government it is straightforward to ask why we observe that they differ in their intensity depending on election timing. There are three main avenues of theoretical considerations to explain this phenomenon laid out below. The first avenue (1) are considerations regarding the available information, the second (2) avenue is the median voter hypothesis and the third (3) is non-standard preference considerations.

(1) The timing of the elections is decisive in to what extent the voter can use the elections to establish her preference for divided government. When elections are held sequentially, the voter can actively condition her vote on the outcome of the first election. If, for instance, a conservative candidate wins the mayoral election, the voter can take a deliberate decision to elect social democrats in the next council election. When the elections are held simultaneously, however, the incentives to behave strategically in this way are blurred as the outcomes of the respective elections are uncertain (see Alesina and Rosenthal (1995)). On the other hand the mechanisms of the incumbency externality effect depend on the precise timing of the interacted elections. When elections are held at the same time, the election campaign effort of a party can, for example, capitalize on synergy effects or on a positive personality of a candidate running for the other election (e.g. Mondak (1990)).[4]

(2) From a standard preferences point of view the median voter[5] may trigger the different behaviour. As discussed above the median voter is likely to vote for one party in the mayor and the other in the council to achieve a policy outcome in the middle. In the case of subsequent elections the median voter knows who won the first election and can vote in the ensuing election accordingly. However, in the case of simultaneous elections the median voters can split their tickets too but as they do not know whom the others vote it is much more unlikely to observe this median voter-divided government effect in the data.

(3) From a non-standard preference/behavioral point of view cognitive dissonance (or: the aim of the voter to minimize the psychic cost of voting[6]) may play an important role. This logic can be applied to the timing of elections as follows:

---

4 It is a reasonably well-documented fact, for example, that electoral campaigns for positions in the US Senate and the House of Representatives have better prospects for individual candidates, if their campaigns run simultaneously with the election for a US president and this race has a charismatic, winning presidential candidate from their party (e.g. Campbell and Sumners (1990), Ferejohn and Calvert (1984)). The same is shown to apply to gubernatorial elections, e.g. Hogan (2005).

5 See Mueller (2007, chap. 5) for an introduction to the concept.

6 see Kirchgaessner (1992) and Kirchgaessner and Pommerehne (1993)

Simultaneous mayor and council elections. If we assume that incumbent mayors have an advantage when running again for office (as Freier (2011) shows) then there must be a positive incumbency externality on simultaneous council elections. This is because voters minimize psychic costs that arise when voting for different parties on the same ballot[7]. Empirically, this theoretical prediction has been tested by Mondak and McCurley (1994) who find that voters employ their evaluations of presidential candidates in the US to decide which House candidate to support in order to increase their cognitive efficiency.

Subsequent elections. If voters are myopic and may have forgotten whom they voted for in the preceding mayoral election or at least if this is less present for some then psychic costs of voting different parties will be lower than in the simultaneous case and a second mechanism of psychic costs may prevail: voters will vote according to their true preferences to minimize psychic costs as Kirchgaessner (1992) and Kirchgaessner and Pommerehne (1993) argue. This leads to a lower incumbency externality. In this case of subsequent elections yet another theoretical reasoning might explain why we do not observe an incumbency effect in the data – voters vote for a program in the case of the mayor election and for representation in the case of the council election[8] With myopic voters and subsequent elections one should then not expect large interactions between the two elections.

Another behavioral/non-standard preference explanation why voters might behave differently when elections are or are not simultaneous is the expressive voter hypothesis (see e.g. Fiorina (1976) and Brennan and Buchanan (1984)). Here voters may vote to express opinion as they are aware that their individual vote does not affect the outcome. In the case of this paper one could imagine that voters want to express that they are good and aware citizens by not voting in favor of unified government (even though their personal interest may be to have one of the parties to control both the mayor office and the council). They might be motivated e.g. by the lessons from the rise of autocratic regimes. In the case of non-simultaneous elections this form of expressive

---

7   Given the incumbency effects for mayors a large number of voters would have to do that if there was no incumbency externality.

8   Blankart and Mueller (2004) present features of two polar cases of representative democracy – pure representative-proportional democracy and pure two party competition – and argue that each has evident advantages over mixed systems. In the pure representative-proportional democracy all sets of voter preferences are directly proportionally represented in parliament which is attained through a transferable vote system. In the pure two party competition there is a single district and run-off elections leading to two parties only. In this system voters choose a program whose implementation they monitor and for which they can easily hold the government accountable. Transferring the idea of these two extreme cases to the local voting system in Germany one finds that the council election is oriented towards representation and proportion (More strongly in those states which allow to vote for individual candidates than in those with closed lists) while the mayor election leans toward two party/competitor competition where voters choose a program (as voting *representation* is hardly possible with just two parties).

voting is easily possible as voters know the result of the other election while with joint elections voting expressively in this sense is difficult as the result of the mayor election is not known when voting for the council and vice versa.

Our analysis is based on a unique and detailed data set of election results at the municipal level in Germany. Overall, we use more than 9,500 elections in the analysis for interdependencies at the local level. To evaluate the effect on higher levels of elections we rely on 18,000 observations for the European elections and 35,000 German federal election observations.

Methodologically, the main analysis relies on a regression discontinuity design to draw causal inference. The crucial argument is that we can identify exogenous variation in the party identity of the mayor by focusing on close election outcomes. We assume that the specific election outcomes are subject to some random component (e.g. shocks in the popularity of the party due to recent media coverage, shocks in turnout due to the weather, see Knack (1994.)). Given that a mayoral election was a very close race, the outcome of that election (the party identity of the mayor) can be seen as a quasi-random event. Lee (2008) was the first to use this methodology to investigate the incumbency advantage for individual seats held by a party in the US House of Representatives.[9] Following Lee's analysis, Ferreira and Gyourko (2009) study the effects of incumbency on a large number of mayoral elections in US cities. They find an effect of incumbency of about 32 percentage points for the probability of reelection. For German mayors, Freier (2011) also documents a substantial party incumbency effect in the order of 38–40 percent in the probability of winning the mayor office.[10]

Following the growing body of literature using the regression discontinuity design in election analysis, Caughey and Sekhon (2010) reassess the study of Lee (2008) and show that the identifying assumptions of the design do not necessarily hold, thus, casting a shadow of doubt on the identification strategy.[11] However, our detailed tests on

---

9   Lee analyzes the effect of obtaining the incumbency status for a party on the probability of winning the race for the district in the present election. He estimates the incumbency advantage to constitute a 45 percentage points higher probability of winning the race for a district. With his quasi-experimental approach, he is the first to produce reliable estimates of the magnitude of the effects of incumbency. Note that, Pettersson-Lidbom (2008) was the first to use the idea of close elections to identify party effects in spending of Swedish municipalities.

10   There are several other studies applying the ideas of the regression discontinuity design to elections. E.g. Chamon, de Mello, and Firpo (2009), Titiunik (2009) for Brazilian municipalities, Eggers and Hainmueller (2009) for Members of Parliament in the UK, Linden (2004), Uppal (2005) for Indian parliamentary elections, Miguel and Zahidi (2004) for national elections in Ghana, Meyersson (2009) for Turkish municipalities, Gagliarducci and Nannini (2009) for Italian politicians, see Caughey and Sekhon (2010) for an overview.

11   They show that there are significant predetermined differences between candidates who just won and just lost their races. Among those differences are that marginal winners have more campaign money, are

the validity of the RDD show no sign that the credibility of the identifying assumptions are of concern in our analysis.

Apart from the main RDD analysis, we consider an additional design that makes use of the precise timing of local elections in the German electoral system. This design relies on second ballots (run-off elections) in cases where the first round of the mayoral race is held simultaneously with the council election and no candidate received the necessary majority. This provides an unique opportunity to evaluate whether the voter subsequently conditions her vote in the run-off election on the outcome of the town council election. Identification can be obtained by conditioning on the results of the first round of the mayor election. Thereby, we can exclude unobservable characteristics (individual mayor candidate characteristics, popularity shocks for individual parties, etc.) and consistently estimate the impact of the town council election result. Given that there is no incumbency externality effects at work, the result can be attributed only to a preference consideration of the voter.

The remaining part of the paper is structured as follows: Section 2 introduces the basic features of local government in Germany that are relevant for the empirical analysis. Section 3 highlights the characteristics of the underlying data. In section 4, we describe the empirical methodology and derive the empirical model, before section 5 presents the results. Conclusions are drawn in section 6.

2.2   Institutional background: voting rules and local government

To understand the implications of the local institutional features for our analysis we present information on the voting systems and rules as well as the key properties of local governments in Germany. The results of this paper are based on elections in eight of the sixteen German states for which data is available and institutions are comparable (see table 2.1 for an overview of the states and elections included).

more likely to belong to the party that won the last election, and are more often the predicted winner in the journal "Congressional Quarterly". The authors conclude that tight elections might differ from other elections, as their tightness is often known to both campaigners and voters, hence, e.g. more money is directed at those tight races since its expected payoff is highest. While these arguments are of great importance for US-House elections which are characterized by detailed media coverage, a multitude of polls and high campaign spending, these arguments do not apply to the elections we investigate: as they are at the local level that is characterized by very small districts (communities and cities) there are hardly ever polls available, relatively low campaign spendings, and media coverage is usually limited to the local section of the regional newspaper.

Table 2.1: Data set – number of observations and elections

	Design 1	Design 2	Center -Left	Center -Right	# communities in 2001	# of election dates[a]
Bavaria	6595		2421	4174	2100	5
Thuringia	495		120	375	992	2
Brandenburg[b]	156	52	109	99	420	1
Rhineland-Palatinate		93	45	48	212	2
Hesse		1399	768	631	430	3
Saarland		108	54	54	52	2
Saxony-Anhalt		280	103	177	1118	1
Saxony		398	115	283	520	1
Total	7246	2330	3735	5841	5844	17

a The council election years are: Bavaria 1984, 1990, 1996, 2002, 2008; Thuringia 1999, 2004; Brandenburg 2008; Rhineland-Palatinate 1999, 2004; Hesse 1997, 2001, 2006; Saarland 1999, 2004; Saxony-Anhalt 2004; Saxony 2008.

b: Brandenburg is the only state in which we have observations in both designs. This is, because larger cities have different term lengths for the mayor and the council election whereas in small communities the term lengths of mayor and council coincide and elections are held simultaneously. *Source*: Own calculation based on the data provided by the state offices for statistical services.

2.2.1 Voting system and rules

There are two important elections at the community level in Germany: elections for the position of the mayor and elections for the members of the town council. In all states under consideration the voters in a community elect the mayor through a majority vote and the council in a proportional election.

In the majoritarian election for the mayor, a party gains control over the mayor's office if the candidate obtains a simple majority of the votes. Mayoral elections are held every five to eight years[12] and are held on fixed state-wide dates in Bavaria, Thuringia, and Brandenburg (part-time mayors) and on community-individual dates in the other states.[13] Another feature that is crucial for the correct implementation of our design is the presence of a second (or run-off) ballot. If no candidate reaches the majority of

---

12 Five years in Brandenburg (part-time mayors) and Thuringia, six years in Hesse and Bavaria, seven years in Saxony and Saxony-Anhalt, eight years in Saarland, Rhineland-Palatinate, and in Brandenburg (full-time mayors).

13 In Brandenburg the elections of the full-time mayors are also community-individual.

50% in the first ballot, a second ballot is held between the two leading candidates.[14] As the second ballot determines the victor in the mayoral race, we use the results of this second ballot if applicable. It is also interesting to note that it can occur that only one candidate runs for office and that, in some cases, parties can join forces to nominate a common candidate (see detailed description in the data appendix).

Council elections are held every four years in Rhineland-Palatinate, five years in Hesse, Saarland, Saxony, Saxony-Anhalt, Brandenburg, and Thuringia[15], and six years in Bavaria. Hence, in some states the term length of the mayor and the council are identical. In these states (Bavaria, Thuringia, and in communities with non-salaried mayors in Brandenburg) the elections for mayor and council are held on the same day. We denote these states as "Design 1" and the states with asynchronous elections as "Design 2". The choice of the two designs is exogenous to our analysis: First, the term length of local institutions and the alignment of elections is subject to state legislation. Hence, the communities have no direct influence on these rules. Second, the choice of a asynchronous or harmonized election scheme typically dates back to the time when the states were founded or results from legal obligations. Rhineland-Palatinate, Hesse, and Saarland introduced the direct election of the mayor only in the 1990s. When doing this the communities had to honor the term of the previous, purely administrative, heads of the local administrations. Their terms were of different length and ended at different dates hence causing mayoral and council elections to be asynchronous until today.

In the analysis we also consider the effect of the mayoral position on elections in other tiers of the state structure. Specifically, we look at elections for the European parliament and the German federal parliament (*Bundestag*). It is important to note that those higher level elections are hardly ever simultaneous with the local elections in any of the data that we collected.

2.2.2 Local government

The political and administrative structure of Germany is organized into four tiers. The four tiers consist of the federal level, sixteen states, about 450 counties and just over 12500 municipalities (as of 2006). While the federal government is involved in nearly all branches of state activity, the remaining tiers each have specific responsibilities.[16] The municipal level takes direct responsibilities for the provision of public goods in

---

14 In the state of Saxony all candidates can join in the second round of a mayor elections and the candidate with the largest vote share wins the office.

15 In Hesse, prior to 2001, every four years.

16 Education, for example, is in the responsibility of the state, whereas counties are generally concerned with the administration of public order issues (police, fire rescue) and health (hospitals, ambulances).

the areas of child care, cultural expenditures, sport and recreational facilities, local infrastructure investments as well as a number of minor tasks. Communities also often oversee public firms that deliver local services (e.g. energy and water supply) and administer mandated spending allocated by higher tiers (like social services, investment in schools, and certain infrastructural investments). In total, the local governments administrates and oversees about two thirds of all state investment. About 40 percent of all state employees work for municipalities.[17]

The mayor and the council jointly govern the community. The responsibilities of the mayor include the daily administration of the community, leading personnel, representing the community and making urgent decisions. The council is in charge of all general decisions of both legislative and administrative quality. It follows that, on the one hand, the mayor needs the support of a majority in the council to realize her policy goals and, on the other hand, any council majority will have a hard time pushing through projects against the will of the mayor. This is true in all states considered in this analysis. The exact distribution of power between the two political institutions at the local level is regulated by state law that specifies the precise nature of the interaction (e.g. does the mayor have an active voting right in council meetings).

While these regulations differ in each state, we stress that these differences in legislation would only matter to our analysis if they were recognized by the voters. A clear indication that this is not the case is that the electoral advantage of mayors in different states is generally very similar (around 38–41 percentage points). Freier (2011) studies the mayor incumbency advantage for German mayors in more detail. He finds no significant difference for the incumbency effects in different German states. However, we further test this assumption implicitly in the results section.

2.3   Data and descriptive statistics

We use data from the German states of Hesse, Rhineland-Palatinate, Bavaria, Saarland, Brandenburg, Saxony-Anhalt, Saxony, and Thuringia. We obtained information on both mayor and town council elections for several years from the statistical office of each respective state. Data for further years and the remaining German states was either not available or cannot be used due to differing institutional design (e.g. in the city-states). We also collected data on the results of European and German federal elections at the municipal level. On the basis of this data set, we are able to link the specific election outcomes in a municipality with information about the party identity of the mayor at the time when the election was held.

---

17   See Bundesbank (2007).

For all mayoral elections in the data we have the number of valid votes as well as the result for each candidate in the race for the mayor's office. From this data we can extract the exact vote share for each candidate (party) and identify how close each election was. For all other elections (town council, European and federal elections), we collected the number of valid votes as well as the votes for each participating party. For the analysis, we are interested in linking the results from the mayoral races with the outcomes from the other elections. We limit the analysis to results for the center-left (SPD – Sozialdemokratische Partei Deutschlands) and the center-right (CDU/CSU – Christlich Demokratische Union/Christlich Soziale Union) party because they are the only parties that participate regularly at all levels of the political structure (for further details see data appendix).

Table 2.1 provides an overview of the main data set in which we link each town council election with the preceding mayoral election in the respective community. Overall we have 9,576 such election pairs in 5,844 communities. The number of observations is derived as follows: In each state, we observe a number of town council election dates (see column 6) when each community (see column 5) in the state elects its town council. In Hesse, for example, we observe community councils elected three times (1997, 2001, 2006) in all 430 communities. For each election we match the preceding mayoral election to the data. One observation for our analysis now is given if we can identify either the center-left or the center-right party to have participated in the town council election *and* there is a result for a candidate of the respective party also in the preceding mayor election (see data appendix for detailed description of the data limitations). It is important to note, that a particular community may thus generate two observations in one election (one for each of the two parties).[18]

As discussed in the section on the institutional background, some states hold council and mayor elections simultaneously (see observations in column 1 denoted 'Design 1') while other have differing term lengths and, hence, different election days and years (column 2 denoted 'Design 2'). We have a total of 7246 election pairs in Design 1 and 2330 in Design 2. Overall the state of Bavaria plays a central role in our data set with 6595 of the 9576 observations. This is due to good data availability combined with a large number of communities.

Table 2.2 presents the number of observations in different subsamples relevant for our analysis. We estimate our models within the 60 percent margin of victory in the mayor election to make sure that extreme cases do not drive our estimates at the threshold via the control function. That means that we exclude all cases where the difference

---

18 Note that those two parties are seldom the only parties running in mayoral or council elections. To respect the fact that the results are nevertheless linked within the same council election, we cluster all standard errors in the analysis at the level of each election within the municipality.

Table 2.2: Data set – defining different samples

	Design 1			Design 2		
	Total	Center -Right	Center -Left	Total	Center -Right	Center -Left
# of observations						
total	7246	4626	2620	2330	1215	1115
within 60% margin	5677	3371	2306	1968	1011	957
# of narrow observations						
within 5% margin	514	335	179	201	111	90
within 2% margin	219	140	79	83	45	38
within 1% margin	95	59	36	43	24	19

Notes: 'Margin' in this table means the difference in percentage points between the winner and the best opponent. For example, in the case of only two candidates a margin of 5 percent means that the winner may have gotten at most 52.5 percent while the other got 47.5 percent. *Source*: Own calculations based on the data provided by the state offices for statistical services.

between the candidate with the most votes and her best opponent is more than 60 percent.[19] Applying this limitation we lose 1569 observations, of which most are cases where only one candidate ran for office. Table 2.2 also gives information on the observations that represent tight races in the mayor election. For example, in the case of only two candidates a margin of 5 percent means that the winner received less then 52.5 percent while the challenger got more than 47.5 percent. For Design 1 we have 514/219/95 tight races in the 5/2/1 percent margin respectively. For Design 2 there are 201/83/43 tight races in the three margins, respectively.

To test the effect of the incumbent mayor's party on higher level elections, we collected data on European and German federal elections in the municipalities. The numbers of observations and the corresponding elections years are presented in table 2.6 in the appendix. As in the case of council elections, the total number of observations is different from the product of the communities times the election date for the same reasons.[20] In general, data for higher government level elections is almost always available (in contrast to local election results). We have a total of 18,000 observations for the European elections and 35,194 observations for the federal elections. Note that the number of actual observations in the estimation tables will be lower as we

---

19 For clarity, consider the following example. In the case of only two candidates we exclude cases where the winner has more than 80 percent of the vote (hence, the second best opponent has 20 percent and the margin of victory is 60 percent). It would be hard to argue that these cases could contribute anything to (even via a flexible control function) the tight races in which we are interested in.

20 However, we did not have to exclude any observation for non participation in the European/federal election as both parties participated in these elections in all communities.

exclude elections pairs with extreme mayor elections (more than 60 percent margin of victory). European elections are held every five years and federal elections every four years. Both elections are almost never held simultaneously with local elections.

2.4 Empirical model and methodology

The main empirical strategy is based on a Regression Discontinuity Design (RDD). The treatment under consideration is the mayor incumbency of a party. We denote treatment with the dummy variable $d_{i,t}^p$, where i refers to the community or town for which we observe elections, t refers to the election year[21] and p refers to the party under consideration. The variable that unambiguously determines treatment in our application is the margin of victory, $v_{i,t}^p$, which is defined as the distance in the vote share of party p in the mayoral election in t to the best opponent. The decisive threshold that the so-called score variable $v_{i,t}^p$ has to cross is $v_0 = 0$. The relationship between $d_{i,t}^p$ and $v_{i,t}^p$ is as follows:

$$d_{i,t}^p = 1 \left[v_{i,t-1}^p > 0 \right] \tag{2.1}$$

This implies that the incumbency is earned if the party won first place in the preceding election. The outcome variables that we are interested in are denoted $y_{i,t}^p$. In particular, we consider the election outcomes of party p in the subsequent elections. Firstly, we measure the vote share of the party in the following town council election. The object of interest here is the evaluation of the effect of an incumbent mayor on the election results in the following town council election for her party. Secondly, we investigate the effect for the party in subsequent elections for both the European parliament and the *Bundestag* (German Parliament).

To estimate the causal effect of incumbency of a party on subsequent election outcomes we follow Pettersson-Lidbom (2008), Lee (2008) and Hainmueller and Kern (2008) (see also Hahn, Todd, and van der Klaauw (2001)). The basic model is given by:

$$y_{i,t}^p = \delta_0 + \delta_1 d_{i,t}^p + c_{i,t} \quad for \quad |v_{i,t-1}^p| < \Delta \tag{2.2}$$

where δ_1 is the parameter of interest. This approach is often denoted as a limited sample approach. The regression relies solely on observations within some small margin Δ close to the threshold. As an alternative to the limited sample approach, we also

---

21 The timing with the t index is specific. The incumbency status of a certain mayor is determined in $t - 1$. Henceforth, the party's candidate holds the relevant mayor position, which is indicated by $d_{i,t}^p$. We use the index t (instead of $t - 1$) to illustrate that the mayor holds this position also when the next election is held in t.

implement a RDD using a control function design:

$$y_{i,t}^p = \delta_0 + \delta_1 d_{i,t}^p + h(v_{i,t-1}^p, \theta) + \varepsilon_{i,t} \qquad (2.3)$$

where $h(\cdot)$ is some function that represents the influence of the margin of victory in the preceding mayor election on the voting outcome $y_{i,t}^p$. In this alternative specification, we run the estimation on the entire sample.[22]

The RDD makes use of quasi-experimental variation by focusing on the observations just around the threshold. For observations close enough to the threshold v_0 the reasoning is that they are comparable and differ only in the treatment status. Essential for the validity of the RDD are two arguments. First, the final vote count leading to the margin of victory $v_{i,t-1}^p$ must contain a random component. If it were true that a party had absolute certainty about the final vote outcome, the design would be invalid. Instead of producing good counterfactual observations on the left and right of the threshold, perfect foresight of the election outcome would enable parties to sort around the cut-off point. The estimates might be affected by a selection bias. We believe, however, that close elections are reasonably subject to some random component (e.g. weather conditions, shocks in the party popularity on an aggregate level and other factors that determine outcomes on the election day, see Knack (1994.)). Secondly, for the RDD to hold, the margin of victory must have a continuous density. The example that Lee (2008) uses to illustrate the need for this assumption is electoral fraud. If one party had the ability to administrate electoral fraud and influence the final vote count in their favor, then in repeated draws the density of the margin of victory would be discontinuous around the threshold. We have no suspicion that electoral fraud is of any concern in local elections in Germany.[23]

By implementing the limited sample approach, one makes direct use of the counterfactual observations argument. By focusing solely on observations that are within this margin, one isolates the causal effect of the treatment. If it was a random event determining the election outcome, there should be no characteristic (be it observable or unobservable) that differs for the observations just to the right and left of the threshold.

The inclusion of the control function $h(\cdot)$ allows for estimation to proceed using the entire sample while maintaining the same identifying assumptions. A correctly speci-

---

22 In practice, we also limit the sample somewhat by excluding observations where the margin of victory is greater than 60 percentage points. Outside this range, observations are often based on elections where only one candidate contested the election. When we include those non-meaningful observations in the analysis, the control function approach shows greater dependence on the specific function that is chosen.

23 Figure 2.5 in the appendix highlights the frequencies observed in the data. Focusing on just the region around the threshold, there is no indication that the frequencies are abnormally high or low just right or left to the deterministic cut-off-point.

fied control function will capture any correlation of $d_{i,t}^p$ with the error term that might be of concern. The issue is that a misspecified control function leads to an inconsistent estimate of the treatment effect. For the control function in our application, we used different parametric polynomial specifications. We offer more detail on how the results depend on the specification of the control function in the results section. Note that all control functions that we use allow for different parameters on either side of the threshold.

In the analysis of the effect of the mayor position on subsequent town council elections we distinguish between two designs relating to the timing of the local elections. Design 1 uses data only on simultaneous mayor and council elections while Design 2 is based on asynchronous elections. The empirical RDD strategy is, therefore, implemented using two distinct subsamples. The distinction is not relevant when analyzing the effect on higher level elections as these elections are never held simultaneously with local elections.

To complement the analysis, we also implement a completely different design in the final part of the empirical investigation. This last part does not rely on a RDD but makes use of another distinct institutional feature in the German electoral system. When mayor elections and town council elections are held simultaneously, there is the chance that the mayoral election is undecided and that a run-off election is needed, which takes place one or two weeks after the first round. By that time the result of the town council election is publicly known. Therefore, the voter can condition her vote on the outcome of the town council election in the second ballot election. We examine the impact of the town council election results on the mayoral run-off election. This can be done consistently because we can use the results from the first round of the mayor election to control for all unobservable characteristics (individual mayor candidate characteristics, popularity shocks for individual parties, etc.) that will affect the election results.

2.5 Results

In this section we highlight the empirical findings. First, we present our estimates from the RDD to identify whether voters are influenced by the mayor's party identity when they elect the local town council. Here, we focus on the implications of the timing of local elections. Secondly, we turn to the estimation of the partisan effect of mayors on elections in higher tiers of the federal structure (German federal elections and European elections). Thirdly, we investigate the additional design in which we analyze the impact of town council election results on run-off mayor elections.

2.5.1 Effect of the mayor's political identity on subsequent town council elections

Table 2.3 highlights the results from the RDD analysis of the causal effect of the mayor's office on the subsequent town council elections. The object of interest, thus, is the election outcome for a party in the town council election after a candidate from that party has either narrowly won or lost the preceding mayoral election. As indicated above the analysis is conducted for observations in Design 1 and Design 2 respectively.

Table 2.3: Interdependency between mayor's office and town council elections

| | Dependent variable: Vote share in TCE in t | | | | | |
	(1)	(2)	(3)	(4)	(5)	(6)
	Panel 1 : Design 1					
d	0.059***	0.056***	0.025	0.052***	0.043***	0.047***
	(0.009)	(0.015)	(0.024)	(0.019)	(0.006)	(0.011)
N	514	219	95	514	5677	5677
R2	0.08	0.07	0.01	0.08	0.26	0.26
	Panel 2: Design 2					
d	0.029*	0.009	0.010	0.015	0.021**	0.010
	(0.015)	(0.022)	(0.033)	(0.029)	(0.010)	(0.017)
N	201	83	43	201	1968	1968
R2	0.02	0.00	0.00	0.03	0.27	0.27
Sample	5 %	2 %	1%	5 %	60%	60%
Control function	none	none	none	linear	linear	3rd order

Notes: Significance levels: * $p < 0.10$, ** $p < 0.05$, *** $p < 0.01$. Standard errors in parentheses are robust and clustered on the level of each individual municipality election. The dependent variable is the vote share of a party (which had a candidate in the preceding mayoral race) in a town council election. The regressions in columns 1–3 are based on a limited sample within the respective margins and include only a constant and the treatment dummy. The estimations in columns 4–6 include a polynomial control function of the degree indicated which is specified to be flexible on both sides of the threshold. *Source*: Own calculations.

Panel 1 in table 2.3 shows the effects when mayor and town council elections are held simultaneously (denoted Design 1). In columns 1–6 we present different implementations of the RDD using both the limited sample approach (columns 1–3) as in eq. 2.2 and the control function approach (columns 4–6) as in eq. 2.3. We observe a sizable and significant effect of around 4.3–5.9 percentage points throughout almost all specifications. This implies, that (on average) a party receives a 4–6 percentage point bonus in vote share in the town council elections when its candidate just won the preceding mayoral election.

Figure 2.1: Design 1

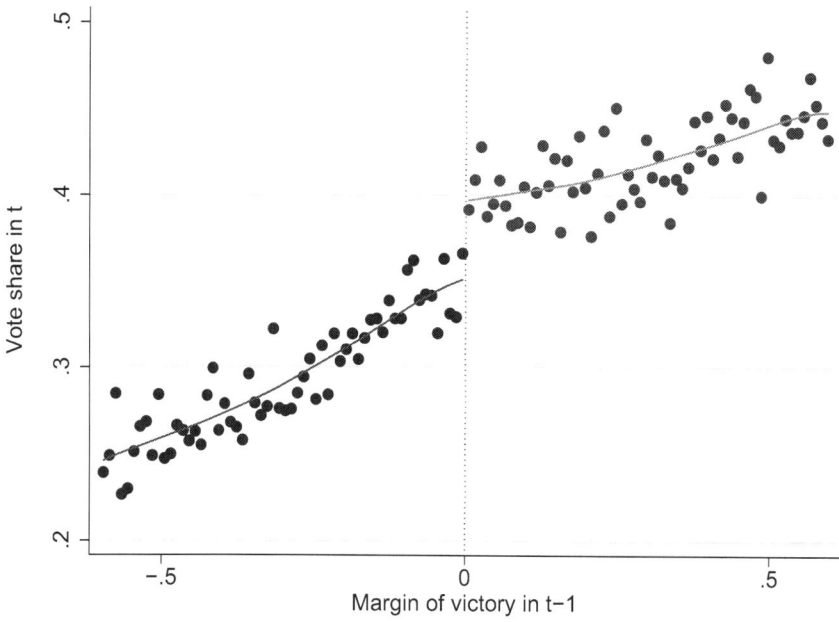

Notes: This figure graphically illustrates the discontinuous jump of the vote share in the town council election for party x when party x narrowly won the mayor election in $t-1$. The data used are those from Design 1. For clarity the data have been grouped in bins, each bin representing an interval of 1 percent in the margin of victory. The line fitted onto the scattered data is based on a local kernel regression using endogenous Epanechnikov weights. *Source:* Own calculations.

The highest effect, with 5.9 percentage points in vote share, is indicated in the limited sample with a 5% margin (column 1), which is arguably still a relatively large margin around the threshold. The result of using a 2% margin (column 2) shows a similar effect of 5.6 percentage points. The only insignificant estimate is displayed in column 3 for the 1% margin, based on very few observations. With the control function approach, the estimates are similar in size. We find an effect of 4.3 (4.7) percentage points using the full sample and a linear (cubic) control function (see columns 5 and 6). Column 4 combines the limit sample and control function approach and estimates the effect using a linear control function within the 5% margin sample. Again the effect is of a similar size and statistically significant. The effect is visualized in Figure 2.1, which illustrates a clear discontinuous jump at the threshold. Table 2.8 in the appendix shows that the effects are present irrespective of the individual parties.[24]

---

24 Point estimates illustrate that the effect might be slightly higher for the center-left party (social democrats), but such differences are not statistically significant. Note that most of the data for De-

The magnitude of this effect is sizable. Depending on the size of the council, an effect of around 5% in vote share implies that the party holding the mayoral position earns 1 or even 2 additional seats. To further illustrate the importance of the effect, we present estimates using the probability of becoming the strongest party in the council (instead of vote share) as an alternative outcome variable. This is particularly interesting as the party holding the most seats in the council is traditionally the first mover when it comes to coalition formation and policy making. Table 2.7 in the appendix illustrates the estimates from this specification. The evidence points to an effect as large as 20% percentage points in the probability of becoming the strongest party in the council.[25]

The pattern of the mayor influence is completely different for observations in Design 2, in which mayor and town council elections are *not* held simultaneously. The estimation results for this subset of the data are presented in table 2.3 (Panel 2) and figure 2.2. We find that when mayor and town council are asynchronously elected we do not observe a consistent effect of the mayor's partisanship on the town council election results. Point estimates are small and positive in the range of 0.9 to 2.1 percentage points but generally insignificant throughout most specifications.[26] Figure 2.2 does not indicate a significant break of the overall trend at the discontinuity.

How are these results to be interpreted with regard to the two main mechanisms previously discussed? We expect the incumbency externality effect to increase the vote share of the mayor's party whereas a divided government effect would decrease the support for the party. We find, that even if there might be a preference effect for divided government, it does not prevail against the externality effect. In both designs the effect of the mayor on the subsequent town council is non-negative.

The substantial disparity between the results from Design 1 and Design 2 indicates that the precise timing of the elections for the two local political institutions (mayor and town council) is crucially important. The observed differences are consistent with the notion that either one or both of the mechanisms exert a differential effect with respect

---

sign 1 are from the state of Bavaria, which is traditionally a conservative party stronghold. This might explain why the effect is slightly higher when a social democrat narrowly makes it into office.

25 Note, that those results are not quite as stable to different specifications of the RDD. In our three preferred specifications we observe an insignificant 18.3 percentage point effect (column 4), one effect of 17.6 percentage points (column 2), and a clearly significant effect of 20.4 percentage points in column 6.

26 The results also do not change if we include state and year dummies to increase efficiency. Moreover, specifications of the RDD, which we do not present here, do not show any indication that could point to a conclusion that there is an effect of the mayor position on the town council elections in Design 2. The difference to the estimation results in Design 1 are sizable and statistically significant in the preferred specifications. In column 2, the difference is 0.0478 points with a standard error of 0.025. It is thus statistically significant at least at the 10 percent level, and when including year fixed effects even at 5 percent level. The same is true for the estimated differences in columns 5 and 6.

Figure 2.2: Design 2

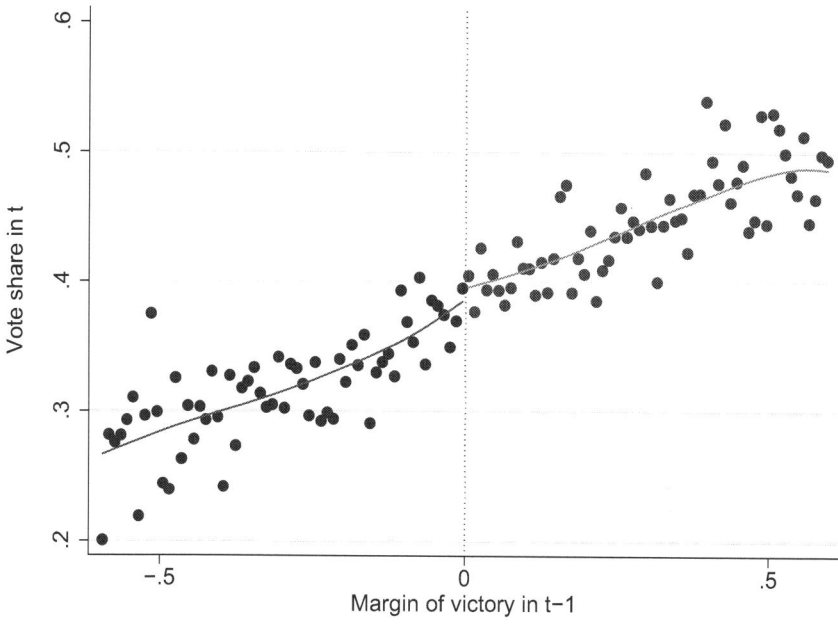

Notes: This figure graphically illustrates the evolution of the vote share in the town council election for party x when party x narrowly won the mayor election in $t - 1$. The data used are those from Design 2. For clarity the data have been grouped in bins, each bin representing an interval of 1 percent in the margin of victory. The line fitted onto the scattered data is based on a local kernel regression using endogenous Epanechnikov weights. *Source:* Own calculations.

to timing and are in line with the other theories discussed in the introduction(myopic voters and psychic costs, program vs. representation and psychic costs, and expressive voting).

It is reasonable to assume that the incumbency externality effect could be larger (more positive) in the case of joint elections. In both designs the party that has access to the mayor's office can profit from the use of this resource (media presence, increased financial resources, time spent with the electorate etc.). However, it is only when elections are held simultaneously that the party can benefit also from synergy effects of joint campaign efforts as well as a potential coattail effect. The differences in the two designs might therefore be consistent with a heterogeneous incumbency externality effect.

However, we also consider the theory that voters prefer divided government as a driving factor for the difference in the effects. According to this theory voters try to balance the government by voting for different parties in different elections, thus the mayor's party would lose support. As pointed out by Alesina and Rosenthal (1995), timing might be of the essence for the opportunity to act on this strategic incentive. When elections are not held simultaneously voters can condition their choice directly on the state in the second institution (here the mayor position). A "pro divided" voter can cast her vote accordingly as one part of the government is already known. When the elections are held at the same time, voters have to form an expectation about the outcome of the second election (here the mayor election). A voter that might otherwise prefer a divided government might decide to cast both votes for the conservatives to prevent an all social democrat leadership. The incentives to behave strategically are weaker under the uncertainty of the other election outcome. Hence, also heterogeneity in the divided government effect might explain the observed differences in Design 1 and 2.

The empirical observations from the two RDD designs are not conclusive as to distinguish between the two competing theories. As both effects might be heterogeneous with respect to timing, we have in essence four parameters, but only two estimates. At this juncture, we can only conclude that (1) the joint effect of the two mechanisms is non-negative under both designs, hence, the divided government effect never prevails; (2) As we observe a positive effect in Design 1, it must be that an incumbency externality effect exists and is positive (at least in this case); and (3) The observed differences in the two designs are consistent with either a larger externality effect or a smaller divided government effect when elections are held simultaneously.

Apart from not being able to pin down the magnitude of the effects, it is very unsatisfying that we cannot yet derive a statement whether a divided government rationale is of importance at all. In the following subsections, (see subsections 5.2, 5.3), we examine additional evidence on the nature of the interaction between the mayoral office, the town council, federal, and European elections. We find proof of a divided government effect from the additional design studying the interaction between council and mayor elections. Although the institutional setting is slightly different, we use this result to further conclude that: (4) Given a negative divided government effect, it must be that an incumbency externality effect exists when the timing of elections is asynchronous. A positive incumbency externality effect of similar size as the divided government effect is needed to explain a zero joint effect. This is interesting, because it shows that the incumbency externality effect is of importance also when we exclude arguments such as joint campaign efforts or joint ballot coattail effects.

2.5.2 Effect of the mayor's political identity on elections for higher levels of government

In table 2.4 we highlight the effects of the mayor position on elections in higher tiers. In particular, we evaluate whether having a mayor of a certain party exerts an effect for her party in subsequent European and German federal elections.[27]

Table 2.4: Interdependency between mayor's office and higher level elections

| | Dependent variable: Vote share in the respective election | | | | | |
| | Obs from Design 1 | | | Obs from Design 2 | | |
	(1)	(2)	(3)	(4)	(5)	(6)
	Panel 1: European Elections					
d	0.008	−0.004	0.009	−0.013	0.021	−0.006
	(0.022)	(0.023)	(0.016)	(0.027)	(0.031)	(0.022)
N	469	1110	12057	86	194	1826
R2	0.00	0.01	0.12	0.00	0.01	0.05
	Panel 2: Federal Elections					
d	0.005	−0.002	−0.002	−0.001	0.008	−0.009
	(0.016)	(0.015)	(0.012)	(0.016)	(0.015)	(0.011)
N	790	2053	22849	160	357	3558
R2	0.00	0.00	0.09	0.00	0.00	0.08
Sample	2 %	5 %	full	2 %	5%	full
Control function	none	linear	3rd order	none	linear	3rd order

Notes: Significance levels: * $p < 0.10$, ** $p < 0.05$, *** $p < 0.01$. Standard errors in parentheses are robust and clustered on the level of each individual election. The dependent variable is the vote share of a party (which had a candidate in the preceding mayoral race) in a higher level election (European, federal election respectively). Columns 1–3 estimate the three preferred specifications for the observations from design 1, while columns 4–6 refer to estimates for observations from design 2. The regressions in columns 1 and 4 are based on a limited sample within a margin of victory of 2 percentage points and include only a constant and the treatment dummy. The estimations in columns 2,3 and 5,6 include a polynomial control function of the degree indicated which is specified to be flexible on both sides of the threshold. *Source*: Own calculations.

The panels 1 and 2 in table 2.4 refer to elections for the European parliament and the German *Bundestag* respectively. We find no significant effect of the mayor's office on either of the two levels. The mayoral position appears to be irrelevant for the electoral outcome of the party in higher tiers throughout all specifications.

---

27 Note that these higher level election are held simultaneously with local elections only in exceptional cases. There are a few communities in Hesse, Rhineland-Palatinate, Saarland and Bavaria where mayoral elections were, in fact held, simultaneously. The number of elections however, is too few to run a meaningful, separate analysis.

Compared to the results of the town council, these outcomes can be clearly interpreted as evidence that there is no incumbency externality of the mayor's office at these levels. We assume that voters do not strategically balance their votes between the local elections and higher level elections. The policy making interaction between communities and the federal government, let alone the European Union, is hardly relevant for an individual voters decision. We would therefore argue that there is no preference effect in this analysis. Thus, any effect would have been a pure incumbency externality effect.

Note that we also subdivided the results for the higher level election outcomes again into the observations from Design 1 and Design 2. We did this to examine whether the results are different at higher tiers along this margin. We observe no differences in those estimates. These findings are reassuring, as we can exclude that specific state differences are driving our results on the mayor's effect on town council elections.

2.5.3 Effect of town council elections on run-off mayoral elections

In this last part of the analysis, we turn away from the RDD and use another institutional feature of the German electoral system. Whenever mayor and town council elections are held simultaneously, there is the chance that the first ballot in the mayor election does not establish an absolute majority winner of the election. In these cases, a second ballot between the two leading candidates is held. This feature in the electoral design presents an interesting opportunity to study the effects of the town council election on the second ballot (run-off) election for the mayor.

Specifically, we investigate whether the vote shares in the town council election affect the vote outcome in the second-ballot election for the mayor. This analysis is interesting as an incumbency externality effect should not play a role in this setting and any remaining influence can hence be attributed to a preference for divided government. If voters prefer divided government, we expect a high vote share in the town council election to decrease the vote share of a candidate of this party in the run-off election. Empirically, we can identify this effect because we also have the information on the first-ballot round results. While it is true that in general, town council election results and second-ballot outcomes are determined by common non-observed variables, any such factors should already be featured in the election result of the first round.

Table 2.5 highlights the results from this analysis. In column 1, we only regress the vote outcome for a party in the run-off mayor election on the result of the same party in the town council election, which was held one or two weeks previously. In this regression one variable simply proxies for the other and we simply pick up that a community

Table 2.5: Run-off mayor elections

| | Dependent variable: vote share in run-off mayor election | | | | | |
	(1)	(2)	(3)	(4)	(5)	(6)
Vote share CE	0.947***	−0.211***	−0.253***	−0.246***	−0.246***	−0.240***
	(0.034)	(0.027)	(0.026)	(0.025)	(0.025)	(0.025)
Vote share main ME		1.365***	2.299***	2.090***	2.117***	2.217***
		(0.020)	(0.075)	(0.077)	(0.090)	(0.091)
Vote share main ME squared			−1.505***	−1.688***	−1.729***	−1.706***
			(0.121)	(0.116)	(0.133)	(0.129)
Dist. to next main ME				0.250***	0.239***	0.162***
				(0.026)	(0.035)	(0.037)
Behind in main ME					−0.004	−0.005
					(0.008)	(0.008)
4 candidates in main ME						0.014***
						(0.004)
5 candidates in main ME						0.036***
						(0.006)
6 candidates in main ME						0.039***
						(0.010)
7 candidates in main ME						0.005
						(0.022)
Constant	0.104***	0.015***	−0.097***	0.008	0.006	−0.044***
	(0.012)	(0.005)	(0.009)	(0.014)	(0.015)	(0.017)
N	1454	1453	1453	1453	1453	1453
R2	0.337	0.818	0.835	0.844	0.845	0.849

Notes: Significance levels: * $p < 0.10$, ** $p < 0.05$, *** $p < 0.01$. Robust standard errors in parentheses. ME: Mayor election, CE: Council election. The dependent variable is the vote share of a party in the second ballot (run-off) election for town mayor. The main variable of interest is vote share of a party in the town council election held one or two weeks before the run-off election of the mayor's office. In further columns we control for the vote share in the first-round mayor election (linear as well as in squares), the distance to the next best opponent, a dummy whether the candidate was behind in the first round and a set of dummies that specifies the number of candidates that participated in the initial mayor election. *Source*: Own calculations.

generally prefers a certain party.[28] In column 2 and 3, we also include the vote share of the party (and its square) in the first round of the mayoral election. This not only controls for any unobservable characteristic that determines the attitude of the voters towards the party, it also controls for the personal characteristics of the candidates in

---

28 Say, for example, that there was a shock in the community before the rounds of local elections that made the voters dislike the conservative party. This will turn up both in the town council election and in both rounds of the mayoral elections.

the mayor elections.[29] We find that in this specification the effect of the town council election turns negative. For an additional 10 % in vote share in the council elections the voters in the community will cast 2.5% fewer votes to a candidate of this party in the run-off election. This effect remains perfectly stable if we include further information on the first-round mayor election such as the distance to the best opponent, a dummy for being second in the first round election and a set of dummies for the number of candidates that participated in round one (see columns 3–5).

We interpret this outcome as clear evidence for balancing behavior of the voters. At least some of the voters prefer not to cast their vote for this party's candidate when the vote share in the town council was high. We conclude that those results are evidence for a negative divided government effect.

2.5.4 RDD validity and robustness tests

In this section we present evidence for the validity of the RDD approach used in the estimations. Additionally to the results reported above, we also implement a number of robustness tests and further specifications in different subgroups.

There are two tests to examine the crucial assumption of random assignment of the treatment around the threshold. The first check is that the group of observations on either side are "perfect" counterfactuals. That implies that any predetermined characteristic of those communities just right and just left of the threshold must be similar on average. A second test to examine the underlying identifying assumption is to look at the frequencies of observations just around the threshold. If treatment is random at the threshold, there should be no systematic difference between the number of observations around the discontinuity. Any significant difference would speak for the ability to sort around the threshold that would invalidate the research design.

Figures 2.3 and 2.4 in the appendix examine this property in the data for five predetermined measures. We investigate whether the communities differ with respect to the voter turnout in the mayor election in $t - 1$, whether the party ran a candidate in the mayor election in $t - 2$, the level of spending in $t - 1$, the unemployment rate in $t - 1$ and the outcome of the town council election in $t - 1$. As the treatment was not yet determined at the moment when we observe these characteristics, there should be no effect on those variables. The figures show that there is no discontinuous jump in any of these measures around the threshold. Figure 2.5 in the appendix presents the frequencies in our data. There is no indication that those frequencies are systematically

---

29 The R^2 clearly indicates that the vote share from the first round is the ideal predictor for the outcome of round two. Note, that the effect on the vote share in round one is larger than 1 as there are, by definition, fewer candidates on the second-ballot.

different around the threshold. Hence, we conclude that the quasi-experimental design is valid according to both of those tests.

Freier (2011) estimates a RDD to evaluate the electoral advantage for German mayors in subsequent mayor elections. The argument is based on a similar design using close elections. He confirms the validity of the RDD with a number of additional tests using several other predetermined variables and frequency tests in different margins from the threshold.[30] He reports no significant differences in either the predetermined variables or frequency plots.

To ensure that the effects measured in the Design 1 analysis are indeed valid and not simply an artifact of random noise we run placebo tests simulating different thresholds determining our treatment. Table 2.9 in the appendix shows the results of two of those tests. In the first test (columns 1–3) we simulate that a party gained access to the mayor's office even when it lost the election with a 5 percentage point margin. In the second placebo, we test the results assuming that the mayor's office could only be obtained if the party won by more than 5 percentage points. Both tests yield the expected result that those devised thresholds -that should not matter for the interaction between mayor and town elections – indeed do not show any significant effects. This provides further evidence for the reliability of the effects estimated above.

To further investigate the robustness of our results, we test a number of additional specifications of the RDD in which we varied the degree of the polynomial control function and experiment with other margins for the limited sample approach. The results always compare well to the estimates reported in the two designs. Further, we investigated whether the type of mayor position (full-time or part-time) made a significant difference. This might be especially interesting since communities in the sample of Design 1 are on average smaller and less likely to have a full-time mayor.[31] To check whether differences in the two designs are simply driven by differences in the community size/contract type of the mayor we run estimations for only those communities in Design 1 that have full-time mayors. The estimation results indicate that

---

30 Freier (2011) reports no differences in the following predetermined variables: Incumbency status of the mayor in the previous two election periods (also 2nd moments), votes share in the last two mayor elections (also 2nd moments), participation in the mayor race in $t - 2$ and $t - 3$, status of the mayor in $t - 2$ and $t - 3$ (full-time or part-time employed), number of candidate in the race for mayor in $t - 1$ and $t - 2$, number of voters in $t - 1$ and $t - 2$, turnout rate in $t - 1$ and $t - 2$. As well as the fiscal information on total expenditures (per capita), total debt, revenue from trade tax, as well as tax power (measured by the ratio of tax revenue to total revenue) each in the year preceding the elections in $t - 1$ and $t - 2$. For the frequency plots, he looks at 1 percent bins in a large margin around the threshold as well as 0.25 percent bins just around the threshold and shows that there is no significant difference.

31 Most of the data for Design 1 is from the state of Bavaria, which has a large number of very small communities, many of which only have part-time mayors.

there is no significant difference between the estimates for full-time mayors only and the estimates in the overall Design 1 sample. If anything, point estimates are slightly higher on average for the full-time mayors, indicating that a differences between the designs might be even larger.

Moreover, for the analysis in Design 2 of the effect on the town council, we split the sample with regard to the time that the mayor and town council will have to govern together. For some observations this time period is only one or two years before a new mayor is elected, for others it is three or more years. This division is of potential interest as the voter might find it even more worthwhile to balance the government if this decision determines the political structure in the community for a long lasting period. However, estimation in these subgroups does not show any significant differences between the individual subgroups and the overall result for Design 2.

Last, but not least, we examine whether the interaction between mayor and town council election is different (in Designs 1 and 2) when we control for the past balance between mayor and council. We asked whether voters behave differently when the past mayor and council majority were of the same party compared to a case were the local government were already divided in the two political institutions. Again, estimation results do not exhibit any significant differences to the effects presented above.[32]

2.6 Conclusions

In this paper we examine interdependencies in voting decisions for different political institutions. In particular, we analyze how voters consider the election result of one political body when they vote for a different institution. We compile a new data set containing community level results for mayoral, town council, federal, and European elections from eight German states to conduct the analysis. Methodologically, we mainly rely on a regression discontinuity design, which uses close election outcomes to identify quasi-random variation in the partisanship of the local mayor.

For the local elections, we find that the party of the incumbent mayor receives a bonus of around 4 to 6 percentage points in the subsequent council election if these elections are held jointly. If the elections for the mayor and the council are on different dates the mayor's party does not benefit from holding the office. In the other direction, we investigate the effect of the council election result on run-off mayor election outcomes. We find that a ten percent increase in vote share in the council election for a party

---

32 Estimation results for all robustness tests and further specifications are available from the authors upon request.

is associated with a decrease of 2.5 percentage points in vote share for the party's candidate in the run-off mayor election.

Throughout the analysis, we link the empirical evidence to two underlying mechanisms: the incumbency externality effect from the mayor's office and a preference effect for divided government. Our findings support the following conclusions. We find that both a positive incumbency externality effect and a negative divided government effect are present in the observed voting behavior. In evaluating the impact of the mayoral position on the next council election, the incumbency externality effect (weakly) dominates the divided government effect, irrespective of timing. The intriguing timing differences are consistent with either a larger externality effect or a smaller divided government effect when elections are held simultaneously.

For elections at the federal and European level, we show that there is no effect of the local mayor's partisanship on these election outcomes. Assuming that there is no incentives to also balance votes between institutions at different tiers, we conclude that there is no significant incumbency externality effect. Voting decisions for the higher tiers are hence independent from the local institution of the mayor.

For the analysis above, we show that interaction in voting behavior is not of significance between different tiers of government, however, within one tier we find substantial interdependencies between political institutions. We presented a number of reliable empirical observations that prove that the mayor's office can be of importance in the next town council election and vice versa. These findings are consistent with two mechanisms that we identify from the theoretical literature. The described effects have a significant influence on government composition and hence policy outcomes. We conclude that one should carefully consider the strategic and psychological aspects in the voters decision making when designing electoral rules, in particular when it comes to timing of elections and run-off procedures.

Appendix

In the appendix we present more detail on the properties and processing of the original data and additional detail on the econometric implementation. The appendix furthermore contains tables and graphs with further descriptives, additional analysis, and validity checks.

We restrict our analysis to the two major parties in Germany (the center-right CDU/CSU and the center-left SPD). We do this for three reasons. First, these two parties participate in most council elections and are the two key sources of mayoral candidates. The remaining mayoral candidates are most frequently from voter lists or even independent candidates. If we wanted to include those candidates we would also need that a voter list that nominates a candidate for the mayor election also runs a list for the following council election to obtain an observation. For independent candidates this is obviously not possible and for voter lists it does not occur very frequently. Furthermore, there is a lot of entry and exit from the political sphere when it comes to voter lists. Second, the votes for both voter lists and independent candidates are often poorly documented in the original data. They are often just coded as 'independent party 1', 'independent party 2' instead of providing the actual party name. This makes it impossible to track them over time. Sometimes the votes for all voter list are even only provided as total sum. Third, the smaller parties FDP, the Greens, and the left party do not frequently run mayoral candidates and are rarely among the top two candidates in terms of votes received. Including these parties would therefore not add much valuable information at the threshold and those cases would be exceptional situations.

Often several parties and voter lists jointly nominate a candidate. In these cases we only count the candidate as affiliated with the center-left or the center-right party when the respective party was mentioned first. E.g. when the party affiliation of a candidate was given by 'CDU/Independent voter group' we would count her as member of the center right party (CDU) while we would not do so if the affiliation was given by 'Independent voter group/CDU'.

The mayoral election in some communities may be counted as two observations. This occurs when the term of the mayor is longer than the term of the council. For example, a mayor is elected in year x, then there could be a council election in year x+1 and another council election in year x+5 before the next mayor election is held in year x+8. We include both cases in the analysis.

As discussed in the section on the data, we may use one election pair twice to generate two observations as we look at both big parties. To prevent that e.g. common shocks in a community at a certain council election bias the standard errors we cluster the standard errors by community and council election year.

There are three different types of ballot structures for the council elections in the investigated states. In the first setting, e.g. in Hesse, each voter has as many votes as there are seats in the council. In the second setting, e.g. in Thuringia, each voter has three votes. In both cases the voters can freely attribute their votes between different candidates, which they can choose from the candidate lists of one or different parties. The voters can allocate up to three votes to one candidate. Alternatively, they can simply assign all votes to a specific party list. To calculate the number of seats of a party all votes received by candidates of this party are added and then compared to the total number of votes of the other parties. For the properties of these two settings there may be more votes than voters in the data. In the third setting voters have only one vote, which they can cast for a list. This is the case e.g. in Saarland.

It can occur that only one candidate runs for the mayoral office. In these elections voters can either accept or refuse the candidate. If, e.g., 90 percent accept the candidate, a margin of victory of 80 percent is recorded in the data. As those elections cannot be compared in any reasonable way to the elections with more than one candidate we exclude them from the analysis. About 15 percent of all mayor elections in our data are single candidate elections.

Table 2.6: Data set – higher level elections

	European elections		Federal elections	
	# Obs	Years	# Obs	Years
Bavaria	15059	'79 –' 09	29656	'49 –' 09
Thuringia	556	'04	1059	'02 –' 05
Brandenburg	201	'04	207	'05
Rhineland-Palatinate	142	'04 –' 09	147	'98 –' 05
Hesse	1122	'04 –' 09	2341	'98 –' 09
Saarland	186	'04 –' 09	292	'98 –' 09
Saxony-Anhalt	319	'04	658	'02 –' 05
Saxony	415	'04	834	'02 –' 05
Total	18000		35194	
# within 60 % margin	13883		26407	
# within 5 % margin	1304		2410	
# within 2 % margin	555		950	

Source: Own calculations, based on the data provided by the federal election office.

Table 2.7: Design 1 – strongest party

	Dep. Var: Probability of becoming strongest party in the council					
	(1)	(2)	(3)	(4)	(5)	(6)
d	0.231***	0.176**	0.106	0.183	0.181***	0.204***
	(0.053)	(0.085)	(0.134)	(0.111)	(0.030)	(0.062)
N	514	219	95	514	5677	5677
R^2	0.05	0.03	0.01	0.06	0.19	0.19
Sample	5 %	2 %	1%	5 %	full	full
Control function	none	none	none	linear	linear	3rd order

Notes: Significance levels: * $p < 0.10$, ** $p < 0.05$, *** $p < 0.01$. Standard errors in parentheses are robust and clustered on the level of each individual municipality election. The dependent variable in all specifications is a dummy variable indicating whether the respective party became the strongest party in the council (based on the obtained vote share). The regressions in columns 1–3 are based on a limited sample within the respective margins and include only a constant and the treatment dummy. The estimations in columns 4–6 include a polynomial control function of the degree indicated which is specified to be flexible on both sides of the threshold. *Source*: Own calculations.

Table 2.8: Design 1 – effects by party

	Center-Right			Center-Left		
	(1)	(2)	(3)	(4)	(5)	(6)
d	0.054***	0.058***	0.032**	0.064***	0.066**	0.080***
	(0.017)	(0.022)	(0.013)	(0.021)	(0.028)	(0.016)
N	140	335	3371	79	179	2306
R2	0.07	0.06	0.13	0.11	0.17	0.32
Sample	2 %	5 %	full	2 %	5 %	full
Control function	none	linear	3rd order	none	linear	3rd order

Notes: Significance levels: * $p < 0.10$, ** $p < 0.05$, *** $p < 0.01$. Standard errors in parentheses are robust and clustered on the level of each individual municipality election. The dependent variable is the vote share of the respective party in a town council election. Columns 1–3 refer to results of the center-right party. Columns 4–6 are estimates for the center-left party. The regressions in columns 1 and 4 are based on a limited sample within a margin of victory of 2 percentage points and include only a constant and the treatment dummy. The estimations in columns 2,3 and 5,6 include a polynomial control function of the degree indicated which is specified to be flexible on both sides of the threshold. *Source*: Own calculations.

Table 2.9: Design 1 – placebo test (-5 percent, +5 percent)

	- 5 percent			+ 5 percent		
	(1)	(2)	(3)	(4)	(5)	(6)
d	0.001	−0.013	−0.010	0.009	0.003	−0.000
	(0.014)	(0.019)	(0.011)	(0.014)	(0.020)	(0.009)
N	211	515	5677	189	478	5677
R2	0.00	0.01	0.26	0.00	0.00	0.26
Sample	2 %	5 %	full	2 %	5 %	full
Control function	none	linear	3rd order	none	linear	3rd order

Notes: Significance levels: * $p < 0.10$, ** $p < 0.05$, *** $p < 0.01$. Standard errors in parentheses are robust and clustered on the level of each individual municipality election. The dependent variable is the vote share of the respective party in a town council election. Columns 1–3 refer to results of the placebo test in which we simulate that a party obtained the mayor incumbency status also if it lost the preceding mayor election with at most 5 percentage points. Columns 4–6 are estimates for the reverse placebo test in which a party needed more than 5 percentage points winning margin to gain the incumbency status. The regressions in columns 1 and 4 are based on a limited sample within a margin of victory of 2 percentage points and include only a constant and the treatment dummy. The estimations in columns 2,3 and 5,6 include a polynomial control function of the degree indicated which is specified to be flexible on both sides of the threshold. *Source*: Own calculations.

Figure 2.3: RDD validity check – predetermined variables

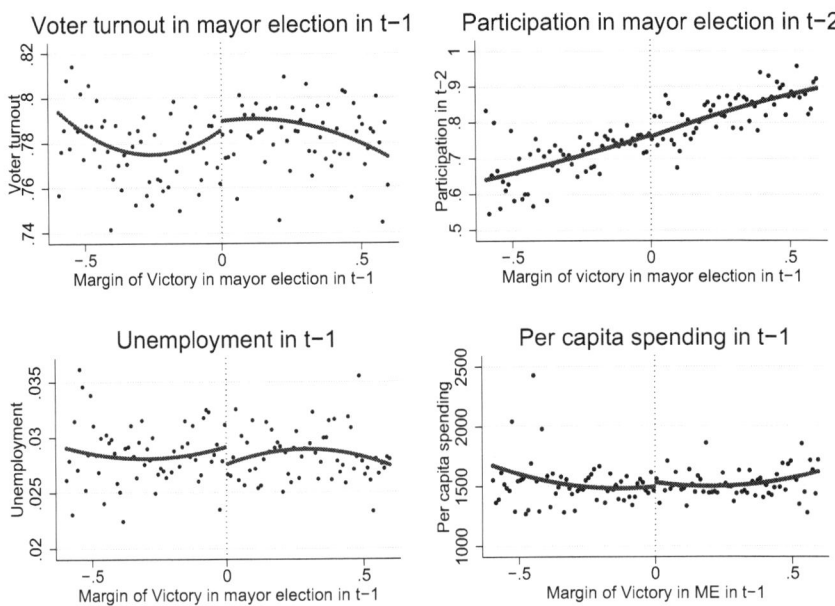

Notes: This figure illustrates that predetermined variables in $t-1$ are not affected by the treatment that occurs at $t-1$. Each bin in the graphs represents an interval of 1 percent in the margin of victory. The line fitted onto the scattered data is a polynomial function of degree two which is flexible on both sides of the threshold. The upper left figure depicts the relationship between the margin of victory in the mayor election and the voter turnout in the the very same election. The upper right figure illustrates the relationship between the mayor election in $t-1$ and the participation in the preceding mayor election (in $t-2$). The lower left graph shows the relationship between a measure of unemployment in the year of the election and the margin of victory in that election. The lower right figure illustrates the relationship between the margin of victory in the mayor election and the aggregate per capita spending of the respective community in the election year. *Source:* Own calculations.

Figure 2.4: RDD validity check – vote share in last town council

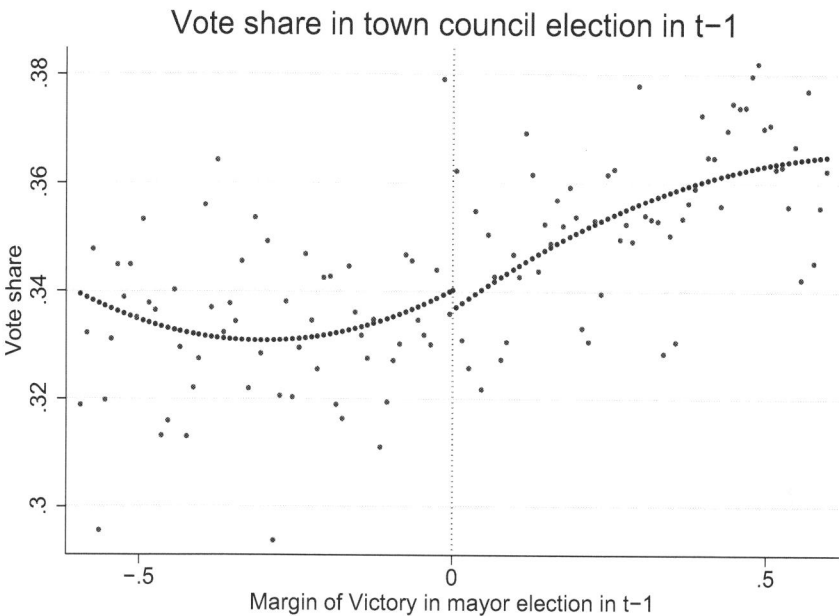

Notes: This figure illustrates that the predetermined variable vote share in the last council election is not affected by the treatment that occurs at $t-1$. Each bin in the graphs represents an interval of 1 percent in the margin of victory. The line fitted onto the scattered data is a polynomial function of degree two which is flexible on both sides of the threshold. *Source:* Own calculations.

Figure 2.5: RDD validity check – frequencies around the threshold

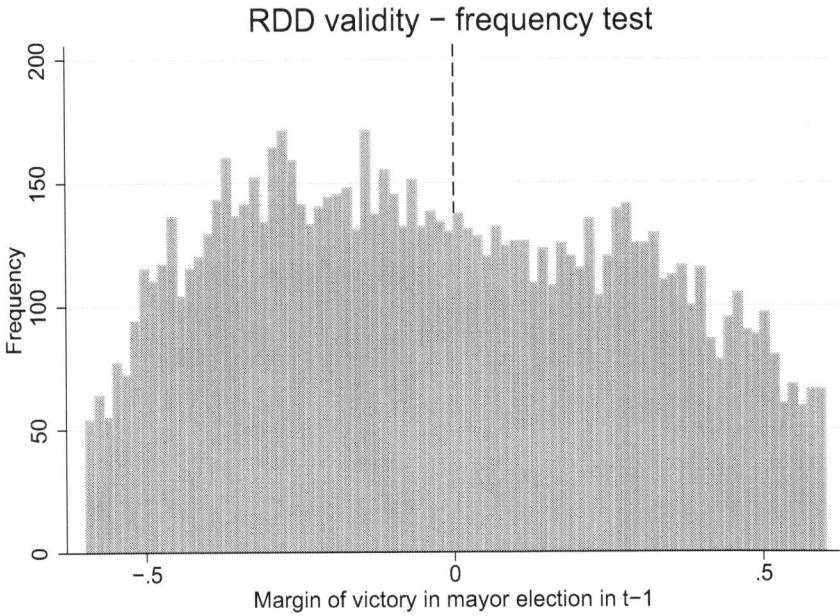

Notes: This figure presents the frequencies of observations in data with respect to the margin of victory. Each bin in the graphs represents an interval of 1.5 percent in the margin of victory. *Source:* Own calculations.

Chapter 3: Incumbency, party identity and governmental lead
Evidence for heterogeneous incumbency effects for Germany[1]

Abstract: Do incumbents in an election have an advantage, and if so, are these advantages heterogeneous across parties or government and opposition? We first present a theoretical discussion on the possible heterogeneity of incumbency effects in a pure two-party system. Then, we estimate the incumbency effect for the direct district candidates in German federal and state elections using a regression discontinuity design (RDD). When studying the heterogeneity in these effects, we find that incumbents from both large parties, the center-right CDU and the center-left SPD, have an advantage only if the SPD is in government. This effect is robust and shows even in state elections that are unrelated to federal elections – calling into question the findings of average incumbency effects in the literature. Because this effect is stronger in the East than in the West and only shows post reunification, we hypothesise that the emergence of the socialist party "The Left" may be behind this heterogeneity.

3.1 Introduction

The electoral advantage of incumbency is perhaps one of the best known and least understood facts of American political life.

Since Abramowitz (1975, p. 668) made this statement, much work has been dedicated to changing this fact. However, there are still new and interesting questions to be investigated: for instance whether there are heterogeneous incumbency effects regarding the party identity or across government and opposition. In this paper, we use data from German federal and state elections to assess this potential heterogeneity in the incumbency effects of district representatives.

We start with some theoretical observations on incumbency effects across parties and government participation in a pure two-party system. The essence is that an interaction

1   This chapter is joint work with Christian Odendahl and Ronny Freier. We would like to thank Charles B. Blankart, Magnus Johannesson, Juanna Jönsson, Per Pettersson-Lidbom, Jesse Rothstein, Björn Tyrefors as well as colleagues at DIW Berlin, Princeton University, Stockholm School of Economics and Stockholm University for helpful suggestions and comments. Furthermore, we would like to thank participants at the the Annual Meeting of the European Public Choice Societey 2010 in Izmir, the Workshop on Political Economy at ifo Dresden in 2009, and at seminars the DIW Berlin, Humboldt University Berlin, and Stockholm School of Economics in 2009. A special thanks goes to Viktor Steiner and Peter Haan who invited us to work at their department for public economics at the DIW Berlin, helped us with contacting the institutions about the necessary data and gave valuable comments and advice. Furthermore, we would like to thank Helke Seitz who provided excellent research assistance with organizing the data. Ronny Freier would like to thank the Hedelius foundation for funding a research visit to Princeton University, Christian Odendahl would like to thank the Hedelius foundation for funding a research visit to the London School of Economics. The usual disclaimer applies.

term for an incumbent that also belongs to the governing party cannot logically capture a full government participation effect on the incumbency advantage. It can only show the *heterogeneity* in this effect across parties. The reason is that one interaction effect is the mirror image of the other. If the incumbents of both parties have the same positive effect of being in government, the interaction term will be zero. This also complicates the interpretation of our estimation results because we cannot know which party was driving the effects.

We estimate the incumbency effects for direct candidates of German federal elections between 1976 and 2009 and state elections between 1993 and 2010 using a regression discontinuity design (RDD). We make use of the fact that direct district candidates are elected by a first-past-the-post system and estimate the effect from observations when a candidate just lost or just won an election. This makes the variation in incumbency status arguably as good as random.

We indeed find incumbency effects, but also important heterogeneity between the two main parties, the center-right Christian Democrats (CDU)[2] and the center-left Social Democrats (SPD)[3]: both parties only benefit from an incumbency effect when the SPD is in government. We explore whether the effect might be driven purely by the SPD because of the increased competition from the left side of the political spectrum. We find three facts in favor of this hypothesis: (1) the effect exists only after reunification, (2) the effect is stronger in the East than in the West of Germany and (3) the vote share of "The Left"[4] party is directly affected.

Our estimation of heterogeneous effects shows that average incumbency effects may not be the whole story. In fact, the average of the effect can be misleading and is largely uninformative about potential mechanisms. The observation that a positive incumbency effect for both parties only exists when the SPD in government suggests that many of the usually stories told to explain the effect may not matter at all. Due to the observed heterogeneity, it is unlikely that the effect in Germany is driven by name recognition, media coverage, general pork barrel spending in the districts or helping the constituents in handling bureaucracy.[5] Instead, we believe that our findings lend support to the hypothesis that political competition is one of the main drivers of incumbency effects (Snyder and Hirano (2009)).

---

2   *Christlich Demokratische Union* (CDU) and its Bavarian Branch *Christlich-Soziale Union* (CSU) are referred to as Christian Democrats or CDU for simplicity.

3   *Sozialdemokratische Partei Deutschalnds* (SPD)

4   *Die Linke* (in English: The Left) was previously called *Partei des Demokratischen Sozialismus* (PDS). 'The Left' is used for simplicity.

5   See for instance Krehbiel and Wright (1983), Cox and Katz (2002), Ansolabehere, Snyder, and Stewart (2000a), Levitt and Wolfram (1997), Cover (1977), Ansolabehere, Snowberg, and Snyder (2006), Cox and Katz (1996), Cain, Ferejohn, and Fiorina (1984) and Bickers and Stein (1996)

Our paper is linked to three incumbency-related strands of literature: to the empirical estimation of incumbency effects in general; to the observation in the literature that incumbency effects seem to be increasing over recent decades; and to papers that try to investigate the heterogeneity of incumbency effects.

A large strand of literature in political science investigates the issue of incumbency empirically.[6] Lee (2008) uses an RDD to estimate the causal effect of incumbency on subsequent election outcomes. Using data from the US House of Representatives, he finds a sizable incumbency effect of a 45 percentage points higher probability of winning the next election. Following the RDD analysis of Lee (2008), Ferreira and Gyourko (2009) study the effects of incumbency for US mayors. They find an effect of incumbency on the probability of winning of about 32 percentage points.

Empirical studies that use close elections as a source of exogenous variation are not without controversy. Caughey and Sekhon (2010) and Grimmer, Hersh, Feinstein, and Carpenter (2011) show that those candidates in the US House that barely lost and those that barely won are by no means identical on average – an important indication that the design in Lee (2008) might not mimic the empirical gold standard, a randomized experiment. Snyder, Folke, and Hirano (2011) argue in response to the critique that it is true that *at* the threshold there should be no difference between winners and losers. However, as a practical matter, being *near* the threshold means that there may be differences simply because cutting a strictly unimodal distribution implies that there will be more probability mass on one side than on the other even when you are reasonably close to the threshold.

There is some empirical literature on incumbency effects also for Germany. Hainmueller and Kern (2005, 2008) use an RDD and federal election data to show an average incumbency effect of 1–2 percentage points (in vote share). Our work is closely related to theirs. For local mayors in Germany, Freier (2011) estimates an effect of 38–40 percentage points in the probability of winning. Meanwhile, there is no known empirical investigation of the incumbency effect in German state elections.

The second question in the literature, which our contribution is connected to, is why the incumbency advantage seems to be increasing over recent decades.[7] In an early paper on the issue, Mayhew (1974, p. 313) hypothesizes:

> *Voters dissatisfied with party cues could be reaching for any other cues that are available in deciding how to vote. The incumbency cue is readily at hand.*

However, Ansolabehere, Hirano, Snyder, and Ueda (2001) and Krehbiel and Wright (1983) reject the hypothesis that persons have replaced parties in this respect. Our

---

6   See for instance Mayhew (1974), Jacobson (1987), Gelman and King (1990), King and Gelman (1991), Ansolabehere, Snyder, and Stewart (2000b) and Ansolabehere and Snyder (2004).

7   See Cox and Katz (2002) for an example and Jacobson (1987) for a discussion of what "increase" actually means and, more importantly, does not mean.

results also indicate that the incumbency advantage has increased in Germany since reunification in 1991. Since party loyalty were less strong in the East, this may be one aspect, but we leave this investigation to future research.

Finally, our paper is related to the literature that tries to identify heterogeneity in incumbency effects. For example, Snyder and Hirano (2009) investigate the heterogeneity of incumbency advantages regarding competitiveness and budget size and find sizeable differences. To the best of our knowledge, the heterogeneity that we investigate – government participation – is not studied in any existing rigorous empirical research design.

One final introductory point: some studies use the vote share, some the probability of winning as an outcome variable and naturally are they closely related. Since probability of winning works better when parties decide not to (re-)run, it has become the more standard outcome variable. However, we show that during large political swings the probability of winning may end up at its boundaries zero and one, which hides any potential incumbency effect.[8] Again, by disregarding this important feature in the probability of winning, average incumbency effects in this measure are potentially very misleading. For that reason, we prefer the vote share as our measure of outcome.[9]

The remainder of the paper is organized as follows. Section 3.2 discusses the logical necessities in estimating heterogeneous incumbency effects in a pure two-party system, and the institutional background for German elections. In section 3.3 we present our empirical strategy, section 3.4 shortly introduces the data we use and section 3.5 presents and discusses the results, the interpretation and some validity and robustness checks. Section 3.6 concludes the analysis.

3.2   Theoretical and institutional background

3.2.1   Theoretical considerations

We begin with some logical observations on incumbency effects and the potential to identify heterogeneity by government participation. To fix ideas, we assume a two-party system and introduce the following notation. There are two parties $j = C, S$, and the outcome variable is the vote share in the next election for the respective parties: Y^C and Y^S. Then:

$$Y^C = \alpha^C + \beta^C g^C + \gamma^C d^C + \delta^C (g^C \cdot d^C), \tag{3.1}$$

---

8   This issue is related to but different from the one identified in Jacobson (1987). Our concern is that the choice of variables may hide an empirical result.

9   Note that in Germany the two large parties, CDU and SPD run in every single election that we observe. Thus, we do not have to be concerned about strategic entry or exit into the district races.

and

$$Y^S = \alpha^S + \beta^S g^S + \gamma^S d^S + \delta^S (g^S \cdot d^S), \tag{3.2}$$

where g^j is the dummy for government participation of party j and d^j is a dummy equal to one if the incumbent is from party j. At first glance, one could imagine bringing one of the two equations to the data (using different districts and different time periods) and estimate the parameters δ^j. Would, e.g., δ^C give us an indication on the heterogeneity in the incumbency advantage when party C is in government? The answer is no. The analysis is complicated by the interaction of parties.

To clarify this, note that, in a two party system, there are three equalities that we know hold:

$$g^C = 1 - g^S$$
$$d^C = 1 - d^S \tag{3.3}$$
$$Y^C = 1 - Y^S$$

If we insert the above equalities into the equation 3.1 and rearrange, the relationship between the parameters for the two parties is as follows:

$$Y^S = \underbrace{[1 - \alpha^C - \beta^C - \gamma^C - \delta^C]}_{=\alpha^S} + \underbrace{(\beta^C + \delta^C)}_{=\beta^S} g^S + \underbrace{(\gamma^C + \delta^C)}_{=\gamma^S} d^S + \underbrace{(-\delta^C)}_{=\delta^S} (g^S \cdot d^S) \tag{3.4}$$

There are two key observations to extract. First, and most importantly, the relationship between parameters on the interaction term is fixed to $\delta^C = -\delta^S$. Somewhat surprisingly, this implies that the parameters δ^C, δ^S cannot capture an effect that incumbents from either party can receive (we cannot have $\delta^j > 0$ for both parties). Thus, an empirical specification that uses models like the ones presented here will not identify a universal government bonus for incumbents.

The intuition for this effect is as follows. Say, both parties are equally able to push their district incumbents only when they are in government. Say further, party C is in government and can make it such that the party receives an additional 5% in votes in the next election in all districts with party C incumbents (because resources by the government were channeled to the district or the incumbents could receive more media attention). Via this mechanism we now observe an incumbency advantage for party C incumbents.

Now assume that party S is in government and can engage in the same behaviour. Districts in which party S is incumbent now receive an additional 5%. This is the same as saying that party S will do worse (relatively) in districts with party C incumbents. Crucially this implies that we would observe that party C incumbents also have an incumbency advantage. Despite the fact that the mechanism is driven by the access to government of the incumbents of party S, we observe that incumbents from both parties

93

have an incumbency advantage. If both have the same government bonus, $\delta^S = \delta^C$ will be zero. If a universal government bonus exists and contributes to the incumbency advantage it will be indistinguishable from other mechanisms.

Say, we find δ^S and δ^C to be significant ($\delta^j \neq 0$). This necessarily implies that there is heterogeneity in how both parties can capitalize on a government bonus. It is only if, e.g., one party can use the government bonus and the other cannot, that we can empirically observe δ^S and δ^C to matter. Note, that similar to above, we can still not say, which of the two parties is actually driving the results.

The second key observation is that the parameters δ^j and γ^j interact in $\gamma^S = \gamma^C + \delta^C$. Assume that γ^C is positive and δ^C is negative and both have the same size in absolute values. That implies that γ^S is zero and δ^S is positive. What at first looks as if party C is punished when in government (while party S gains) can also be interpreted as showing that both have an incumbency effect when party S is in government: γ^C for party C and γ^S plus δ^S for party S. This is the way we interpret our results below. Stated differently, when we hold the governing party constant, the incumbency effects of one party is the mirror image of the effect for the other. For more clarity, we supply a graphical interpretation of these considerations in the appendix.

Turning from the simple example to the actual data, we should note that the German system includes more than two parties. However, there are two major parties (CDU and SPD) that participate in every district during federal elections. Almost all directly elected candidates come from one of the two major parties. Hence, we expect the results to be a noisy representations of the above logical observations.[10]

3.2.2 Electoral system

The German electoral system at the federal and state level is a mixed-member proportional system. The intention of such a system is to have proportional representation in parliament without sacrificing local representation and accountability of the legislators. Therefore, voters make two distinct choices on election day. First, they cast their ballot for the representative of their district (hereafter *direct candidate*) in a first-past-the-post system. Second, they elect the party for the proportional representation in parliament (hereafter *second ballot*).

There are twice as many seats in the federal parliament (*Bundestag*) as there are electoral districts. The second ballot determines the number of seats that a party can fill

---

10 Cox and Katz (2002) analyze the incumbency advantages for Republicans and Democrats separately and find interpretable differences. However, in a pure two-party system one should be the mirror image of the other. Their results and interpretation is therefore at odds with our theoretical considerations.

in total, and it is calculated with the Sainte-Laguë algorithm.[11] Direct candidates always get their seat; the remaining seats are filled through the party lists. If there are no remaining seats, that can happen if, a party has more winning direct candidates than there are seats for it, the party will get one more seat in the federal parliament, a so called overhang seat (*Überhangmandat*).[12]

3.3 Empirical strategy

The empirical challenge for estimating incumbency effects is that incumbency is not exogenous: comparing the vote share of those districts with CDU incumbents to those with SPD incumbents will tell us nothing causal about the effect of incumbency. We therefore rely on a regression discontinuity design (RDD) to isolate exogenous variation in the incumbency status.[13] The model that we use for our estimation is

$$y_{i,t+1} = \alpha + \beta_t + \gamma d_{i,t} + \delta d_{i,t} g_t + h(v_{i,t}, d_{i,t}, g_t; \theta) + \phi_s + \varepsilon_{i,t} \qquad (3.5)$$

We run a separate regression for both parties, CDU and SPD, but leave out the superscript p for better readability. For the same reason, we also leave out the superscript s denoting the state that a district belongs to. The outcome variable $y_{i,t+1}$ is the vote share of that party's direct candidate in the next election $t+1$ in district i. In later specifications we also use the probability of winning or the vote share of the second ballot in the next election as an outcome variable.

The coefficients of interest are γ and δ, where $d_{i,t}$ is the incumbency or treatment dummy and g_t denotes whether the party in question was in government or not. The β_t replaces the stand-alone g_t term as these election fixed effects β_t are collinear with the government dummy.

The function $h(\cdot)$ is the control function of the margin of victory, $v_{i,t}$; that is, the difference in vote share between the candidate in question and the best opponent. This

---

11 This algorithm divides the total number of votes by the total number of seats. The resulting quotient is the "price" for each seat. In a next step, the number of votes that each party receives (their "budget") is divided by this quotient or "price" to get the exact number of seat that this party should receive with perfect proportionality. Using standard rounding, these exact numbers are then turned into integers.

12 The exact calculation in the federal election is complex, as the algorithm applies separately to each state. The resulting overhang seats in the federal election are not compensated for, which implies that proportionality can be violated. In 2009, the federal election resulted in 24 overhang seats (out of a total of 622 seats), all for the CDU (or CSU in Bavaria), whereas in 2005 there were 7 for the CDU and 9 for the SPD. In state elections, these overhang seats are usually compensated for by giving other parties additional seats, too. The details regarding these so called leveling seats (*Ausgleichsmandat*) vary.

13 Others use a similar design using close elections in order to estimate causal effects of political outcomes. Lee, Moretti, and Butler (2004) and Pettersson-Lidbom (2008) are among the first, Hainmueller and Kern (2008), Freier (2011), Freier and Odendahl (2011), Ade and Freier (2011), are examples in the context of Germany. Ade and Freier (2011) is also contained in this dissertation (chapter 2) in a slightly different version. See Imbens and Lemieux (2008) for a more general treatment of RDDs.

margin of victory can be positive or negative, depending on whether the candidate of that party won or lost. A margin of victory close to zero implies a very close race and the relationship between $d_{i,t}$ and $v_{i,t}$ is as follows:

$$d_{i,t} = 1\,[v_{i,t} > 0] \tag{3.6}$$

The function $h(\cdot)$ is fully interacted with the incumbency and government dummies. While interacting the control function with the treatment dummy $(d_{i,t})$ is common practice, the interaction with the government dummy g_t serves an important purpose, too. We allow the effect of the vote share in t to have a different impact on the vote share in $t + 1$ depending on whether the party in question is in government or not. This mimics the approach of estimating the incumbency effect in separate samples for being in government or not. Finally, we include state fixed effects ϕ_s.[14]

After this short description of our empirical approach, we discuss the RDD approach and its assumptions before turning to the issue of whether we can causally interpret the interaction term. In general, RDDs have a forcing variable v that may or may not be correlated with unobserved variables that affect the outcome y. In our case, the margin of victory is the forcing variable v and is correlated with a general preference for one or the other party. Our outcome is vote shares in the next election, which is clearly related to both preferences and the margin of victory. However, there is a discontinuous jump in the party identity of the winner. So even though v is related to y, it is so *continuously*, which implies that the jump in our treatment variable is exogenous.

Our design is therefore based on the assumption that the expectations of the potential outcomes y_0 and y_1 in a Rubin Causal Model are continuous in the forcing variable v.[15] That is, the vote share of the CDU in the next election should be continuously related to the current margin of victory v of the CDU candidate in both worlds: whether the CDU candidate wins or loses.

For example, one concern is that parties could be able to sort around either side of the threshold $v = 0$. That is, if there is some unobservable factor that makes CDU candidates the winner in some close races but not others, the design would be invalid because potential outcomes would not be continuous in v.

It is impossible to test this key assumption directly since we cannot observe the outcomes in both worlds, when the CDU candidate wins and loses. However, we can offer auxiliary methods to assess whether it is plausibly satisfied.

---

14 There are 16 states, including three city-states, in Germany, with a total of between 250 and 325 districts. For example, the city-state of Berlin has 12 districts.

15 See Imbens and Lemieux (2008) for details.

Another concern is that parties strategically place candidates in contested districts. There are two arguments in favor of our approach. First, both parties would strategically place candidates. Second, the direct candidates are usually of a local breed, which limits the scope for the party to strategically place a specific candidates. What is more, this would not necessarily invalidate our design: if it is still random whether they lose or win if the race is close, our results remain internally valid. External validity is a different matter, but the two arguments in favor of our approach mitigate a potential problem here.

The inclusion of a control function is essential, unless we are very close to the threshold. A correctly specified control function will capture any correlation of $d_{i,t}$ with the error term that might be of concern. In our estimations we use a sample limited to observations within a 2% margin of victory without a control function, the 5% margin sample with a linear control function, and the whole sample with a 4th order polynomial control function.

The effect that we are estimating is of course local in nature: we are only using close election outcomes for identification. However, because of the first-past-the-post system the vote share of winners ranges from around 30% to 47% because the smaller parties typically nominate a direct candidate as well.

It is important to note that we are estimating the incumbency of *parties* and not of specific candidates. While it might at first appear to be more intuitive to study the incumbency effects of specific candidates that run for consecutive elections, such an analysis requires significantly more data and econometric modeling.[16] The major issue complicating the analysis is the endogenous choice of the candidates to exit the race. A candidate that considers it unlikely to win next time will choose to opt out, while a sure winner may be more likely to stay in the race. This would bias our results because we can only look at those that stayed in the race. Incumbency (or (re-)running) would then be related to the expected vote in future elections.[17]

By focusing on party incumbency we eliminate this problem. Our incumbency measure, also used by Lee (2008) and Hainmueller and Kern (2008), includes the personal incumbency effect without bias as well as potential spillovers to a new candidate from the same party.

We now turn to the causal interpretation of the interaction term. Our RDD setting allows us to estimate a causal effect of incumbency in each of the four possible samples separately: CDU plus CDU in government, CDU plus SPD in government, SPD plus

---

16   See Gelman and King (1990) for a full discussion of the personal incumbency advantage.

17   Cox and Katz (2002) discuss this issue in detail, while Ansolabehere and Snyder (2004) show that it is less of a problem in US elections.

CDU in government and SPD plus SPD in government. Under the assumptions discussed above, each of these effects compares bare CDU winners to bare CDU losers (and likewise for the SPD). When we interpret the interaction effect causally, we in effect *compare* the effects in these four different samples.

This comparison is problematic insofar as there may be other aspects affecting the incumbency effect and that are correlated with the party in government. When we offer interpretations for heterogeneous incumbency effects, we always do so with the caveat in mind that government participation may not be the whole story. However, one of our robustness test – estimating the same interaction effect in 13 election periods between 1994 and 2010 from eight different German state elections – shows that the effect is similar. This increases our confidence that government participation may be the decisive factor in the comparison. We return to this issue in section 3.5.3.

3.4 Data

We use official election data for federal and state elections. In table 3.1 we summarize the data for the federal elections. Starting with the election in 1976, there are nine government terms, with the last election in 2009. Since the last government term saw a so called "grand coalition" of the center-right CDU and the center left SPD, we only include the last period in robustness tests. Three terms ended before the official four years were over: in 1983 a government change led to new elections, in 1990 the reunification required a shorter duration and in 2005 chancellor Schröder called for a federal election after his unpopular Agenda 2010 reforms led to landslide victories for the opposition in several state elections.

One concern with the data is redistricting of the electoral districts, in particular before the 2002 election.[18] We exclude observations of districts that had seen substantial changes in the structure of the voting population. The number of observations reported in table 3.1 may therefore deviate from the absolute number of districts. Column 3 of table 3.1 contains the leading party in the government coalition.[19] Columns 4 and 5 show the number of direct seats that both parties have won. The final two columns show, for the CDU only, how many of the races were close: 199 using a 2% margin and 514 using a 5% margin. Since the leading candidates in almost all districts are from CDU or SPD, this also gives an indication of how many were close for the SPD.

---

18 For the 2002 election, the number of districts was reduced to 299 from 328. We analyzed this reform and found that 238 districts remained structurally unchanged. To make sure that the inclusion of these observations does not drive our results, we exclude this year from robustness tests but results remain unchanged.

19 The first and the last government term is special in this respect. In the 1980–83 period, the government changed after three years from a SPD-FDP coalition to a CDU-FDP coalition. The latter coalition, however, only governed for four months before an early election took place, so we coded the period as "SPD". In the 2005–09 period, Germany had a so called "grand coalition" that consists of the two large parties CDU and SPD. This period is coded as both CDU and SPD.

Table 3.1: Descriptives – federal elections

Period	Obs.	Head of Government	Seats won CDU	Seats won SPD	Tight elections (CDU) 2% margin	Tight elections (CDU) 5% margin
'76-'80	161	SPD	98	63	18	41
'80-'83	248	SPD[a]	121	127	20	49
'83-'87	248	CDU	180	68	22	57
'87-'90	248	CDU	169	79	21	51
'90-'94	322	CDU	232	89	24	60
'94-'98	325	CDU	221	100	25	71
'98-'02	238	SPD	97	140	20	60
'02-'05	296	SPD	125	168	22	61
'05-'09	279	CDU[b]	138	137	27	64
	2365		1381	971	199	514

a After the first two years of the four year term the coalition partner of the SPD, the FDP, decided to cooperate with the CDU and elected a CDU chancellor. In order to morally legitimize the new government called for early election in 1983. Overall the the CDU led government was in power for only four months before the premature election. Hence the SPD headed the government for most of the period and we coded the period as SPD governed.
b Coalition government of CDU and SPD, led by the CDU. *Notes: Source:* Own calculations based on the data provided by the state offices for statistical services.

Only in recent years has the SPD seen a few more tight races in districts where they had competition from third parties.

During our robustness tests , we also estimate incumbency effects and government participation at the state level. The descriptive statistics for these are given in table 3.4 in the appendix.

3.5 Results

3.5.1 Main results

The results of our main estimation are presented in table 3.2. The upper panel shows the results for the estimation using only the center-right party (CDU), the lower panel the results using the center-left party (SPD). We estimate three different specifications that we repeat for each of the different cases. The first only uses data from observations within a 2 percentage points margin around the threshold, the second specification uses data with a five percentage point margin and also includes a linear control function, and the last uses the full sample while making use of a fourth order control function. Without a government interaction term, the effects for both CDU and SPD should have the same size and sign in a pure two-party system, as outlined in section 3.2. The first three columns of table 3.2 show that this holds true even in the German system that is not a pure two-party system. The first line shows the estimates for the CDU in all periods that we consider, that is, 1976–2009. They compare well to the first line in the lower panel for the SPD. The bottom estimates of both panels show the average incumbency effect for the period 1990–2005. Our estimates are in the same ballpark as those of Hainmueller and Kern (2005).

Turning to the heterogeneity in the effects in columns 4–6, we find that the CDU and the SPD have a positive incumbency effect in periods when the SPD was in government: in column 4, the CDU candidate gains 2.9% points in the subsequent election after when a CDU candidate barely won the past direct candidate election, but is not in government, whereas the SPD gains 3.5% points (treatment estimate plus interaction term). These effects compare well to alternative specifications in columns 5 and 6. When the CDU is in government, the effects for both parties are insignificant.

The lower part of both panels show the same effects for the later period 1990–2005, that is, after reunification. The effects are noticeably larger, albeit not significantly so. Comparing the effects also to the subperiod from 1976–1990, we find that the overall effect is entirely driven by the later subperiod. In fact, for the early period, even the average incumbency effect cannot be consistently found.[20] We return to those before and after reunification differences in the discussion of the results in section 3.5.2.

We can also inspect these effects graphically. Figure 3.1 shows the incumbency effect from the perspective of the CDU. When the CDU is *not* in government, there is a sizable jump of roughly 3 percentage points in the vote share during the next election. This compares well to the stylized figure 3.4 in the appendix. Figure 3.2 contains the same effect when the CDU is in government. As the estimation results suggest, there is no incumbency effect.

So far, we consider the vote share as our outcome variable. How these gains in vote share translate into a probability of winning is what we turn to next. Table 3.3 is structured in the same way as table 3.2. In columns 1–3, we see an average incumbency effect of roughly 22 percentage points in the probability of winning, which again is in the same ballpark as those in Hainmueller and Kern (2005). Columns 4–6 show that the incumbency effect on the probability of winning is only present if the SPD is in government: 43.8% points for the CDU candidate, and 34.7% points for the SPD candidate. All effects are stable across different specifications.[21]

However, there is a problem with using the probability of winning as an outcome variable: it is bounded at zero and one. While this is theoretically true for the vote share

---

20 That is not to say that an average incumbency effect does not exist. However, it is noticeable that we cannot pick it up in the data consistently before but can after reunification.

21 For the period before 1990, the average incumbency effect using the probability of winning as an outcome is roughly the same (not shown). However, the interaction term is insignificant.

Table 3.2: Federal elections – party incumbency and government participation

	Incumbency			Gov. Participation		
	(1)	(2)	(3)	(4)	(5)	(6)
	Panel 1: Center-right party / CDU					
All elections 1976–2009						
Treatment (d)	0.017***	0.010*	0.015***	0.029***	0.017*	0.021***
	(0.004)	(0.005)	(0.004)	(0.008)	(0.010)	(0.008)
Interaction (g*d)				−0.019**	−0.011	−0.013
				(0.009)	(0.011)	(0.009)
Period from 1976–1990						
Treatment (d)	0.015***	0.005	0.010*	0.014*	−0.002	0.006
	(0.005)	(0.007)	(0.006)	(0.008)	(0.008)	(0.008)
Interaction (g*d)				0.002	0.011	0.006
				(0.011)	(0.012)	(0.011)
Period from 1990–2005						
Treatment (d)	0.020***	0.015*	0.020***	0.041***	0.032**	0.037***
	(0.007)	(0.008)	(0.007)	(0.015)	(0.015)	(0.012)
Interaction (g*d)				−0.036**	−0.030*	−0.030**
				(0.016)	(0.017)	(0.014)
	Panel 2: Center-left party / SPD					
All elections 1976–2009						
Treatment (d)	0.023***	0.013**	0.011**	0.010	0.000	0.002
	(0.004)	(0.005)	(0.005)	(0.007)	(0.008)	(0.008)
Interaction (g*d)				0.025***	0.024**	0.017*
				(0.009)	(0.011)	(0.010)
Period from 1976–1990						
Treatment (d)	0.022***	0.011	0.007	0.016*	0.012	0.008
	(0.005)	(0.007)	(0.006)	(0.008)	(0.012)	(0.010)
Interaction (g*d)				0.014	−0.001	−0.003
				(0.012)	(0.014)	(0.012)
Period from 1990–2005						
Treatment (d)	0.024***	0.015*	0.012*	0.009	−0.007	−0.006
	(0.007)	(0.009)	(0.007)	(0.008)	(0.010)	(0.010)
Interaction (g*d)				0.037***	0.051***	0.040***
				(0.013)	(0.016)	(0.014)
N (Panel 1/ Panel 2)	199/201	514/524	2365	199/201	514/524	2365
Controlfunction	No	linear	4th order	No	linear	4th order
Sample	2% margin	5% margin	full	2% margin	5% margin	full
Year and state dummies	Yes	Yes	Yes	Yes	Yes	Yes

Notes: Significance levels: * $p < 0.10$, ** $p < 0.05$, *** $p < 0.01$. Standard errors in parentheses are robust. The dependent variable is the vote share of the respective party in t. The regressions in columns 1–3 indicate the pure party incumbency effect. Columns 4–6 also include the interaction between treatment (winning the district in $t - 1$) and whether the party is in charge of government activity. Estimates in panel 1 are for the center-right party (CDU) and panel 2 show the results for the center-left party (SPD). Sample restrictions and control functions of the margin of victory are indicated below. Any polynomial control function of the degree indicated is specified to be flexible on both sides of the threshold. *Source*: Own calculations.

Figure 3.1: Incumbency effect for the CDU – CDU *not* in government

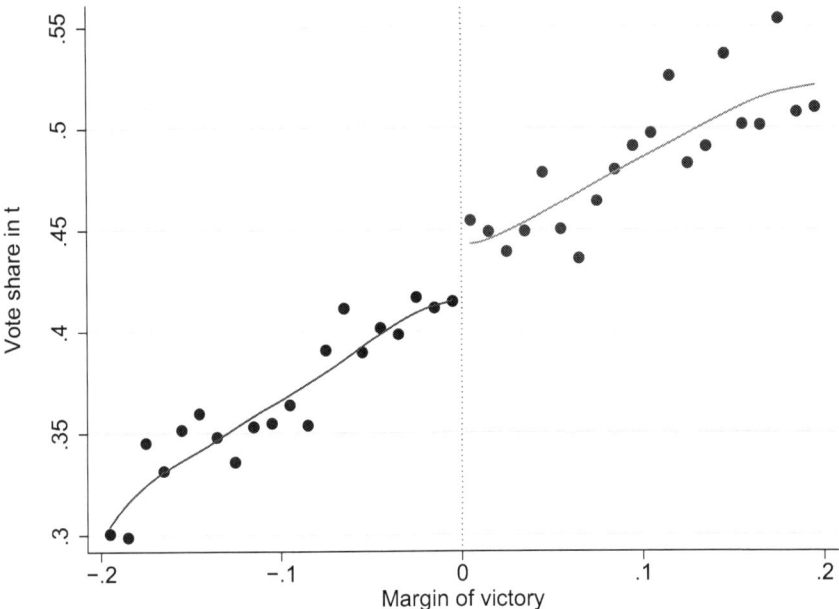

Notes: This figure presents the jump in the vote shares at the zero margin of victory threshold. The data is grouped in bins of 1% in the margin of victory. The line is based on a local kernel estimation using Epanechnikov weights. *Source:* Own calculations.

as well, it is not of practical importance there. For the probability of winning on other hand, this can pose a serious problem for the estimation. Figure 3.3 displays the incumbency effect on the probability of winning for a specific election pair graphically. The left hand side shows the probability of winning in 2009 for SPD incumbents from 2005. The probability of winning would yield an incumbency effect of zero, so what happened?

The explanation is that there was a large shift in the political landscape in 2009 (the outcome variable for these graphs is from 2009), when the SPD lost many seats to the CDU. At the margin, that means that *nobody* in the SPD that won with up to a 2% points margin in 2005 reclaimed their seats. The mirror image of this is that *everyone* from the CDU with up to −2% points margin of victory in the 2005 election, won a seat. The essence of this is that large political swings can bring the probability of winning to its lower and upper bounds.

Figure 3.2: Incumbency effect for the CDU – CDU in government

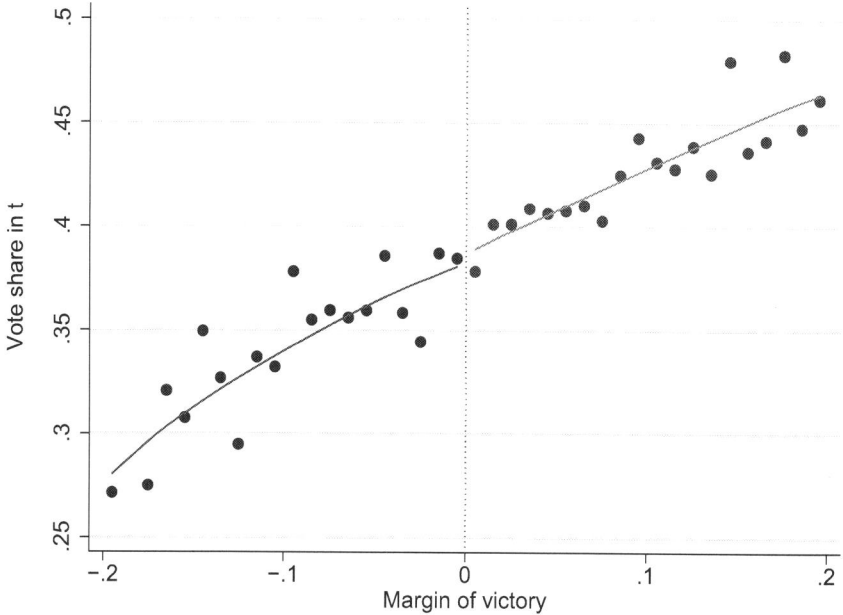

Notes: This figure presents the (lack of a) jump in the vote shares at the zero margin of victory threshold. The data is grouped in bins of 1% in the margin of victory. The line is based on a local kernel estimation using Epanechnikov weights. *Source:* Own calculations.

This can potentially be problematic for any study that uses the probability of winning as the outcome variable. If the probability of winning is at its boundaries at times of large political swings and not at others, the interpretation of an average incumbency effect in this measure is misspecified. As pointed out in figure 3.3, there can be times in which an incumbency advantage may exist (in vote share, see right panel), however, the probability of winning cannot pick it up. This is why the vote share is our preferred outcome measure.

3.5.2 Discussion

The theoretical observations in section 3.2 above show that the interaction term can only capture heterogeneity, not a full government effect on incumbency. Moreover, we saw that both parties have an incumbency effect when the SPD is in government, but none when the CDU is in government. Whether the CDU or the SPD is driving the former effect – one must be roughly the mirror image of the other – and what might be the underlying reason for the heterogeneity, is the question we explore next.

Figure 3.3: Probability of winning vs. vote share as an outcome variable, SPD in 2009

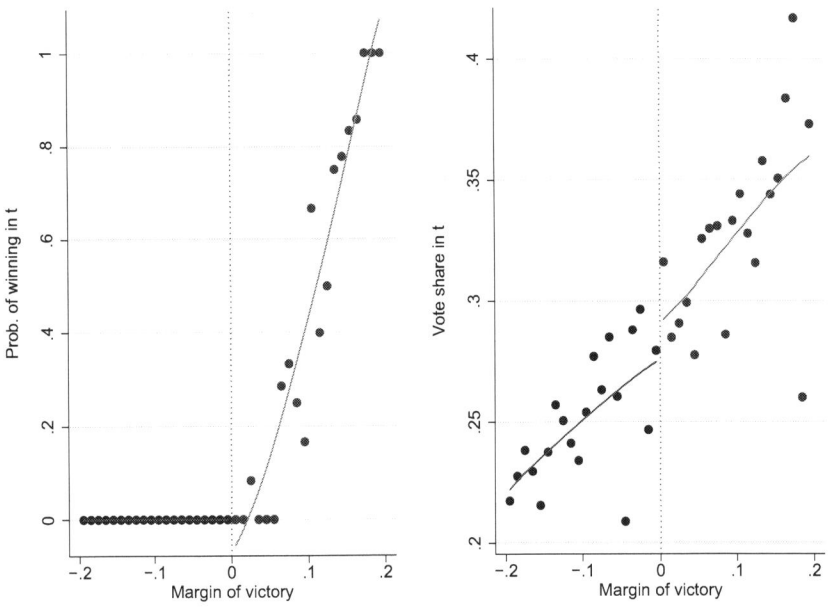

Notes: The left part displays the probability of winning by margin of victory for SPD incumbents in 2005, using the 2009 election results as outcome variables, the right hand part the vote share. *Source:* Own calculations.

Our hypothesis is that the social democrats (SPD) are driving the effect and that the increased competition by a far-left party that emerged after reunification is the reason behind the heterogeneity. After the fall of the wall in 1989, the SPD soon faced a serious competitor from the left, the post-communist party The Left (*Die Linke*/PDS). We believe that in this setting SPD-district representatives are only successfully in district races against CDU and The Left if they hold the incumbent position *and* have the backing of the government. It is only then that these representatives may successfully promote the district's interests in actual decision making while they were weak and easy to attack in all three other cases.[22]

---

22 The literature also suggests that political competition may well be the reason for an incumbency advantage. Snyder and Hirano (2009) find that the incumbency effect is larger in competitive districts. Stein and Bickers (1997) suggest that incumbents in competitive districts may use the resources of office to a larger extent, which is in part confirmed in other contexts, for instance for competitively elected judges in Gordon and Huber (2007).

Table 3.3: Federal elections – probability of winning

	Incumbency			Gov. Participation		
	(1)	(2)	(3)	(4)	(5)	(6)
	Panel 1: Center-right party					
Period 1976–1990						
Treatment (d)	0.262**	0.233*	0.316***	0.235*	0.173	0.292***
	(0.103)	(0.125)	(0.118)	(0.118)	(0.116)	(0.105)
Interaction (g*d)				0.039	0.076	−0.074
				(0.198)	(0.217)	(0.184)
Period 1990–2005						
Treatment (d)	0.241**	0.226**	0.161*	0.438***	0.382**	0.312***
	(0.095)	(0.098)	(0.083)	(0.164)	(0.159)	(0.120)
Interaction (g*d)				−0.342*	−0.277	−0.316**
				(0.190)	(0.195)	(0.157)
	Panel 2: Center-left party					
Period 1976–1990						
Treatment (d)	0.262**	0.233*	0.316***	0.274*	0.249	0.218
	(0.103)	(0.125)	(0.118)	(0.146)	(0.176)	(0.148)
Interaction (g*d)				−0.039	−0.076	0.074
				(0.198)	(0.217)	(0.184)
Period 1990–2005						
Treatment (d)	0.235**	0.215**	0.193**	0.091	0.064	0.012
	(0.092)	(0.098)	(0.083)	(0.100)	(0.112)	(0.100)
Interaction (g*d)				0.347*	0.347*	0.333**
				(0.188)	(0.194)	(0.156)
Controlfunction	No	linear	4th order	No	linear	4th order
Sample	2% margin	5% margin	full	2% margin	5% margin	full
Year and state dummies	Yes	Yes	Yes	Yes	Yes	Yes

Notes: Significance levels: * $p < 0.10$, ** $p < 0.05$, *** $p < 0.01$. Standard errors in parentheses are robust. The dependent variable is the probability for the party of winning the district in t. The estimates are for the sub period 1990–2005. The regressions in columns 1–3 indicate the pure party incumbency effect. Columns 4–6 also include the interaction between treatment (winning the district in $t-1$) and whether the party is in charge of government activity. Estimates in panel 1 are for the center-right conservative party and panel 2 show the results for the center-left social democrats. Sample restrictions and control functions of the margin of victory are indicated below. Any polynomial control function of the degree indicated is specified to be flexible on both sides of the threshold. *Source*: Own calculations.

There are three key arguments supporting our hypothesis. First, the heterogeneous incumbency effect is really only observable after reunification (as argued before), second, it is stronger in East Germany and third, we can show that district incumbency for the SPD has a direct negative effect on the votes share of The Left.

Regarding the first argument, we have already highlighted the differential effects for the period before and after 1990 in tables 3.2 and 3.3.

The second argument that the effects are stronger in the east is shown by table 3.5 in the appendix. The effects in the East are between 2 and 5 times as high, albeit not as robust across different specifications, while the effects in the West are still significant and reasonably robust. What is special about Eastern Germany is the vote share of the socialist party The Left. Figure 3.6 in the appendix shows that the median in the East was between 10% and 30%, while in the Western districts it was below 5% until 2009 when they reached around 7%.

The third point, that an SPD incumbent had a negative impact on the vote share of The Left, is presented in table 3.6 in the appendix. We read this table from the perspective of an SPD incumbent: treatment d is defined as winning a seat for the center-left SPD, and the government dummy g indicates whether the SPD was in government. The outcome, however, is the direct candidate and second ballot vote share of The Left, not of the SPD. The results show that the SPD incumbency effects when the SPD is in government might have been partly at the expense of the left party, even though the effect is not stable across all specifications.

Summing up, there is considerable evidence for our hypothesis that the SPD, under increasing competition, may have scaled up its efforts in districts with winning SPD candidates. Thus, increased competition from the far left may drive the heterogeneous incumbency effect: Not only are the effects bigger in the East, where The Left has its strongholds, and higher after 1990, but also there is a negative effect of SPD incumbents on The Left vote share. A further indication that these observations are not casual is that we find the same heterogeneous effects for state elections (see table 3.8 in the appendix).

Although we believe that there is support for our hypothesis we emphasize that all those arguments can only give an indication. The RDD analysis in subgroups (east-west, before and after 1990) does not explain what determines the differences between these groups but only shows that they exist. In principle, one could argue that other than the above presented mechanism could cause the different results for the subsamples. To rule out some alternative explanations, we investigated whether candidate characteristics differ by whether SPD or CDU is in government. For that, we coded the biographies of all close winners in our sample.[23] We ask whether either one of the following four alternative hypotheses could play a role in the observed differences: 1.) Increase in the share of women in parliament, 2.) changes on ties of candidates to their local constituency, 3.) differences of qualification level of the candidates and

---

23 We took the biographical information from the periodical publication *"Kürschner's Jahrbuch"* in which all members of parliament of a given period are briefly introduced. We did this for every district that was decided within a margin of victory of 2 percentage points, which we believe is a close margin. Unfortunately, we only observe these characteristics for the winner of close races, and we cannot consistently compare these characteristics also for the losers. This implies, that we cannot directly introduce those variables in the RDD analysis.

4.) tenure in the parliament and party. The results are presented in table 3.9 in the appendix.

First, we look at the share of women by party and governmental lead. Voters might be biased towards women as politicians, and women could receive less of an incumbency advantage as a result. Also, there have been changes in the structure of female participation in parliament during the period of observation. However, while it is true that the SPD has a higher share of women among the winners of close races, there is no difference between times in which the CDU or SPD had the governmental lead. We conclude that the observed heterogeneity in the incumbency effects cannot be explained by the number of female candidates in the races.[24]

Moreover, we coded whether a candidate was born in the district as a proxy for the local ties of a candidate. Although the difference in shares is not negligible (particularly for the SPD), those differences are not significant.

We also investigate two measures of candidate quality, the share of university graduates and the share of candidates that hold important positions in the party or the government.[25] There is no indication that candidates of SPD and CDU were different depending on who was in charge of the government.

Lastly, we coded the seniority of the candidates both within the parliament and in the party. We have information on how many periods and years a candidate has served in the parliament (at the time of winning the close race) and about the years of membership with the party. Also, here we do not observe any differences.

We also repeated this analysis for the later period (1990–2005) only for which we find strong heterogeneity effects (not reported). Also in this period, we do not observe significant differences of candidate characteristics by governmental lead.[26]

Overall, the analysis of the candidate characteristics does not hint at an alternative explanation as to why we observe the heterogeneous incumbency effects. While this does not directly imply that our preferred hypothesis is indeed correct, it makes it more likely that this is the case.

---

24 Note, that the share of women indeed increased sharply after 1990 in the SPD. However, within the subperiod from 1990–2005 there is no significant differences in the number of women among close winners by governmental lead.

25 We coded a candidate to be in an important position if she was holding a position in the cabinet, as a undersecretary in a ministry, was active in the board of the party, heading a parliamentary committee or was the spokesperson of the party.

26 Among all the characteristics we observe one significant difference (only at 10 percent level). Results are available from the authors upon request.

Moving from the specifics of our interpretation to broader political economics questions, our results show that positive and significant estimates of an incumbency effect may not show what they seem to show. In our case, the average incumbency effect for both parties may lead readers to believe that both have an incumbency effect. Yet the effect differs by party and government participation as we have seen. The theoretical explanations as to why these effects exist (e.g. media coverage, name recognition) may therefore be very different once we consider heterogeneity.

3.5.3 Robustness and Validity

In this final subsection, we offer some robustness and validity checks for our main results. A first robustness check is whether these results hold for state elections as well – a government level in Germany not been covered so far by other empirical studies on the subject. State elections work in a similar way as federal election with the added complication that if there are overhang seats, the other parties are compensated in some way such that the proportionality is roughly preserved. This in turn implies that direct candidates change the final result of the election to a lesser extent. Moreover, the direct candidates – especially in the Eastern states – do come from parties other than CDU and SPD, moving us further away from a pure two party system.

Table 3.8 in the appendix provide the results for the state elections that confirm our analysis on the federal level. For the center-right party (CDU), the effects are very robust and slightly larger than the federal effects.[27] For the center-left party (SPD), the effects are not as stable, which indicates that on the state level the party system is more diverse even for the direct candidates. However, they still indicate that being in government is – in relative terms – beneficial for SPD incumbents: when the SPD is not in government, the incumbency effect is an insignificant -4.5% points in column (6); when the SPD is in government, the effect is 3.9% and insignificant as well. However, the difference between the two is significant.

The results for the second ballot of the election, can also serve as a further robustness test. In table 3.7 in the appendix, we find that a spillover effect of incumbency (incumbency externality effect) towards the second ballot exists and go in the same direction as our main results. The effects for the CDU are very robust: the average incumbency effect is slightly positive and significant but when disaggregated by government participation, the incumbency effect is only positive when the opposition is in government. For the SPD, the effects are less strong and robust, but have the same sign as those for the direct candidates.[28] The fact that the SPD results are less clear in the second vote

---

27 Note that the state elections come from the post-reunification period only. Therefore, the correct comparison is the lower panel of the federal table.

28 For the second ballot, Germany clearly has a multi-party system, which brings us even further away from the two-party considerations above.

is somewhat puzzling. Unfortunately, we did not find a fully consistent story in the data, that could help us to understand this observation.

In two further robustness checks, we exclude the 1998–2002 period and include the 2005–2009 period respectively. There are two concerns with the 1998 election and the vote share outcomes in 2002. First of all, 1998 was a major swing in the political landscape, away from the CDU towards the SPD and the Greens. Second, there was a major redistricting in 2002. While we drop observations that were difficult to match to older districts, there could still be a selection effect. In the 2005–2009 period, the governing ("grand") coalition consisted of the two major parties, CDU and SPD. When we drop the election in 1998 (that is, we drop those that run as incumbents in 2002), the results are unchanged and, if anything, stronger (table not included). When we include the 2005 election (and therefore, the 2009 outcomes), the results remain unchanged (not shown).[29]

Turning to the validity of our original design, we conduct a placebo test in which we set the threshold of the margin of victory to -5% and $+5\%$ respectively. In other words, if we set the threshold to -5%, we are comparing losers to losers, and if we set it to +5% we are comparing winners to winners. The results for the period 1990–2005 using only the center-right party (CDU) are given in table 3.10 in the appendix. There are no stable effects of incumbency, especially for the specification using the interaction term.[30]

Further validation of our design comes from a histogram that shows the frequency of margins of victory. While not sufficient, such a frequency comparison gives an indication of whether close election occur with equal frequency on both sides of the threshold – an important aspect of whether the variation around the threshold is as good as random. The top panels of figure 3.7 show the distribution of margins of victory for the full sample (left) and zooming in on the range between +/-10% (right). The lower panels show the frequencies by government participation in the subsequent period, zooming in on the sample +/-20%. In all four panels there are no noticable differences in the distribution to either side of the threshold.

A final test for the validity of the RDD is to check whether observations on either side of the threshold are balance in observable characteristics. Caughey and Sekhon (2010) suggest that the two variables are of specific interest: the predetermined vote share in the previous election and the past incumbency status. Figure 3.8 illustrates that we find no significant differences in the distributions of these variables. The upper two graphs show the binned averages in the mean, while the lower graphs focus on the second

---

29 When we include the 2005–2009 period, we code the government interaction as SPD in government and CDU in government. Results are available from the authors upon request.

30 The results are similar to those using the SPD, or using +/-2% and +/-10% as placebo thresholds (not shown).

moment of the distribution. Overall, the tests of frequencies, placebo treatment, and predetermined variables indicate that our research design is valid.

3.6   Conclusion

In this paper, we analyse the heterogeneity of incumbency effects for direct candidates in German federal elections. We find the same average effect for both parties that is previously identified in the literature. However, when we disaggregate the effects into government participation and opposition, we find noticeable differences between the two major parties: both parties have an incumbency effect only when the center-left party SPD is in government. This effect holds up in a wide range of specifications and even in state elections that are unrelated to federal elections.

As we show theoretically, it is impossible to identify an overall government participation effect because in a two party system, one incumbency effect is the mirror image of the other: if candidates of the governing party have an incumbency advantage, the opposition candidates have a likewise advantage because losers of one party reflect winners of the other. What we therefore identify is a heterogeneity in the government participation effect.

We also explore what might explain the heterogeneity in the incumbency effect. Based on additional evidence we argue that the increased pressure of the former communist party "The Left" on the center-left SPD after reunification may have induced the SPD to use its direct candidates more to its advantage when in government.

Beyond the main findings of the paper the results also expose a weakness in the current literature: average incumbency effects may not tell you much regarding the theoretical effects behind them. The observation we make that a positive effect for both parties is only present if the SPD is in government challenges the customary view that name recognition, presence in the media and pork-barrel spending matter for the incumbency advantage. Investigating the heterogeneity of these effects is therefore a promising avenue for future research.

Appendix

Graphical representation of the theoretical consideration

A graphical representation of the theoretical observation in section 3.2.1 may be helpful for an intuitive understanding. Let us assume that the incumbent can generate benefits for her district if, and only if, her party is in government. We further maintain the assumption of a pure two-party system. What we expect to see is the following (figure 3.4): if party C is in government, those candidates of party C that barely win (area II) compared to those that barely lost (area I) will experience an incumbency

Figure 3.4: Incumbency effect – from party C's standpoint

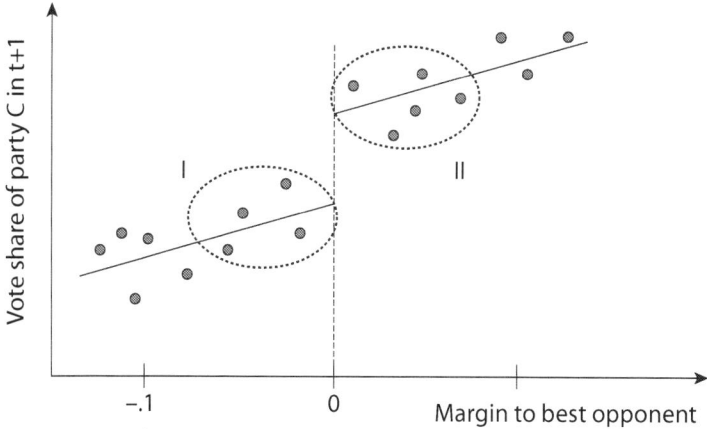

advantage at the next election because their party is in government. The winners in area II are driving the results so to speak.

Somewhat surprisingly, we can use the same figure for party C candidates if party C is *not* in government. The losers in area I are now driving the results because their opponents are from party S and are barely winners. Since party S is in government, they receive an incumbency advantage in the next election compared to candidates of party S that barely lost. The opponents of those that barely lost are from party C and therefore we see an incumbency effect for those party C winners even though the winners from party S were, in fact, driving the results. The figure therefore shows that when both parties' incumbents benefit from being in government, the interaction term above will be zero.

How would heterogeneity show in this figure? Assume once more that γ^C is positive and δ^C is negative and both have the same size in absolute values. If party S is in government, figure 3.4 still shows the effect of party C, captured by γ^C. Figure 3.5 then shows the effect when party C is in government, captured by γ^C plus the negative δ^C. In this figure, the party C winners in area II are the party S losers when party C is in government. Party S incumbent winners in area I therefore experience no incumbency effect, captured by γ^S. Going back to figure 3.4, however, we notice that party S winners do have a large incumbency effect when they are in government, as the party C losers in area I are the winners of party S, captured by γ^S plus δ^S.

Figure 3.5: Incumbency effect – again from party C's standpoint

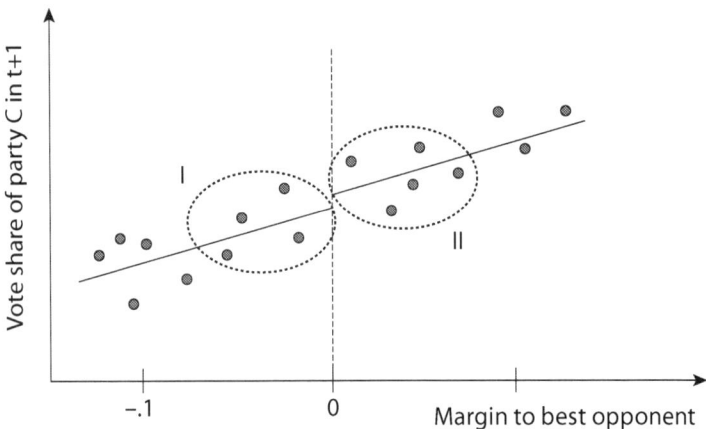

Tables and Figures

Table 3.4: Descriptives – state elections

State	Term	Obs.	Head of Government	Seats won CDU	Seats won SPD	Tight elections (CDU) 2% margin	Tight elections (CDU) 5% margin
Bav	'03-'08	91	CDU	91	0	0	1
Brand	'99-'04	44	SPD	2	37	4	10
Brand	'04-'09	44	SPD	4	17	4	8
Hesse	'03-'08	51	CDU	49	2	2	8
NRW	'05-'10	127	CDU	89	38	7	24
LS	'98-'03	100	SPD	16	84	7	17
LS	'03-'08	45	CDU	43	2	2	5
RP	'01-'06	51	SPD	21	30	6	20
SAAN	'94-'98	34	CDU	25	8	7	17
SAAN	'98-'02	34	SPD	2	32	2	4
SAAN	'02-'06	22	CDU	21	1	0	1
Thur	'99-'04	44	CDU	44	0	0	0
Thur	'04-'09	44	CDU	39	0	4	6
		731		446	251	45	121

Notes: Abbreviations: Bav – Bavaria, Brand – Brandenburg, NRW – North Rhine-Westphalia, LS – Lower Saxony, RP – Rhineland-Palatinate, SAAN- Saxony-Anhalt, Thur- Thuringia
Source: Own calculations based on the data provided by the state offices for statistical services.

Table 3.5: Effects by region: incumbency in the former East and West

	Former East			Former West		
	(1)	(2)	(3)	(4)	(5)	(6)
	Panel 1: Center-right party					
Treatment (d)	0.128***	0.040	0.064*	0.036**	0.029*	0.035***
	(0.008)	(0.032)	(0.034)	(0.015)	(0.017)	(0.012)
Interaction (g*d)	−0.137***	−0.037	−0.074	−0.028*	−0.030*	−0.032**
	(0.009)	(0.034)	(0.046)	(0.016)	(0.018)	(0.014)
N	12	32	216	76	213	927
	Panel 2: Center-left party					
Treatment (d)	−0.002	−0.027	−0.038	0.016**	0.005	−0.003
	(0.042)	(0.031)	(0.038)	(0.007)	(0.008)	(0.008)
Interaction (g*d)	0.105	0.158**	0.094*	0.023**	0.018	0.029**
	(0.074)	(0.060)	(0.049)	(0.010)	(0.013)	(0.012)
N	13	34	216	76	213	927
Controlfunction	No	linear	4th order	No	linear	4th order
Sample	2% margin	5% margin	full	2% margin	5% margin	full
Year and state dummies	Yes	Yes	Yes	Yes	Yes	Yes

Notes: Significance levels: * $p < 0.10$, ** $p < 0.05$, *** $p < 0.01$. Standard errors in parentheses are robust. The dependent variable is the vote share of the respective party in t. The estimates are for the subperiod 1990–2005. Panel 1 refers to results of the center-right conservative party. Panel 2 presents estimates for the center-left. Columns 1–3 are for the subsample of election districts in the former East while columns 4–6 refer to the former West. Sample restrictions and control functions of the margin of victory are indicated below. Any polynomial control function of the degree indicated is specified to be flexible on both sides of the threshold. *Source*: Own calculations.

Table 3.6: Effect on the left party

	Vote outcome of the left party					
	Majoritarian vote			Proportional vote		
	(1)	(2)	(3)	(4)	(5)	(6)
Probability of winning						
Treatment (d)	0.000	0.017	0.005	0.002	0.014	0.005
	(0.005)	(0.012)	(0.010)	(0.003)	(0.009)	(0.007)
Interaction (g*d)	0.000	−0.030*	−0.019	0.001	−0.024**	−0.018*
	(0.005)	(0.016)	(0.014)	(0.003)	(0.012)	(0.011)
N	92	260	1181	92	260	1181
Controlfunction	No	linear	4th order	No	linear	4th order
Sample	2% margin	5% margin	full	2% margin	5% margin	full
Year and state dummies	Yes	Yes	Yes	Yes	Yes	Yes

Notes: Significance levels: * $p < 0.10$, ** $p < 0.05$, *** $p < 0.01$. Standard errors in parentheses are robust. The dependent variable is the vote share of the left party in t in the SPD design (margin of victory of the social democrats). The regressions in columns 1–3 indicate the effect on the majoritarian vote in different specification while columns 4–6 show the effects on the proportional vote. Treatment d indicates that a SPD candidate won the district. The interaction $(g * d)$ means that the SPD incumbent has access to the government. Sample restrictions and control functions of the margin of victory are indicated below. Any polynomial control function of the degree indicated is specified to be flexible on both sides of the threshold. *Source*: Own calculations.

Figure 3.6: Vote share for the direct candidate of the Left party

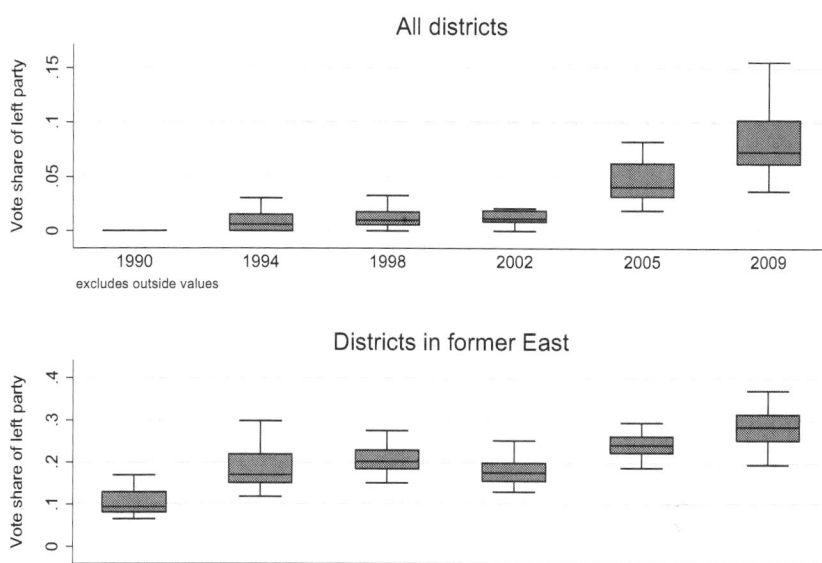

*Notes: Source:*Own calculations.

Table 3.7: Federal elections – party incumbency and government participation in the proportional vote

	Incumbency			Gov. Participation		
	(1)	(2)	(3)	(4)	(5)	(6)
	Panel 1: Center-right party					
Treatment (d)	0.018**	0.010	0.018**	0.039**	0.028	0.034***
	(0.007)	(0.009)	(0.007)	(0.015)	(0.018)	(0.012)
Interaction (g*d)				−0.037**	−0.032*	−0.028**
				(0.016)	(0.019)	(0.014)
N	91	252	1181	91	252	1181
	Panel 2: Center-left party					
Treatment (d)	0.016**	0.012*	0.005	0.009	0.004	0.000
	(0.006)	(0.008)	(0.007)	(0.009)	(0.010)	(0.010)
Interaction (g*d)				0.016	0.018	0.014
				(0.014)	(0.015)	(0.014)
N	92	260	1181	92	260	1181
Controlfunction	No	linear	4th order	No	linear	4th order
Sample	2% margin	5% margin	full	2% margin	5% margin	full
Year and state dummies	Yes	Yes	Yes	Yes	Yes	Yes

Notes: Significance levels: * $p < 0.10$, ** $p < 0.05$, *** $p < 0.01$. Standard errors in parentheses are robust. The dependent variable is the vote share of the respective party in the proportional vote (*Zweitstimme*) in t. The estimates are for the sub period 1990–2005. The regressions in columns 1–3 indicate the pure party incumbency effect. Columns 4–6 also include the interaction between treatment (winning the district in $t − 1$) and whether the party is in charge of government activity. Estimates in panel 1 are for the center-right conservative party and panel 2 show the results for the center-left social democrats. Sample restrictions and control functions of the margin of victory are indicated below. Any polynomial control function of the degree indicated is specified to be flexible on both sides of the threshold. *Source*: Own calculations.

Table 3.8: State elections – party incumbency and government participation

	Incumbency			Gov. Participation		
	(1)	(2)	(3)	(4)	(5)	(6)
			Panel 1: Center-right party			
Treatment (d)	0.026**	0.036*	0.025**	0.052***	0.041**	0.057***
	(0.012)	(0.020)	(0.013)	(0.017)	(0.020)	(0.019)
Interaction (g*d)				−0.053**	−0.065**	−0.065**
				(0.020)	(0.026)	(0.025)
N	45	121	731	45	121	731
			Panel 2: Center-left party			
Treatment (d)	0.008	−0.005	0.007	−0.023	−0.051	−0.045
	(0.013)	(0.016)	(0.013)	(0.029)	(0.036)	(0.037)
Interaction (g*d)				0.047	0.072*	0.084**
				(0.031)	(0.039)	(0.040)
N	51	129	731	51	129	731
Controlfunction	No	linear	4th order	No	linear	4th order
Sample	2% margin	5% margin	full	2% margin	5% margin	full
Election dummies	Yes	Yes	Yes	Yes	Yes	Yes

Notes: 'Margin' in this table means the difference in percentage points between the winner and the next best opponent. For example, in the case of only two candidates a margin of 5 percent means that the winner may have gotten at most 52.5 percent while the other got 47.5 percent. *Source*: Own calculations based on the data provided by the state offices for statistical services.

Table 3.9: Winners of close races by governmental lead

	Lead CDU		Lead SPD		Difference	
	SPD	CDU	SPD	CDU	SPD	CDU
1. Gender						
Share of women	0.26	0.04	0.23	0.06	0.03	−0.02
					(0.76)	(0.74)
2. Local Ties						
Share born in district	0.58	0.48	0.41	0.61	0.17	−0.13
					(0.11)	(0.23)
3. Qualification						
Share with university degree	0.72	0.68	0.68	0.75	0.04	−0.07
					(0.69)	(0.49)
Share with important positions	0.30	0.26	0.30	0.22	0.00	0.04
					(0.94)	(0.69)
4. Seniority						
# of periods in parliament	2.58	3.30	2.61	2.69	−0.03	0.61
					(0.93)	(0.14)
# of years in parliament	5.74	8.36	6.36	6.53	-.62	1.83
					(0.64)	(0.24)
# of years in the party	21.30	24.57	23.22	23.96	−1.92	0.61
					(0.34)	(0.81)
# of Obs	43	50	44	36		

Notes: The data covers the full sample from 1976 to 2009. Standard errors for the difference are reported in parenthesis. Significance levels: * $p < 0.10$, ** $p < 0.05$, *** $p < 0.01$.

Table 3.10: Placebo tests – majoritarian vote of center-right party in federal elections

| | Dep. Variable: vote share in majoritarian vote for center-right party | | | | | |
| | Incumbency | | | Gov. Participation | | |
	(1)	(2)	(3)	(4)	(5)	(6)
	Panel 1: Minus 5 percent					
Treatment (d)	0.008	0.000	−0.002	0.013	0.009	0.000
	(0.005)	(0.007)	(0.006)	(0.010)	(0.013)	(0.011)
Interaction (g*d)				−0.008	−0.015	−0.004
				(0.011)	(0.014)	(0.013)
N	112	256	1181	112	256	1181
	Panel 2: Plus 5 percent					
Treatment (d)	0.002	−0.011*	−0.012*	0.004	−0.010	−0.009
	(0.006)	(0.007)	(0.007)	(0.009)	(0.009)	(0.009)
Interaction (g*d)				−0.004	−0.001	−0.003
				(0.011)	(0.013)	(0.015)
N	98	237	1181	98	237	1181
Controlfunction	No	linear	4th order	No	linear	4th order
Sample	2% margin	5% margin	full	2% margin	5% margin	full
Year and state dummies	Yes	Yes	Yes	Yes	Yes	Yes

Notes: Significance levels: * $p < 0.10$, ** $p < 0.05$, *** $p < 0.01$. Standard errors in parentheses are robust. The dependent variable is the vote share of the respective party in t. Panel 1 refers to results of the placebo test in which we simulate that a party obtained the district incumbency status also if it lost the district race with at most 5 percentage points. Panel 2 presents estimates for the reverse placebo test in which a party needed more than 5 percentage points winning margin to gain the incumbency status. The regressions in columns 1–3 indicate the pure party incumbency effect. Columns 4–6 also include the interaction between treatment (winning the district in $t-1$) and whether the party is in charge of government activity. Sample restrictions and control functions of the margin of victory are indicated below. Any polynomial control function of the degree indicated is specified to be flexible on both sides of the threshold. *Source*: Own calculations.

Figure 3.7: RDD validity – frequency histograms

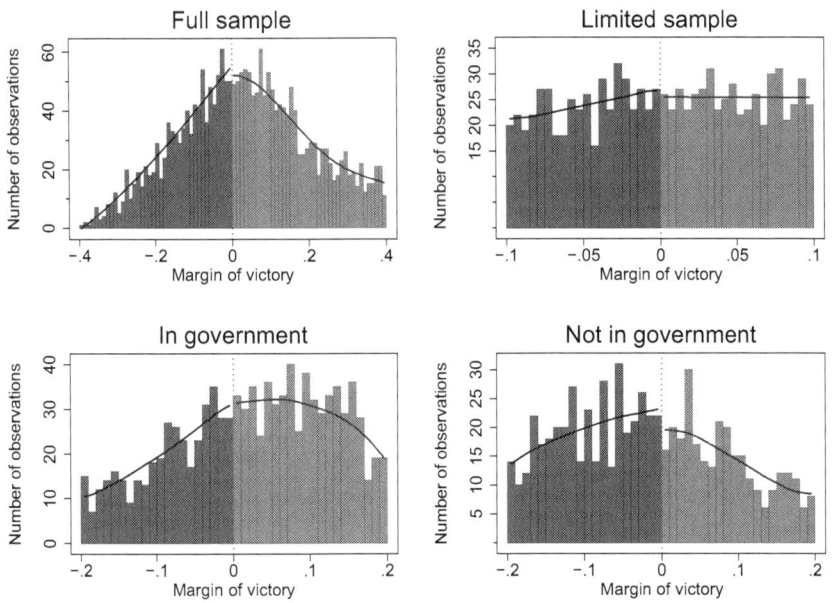

Notes: This figure presents the frequencies of observations in the data with respect to the margin of victory.
Source: Own calculations.

Figure 3.8: RDD validity – predetermined variables

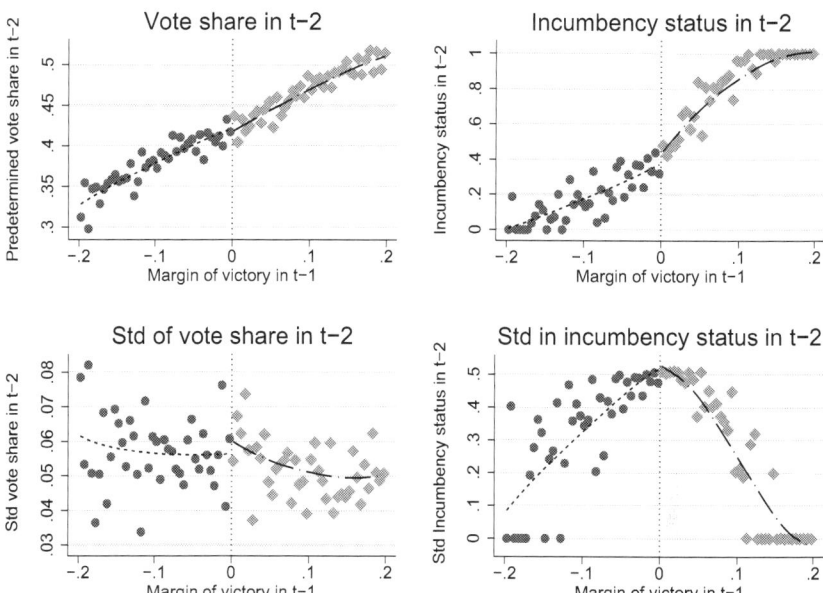

Notes: The figures show the relationship between the margin of victory for the CDU in $t-1$ and two predetermined variables: vote share and incumbency status both in $t-2$. For clarity the data have been grouped in bins, each bin representing an interval of 0.5 percent in the margin of victory. We display only the observations within a margin of victory of 0.2 to draw the focus on the decisive threshold. The upper two graphs show the first moments, while second moments of the variables are displayed in the lower graphs. The lines fitted onto the data is based on a local kernel regression using endogenous Epanechnikov weights. We also estimate the effects on the predetermined variables in regressions similar to the ones presented in table 3.2 and we found no significant differences in the predetermined variables. *Source:* Own calculations.

Chapter 4: When can we trust population thresholds in regression discontinuity designs?

A comment on Egger and Koethenbuerger (2010)[1]

Abstract: A recent literature has used variation just around deterministic legislative population thresholds to identify the causal effects of institutional changes. This paper reviews the use of regression discontinuity designs using such population thresholds. Our concern involves three arguments: (1) simultaneous exogenous (co-)treatment, (2) simultaneous endogenous choices and (3) manipulation and precise control over population measures. Revisiting the study by Egger and Koethenbuerger (2010), who analyse the relationship between council size and government spending, we present new evidence that these three concerns do matter for causal analysis. Our results suggest that empirical designs using population thresholds are only to be used with utmost care and confidence in the precise institutional setting.

4.1 Introduction

Scholars in political economy devote much attention to the causal identification of the effects of fundamental rules and features of governmental organization (e.g. Persson and Tabellini (2002)). Estimating the causal effects of institutional designs and constitutional rules, however, is generally a difficult task for a number of reasons (see Acemoglu (2005)). The main challenges are that institutional rules are usually endogenous and seldom change, that different aspects of constitutional designs often correlate and change simultaneously and that data analysis is often limited by small samples. The new interest has therefore turned to subnational levels and statistical methods from the program evaluation literature in the attempt to use quasi-random variation in specific rules to estimate their impact.

One specific class of designs being used in a range of different applications are regression discontinuity designs that focus on population thresholds. Pettersson-Lidbom (2006) and Egger and Koethenbuerger (2010) investigate whether the municipality's council size, which changes at deterministic population thresholds, affects local gov-

1 This chapter is joint work with Ronny Freier. Acknowledgments: We would like to thank Charles B. Blankart, Peter Haan, Magnus Johannesson, Juanna Joensen, Henrik Jordahl, Erik Lindqvist, Christian Odendahl, Viktor Steiner and David Strömberg as well as colleagues at Stockholm School of Economics and DIW Berlin. Comments at the Applied Microeconomics Seminar at Stockholm School of Economics are also gratefully acknowledged. We would like to thank Peter Egger and Marko Koethenbuerger for making their data available online and Viktor Steiner and Peter Haan who invited us to work at their department for public economics at the DIW Berlin. Ronny Freier would like to thank the Jan Wallander and Tom Hedelius scholarship for continued funding. The usual disclaimer applies.

ernment spending.[2] Regression discontinuity designs, based on population thresholds, are also used to study performance of politicians when salaries increase (Gagliarducci and Nannicini (2009) and Ferraz and Finan (2009)), the effect of fiscal transfers on local elections (Litschig and Morrison (2010)), corruption and the quality of politicians (Brollo, Nannicini, Perotti, and Tabellini (2009)), as well as the impact of representative democracy versus direct democracy on government spending (Hinnerich and Pettersson-Lidbom (2010)).

In this paper, we devote attention to the specific challenges of using population thresholds for reliable causal inference. Our concern is threefold: (1) The first challenge is that the population threshold used may not only define the treatment considered but also additional simultaneous exogenous co-treatments. (2) The identification and interpretation of the treatment effect is further complicated as additional endogenous choices on other institutions are often taken simultaneously. The timing of events is likely to coincide as it is often at specific times that changes are implemented (e.g. at the beginning of an election period). (3) Given that the official population count is usually observable at any moment, the specific concern is that the precise number can be manipulated. In the empirical analysis, we revisit the study by Egger and Koethenbuerger (2010) and present new evidence on the importance of these concerns.

Researchers using quasi-experimental designs recognize the importance of ensuring that a particular treatment effect stands in isolation to other confounding simultaneous treatments. In applications using difference-in-difference designs it is common practice to make an explicit argument that the treatment group is not simultaneously affected by additional treatments. Similarly, for the use of instrumental variables, special care is taken in arguing that the instrument is only of importance to the specific treatment under investigation (see Acemoglu (2005)).[3] We argue that this problem is critical when using regression discontinuity designs with population thresholds. Population count is an intuitive and easy way for higher level governments to impose differential rules on lower tier structures. Hence, it is very likely that the same thresholds might be used in different dimensions of rules and institutions.

According to Bavarian state law the number of town council members must increase at 10 different population thresholds. However, researching the details of Bavarian laws and bylaws we find that the same thresholds also determine large changes in both local

---

2   Both studies use rules (given by the federal or state law) that set the number of members of legislature based on population count of the locality. Those contributions are perceived to be of great importance as they focus on causal identification. For further studies on this topic compare e.g. Baqir (2002) for cities and counties in the US, Gilligan and Matsusaka (2001) for state and local governments in the US, Schaltegger and Feld (2009) for Swiss cantons.

3   Acemoglu (2005) discusses the fundamental problem for the standard instrumental variable approach: that the instrument used for e.g. an institutional setting may not only be an instrument for the institution under investigation but also for a different institution. In this case it is not clear what effect is estimated.

institutions (e.g. referendum quotas, politicians wages) and communal finances (e.g. additional funds from the state government). In total, we find 14 additional legislative laws or bylaws that induce differential rules by population size at the same thresholds. Applying these rules, we show that a part of the spending effect at population thresholds is financed by increases in state grants and additional revenue from fees.

The second challenge in using population thresholds for identification is the timing of changes in the treatment and changes of other endogenous choices. Local institutions are often changed simultaneously at the beginning of new electoral cycles. In Bavaria, e.g., apart from the change in council size set by the exogenous rule, communities must make various (endogenous) decisions just before the next election cycle starts. Those decisions involve, for example, the nature of the mayor position (full-time or part-time) as well as what new tasks the community wants to be responsible for. For the identification of a specific treatment effect, this problem becomes twofold: First, because timing coincides it is harder for the researchers to disentangle the effect in question and, in small samples, pure statistical variation is more likely to introduce bias in the estimation. Second, the interpretation of the effect might crucially hinge on the timing and interdependency of the treatment changes and the choice making. We supplement the data of Egger and Koethenbuerger (2010) with information on one such endogenous decision (work status of the mayor) and no longer find a significant spending effect at the council size thresholds.

Our final concern is that the population count may be precisely manipulated. As population thresholds are critical for the remuneration of government personnel, for allocation of finances from other government levels, as well as for the council size, there are large incentives for sorting around the respective population thresholds. The concern of sorting on the precise threshold is well-recognized in the literature on regression discontinuity design (RDD) (see Lee and Lemieux (2009), McCrary (2008)). For population thresholds this is of particular concern as in Germany the number of inhabitants is by no means a surprise, but rather a regularly updated and publicly known number. Hence, whenever a community comes close to a threshold the administration can purposefully manipulate the number and precisely sort on the desired population count. For Bavarian municipalities during the period of observation we find evidence that there is sorting around the population thresholds. Thus, the spending effects found by Egger and Koethenbuerger (2010) could be potentially biased by selection effects.

Given the results of our empirical analysis, we conclude that researchers must be cautious when using population thresholds for identification in regression discontinuity designs. To be covered against the threats of simultaneous exogenous co-treatment and simultaneous endogenous decisions, researches must acquire deep institutional knowledge while checking legal norms and customs thoroughly. Furthermore, testing of the key identifying assumptions of RDD is required.[4]

This study proceeds as follows. Section 2 introduces the empirical model and the underlying identification assumptions. Section 3 presents the institutional setting and the specific use of population thresholds in Bavarian law, before Section 4 highlights our results and draws comparisons to the findings reported by Egger and Koethenbuerger (2010). Section 5 concludes the analysis.

4.2 Empirical model and methodology

In this section, we consider the empirical methodology that is involved in the use of deterministic population thresholds in regression discontinuity designs (RDD). After discussing the basic empirical setup, we clarify the identifying assumptions needed to allow for causal inference of the treatment effect in question.

4.2.1 Basic model

Assume, for simplicity, that we consider a case in which a treatment is determined at a single population threshold. Define $v_{i,t}$ as the distance of the number of inhabitants in location i at time t from the threshold. Assume further that the treatment (e.g. number of council members) is discontinuously determined at the threshold (sharp discontinuity design). The relationship between treatment $d_{1_{i,t}}$ and $v_{i,t}$ is as follows:

$$d_{1_{i,t}} = 1\,[v_{i,t} > 0] \qquad (4.1)$$

The estimation equation specifying the RDD then reads as follows:

$$y_{i,t} = \delta_0 + \delta_1 d_{1_{i,t}} + h(v_{i,t}, \theta) + \varepsilon_{i,t} \qquad (4.2)$$

where $y_{i,t}$ is the outcome in question (e.g. local government spending), δ_1 is the parameter of interest and $h(\cdot)$ is a flexible function that represents the underlying general relationship between the distance to the threshold (hence population size) and the outcome variable. This simple framework can also be easily adjusted to accommodate the fact that treatment is changing at multiple thresholds (see Egger and Koethenbuerger (2010)).

---

4   Caughey and Sekhon (2010) revisit the empirical evidence presented in Lee (2008), who uses a RDD on close election outcomes. The former rigorously investigate the RDD assumptions and find that, for the US House of Representatives, observations in close elections still exhibit crucially unbalanced predetermined variables that are likely to invalidate the research design.

4.2.2 Identifying assumptions

The parameter δ_1 is an unbiased estimate of the treatment effect under the critical assumption of continuity(see Lee and Lemieux (2009)). It is only if all observable and unobservable covariates, except treatment, are distributed continuously around the threshold that one can assume to have valid counterfactual observations on either side. If observations just right from the required population count are systematically different from the ones just to the left, then identification fails.

The first implication of the continuity assumption is that we must ensure that there exist no further co-treatments. It is obvious that causal inference of an individual effect cannot be upheld when other treatments are simultaneously determined at the same threshold. Formally, the existence of co-treatment implies the following. Let a second treatment, $d_{2_{i,t}}$, be determined at the same threshold v_0:

$$d_{2_{i,t}} = 1 \left[v_{i,t} > 0 \right] \tag{4.3}$$

The individual effects of $d_{1_{i,t}}$ and $d_{2_{i,t}}$ cannot be identified. The second treatment is omitted in eq. (4.2) and the flexible function in v cannot control for it as the threshold coincides. Even if the second treatment is observable, one cannot include it in the regression due to multi-collinearity. The researcher can only identify a joint effect. If one has several thresholds and differences in when certain treatments apply, one may hope to disentangle the isolated treatments. However, the major concern is when and if we fail to recognize the existence of additional (co-)treatments. Although an outcome was in fact induced by several changing factors, we instead falsely attribute the effect to only one treatment.

It is important to note that co-treatment is of particular concern because standard RDD tests are not very likely to detect it. If a second treatment is implemented at the same threshold, distribution tests of predetermined covariates cannot be expected to detect such differences. Further, there is no reason to believe that a direct test of the distribution of the score variable (McCrary (2008)) will be of help.

For population thresholds the problem of co-treatments has to be critically reviewed on a case by case basis. Population thresholds are tools for legislatures to induce differences in laws and bylaws by the population size of local entities. Thus, the same thresholds are likely used in several legislative rules.

Apart from exogenous co-treatments, we consider the precise sorting around thresholds to be of particular concern when using population count in RDD. Lee (2008) shows that it is sufficient to show that there is a random component in the scoring variable to uphold the continuity assumption. If agents cannot precisely control the variable that determines the treatment, then in some neighborhood of the threshold, assignment of treatment is effectively random. This random assignment close to the threshold directly implies continuity.

Thus, any RDD application relying on this argument must investigate whether agents can precisely sort around the threshold. For population count this issue is indeed crucial. The official population of a municipality in Germany is known at any given time. Day to day changes in the population number are very small and even well ahead of the defining deadline, the precise population number can be well anticipated by the authorities of the municipality.[5]

If the agent can indeed ensure that she ends up just to the right of a certain threshold then the continuity assumption is likely to fail. Instead of valid counterfactuals, observations on either side are likely to differ. Variables that drive the selection will be systematically different on both sides and confound the treatment effect estimate.

One advantage of the RDD is that the sorting argument can be tested in a number of different ways. McCrary (2008) suggests a direct test of the distribution of the score variable. If it is profitable for agents to sort on a threshold and the possibility of doing so exists, then one should observe a higher frequency of observations on one side rather than on the other. Also, we can look at the distribution of predetermined variables which – given local randomization – should not systematically differ around the thresholds.

Our last concern is a particularity of the use of population thresholds. Typically, a legal rule that applies a population threshold defines a definite point in time when the population count is taken. This point in time is often distinct from the actual implementation of the new rule. For example, for Bavarian municipalities council size is determined by a population count about a year before the council election.[6] This year, however, is also the time during which important institutional decisions are made. The municipal council, for example, decides whether the next mayor will be part- or full-time and / or whether the local authorities will be responsible for specific services.

These endogenous decisions can be problematic in two different ways. First, interpretation of the effect can be complex. Say, a municipality knows that it will increase the council size in one year. It must decide whether the future council will become responsible for certain tasks (e.g. water management). Their decision to do so might depend on the anticipated council size. A larger council might, for example, be able to support

---

5 Caughey and Sekhon (2010) make the point that it is important to assess the magnitude of the random component in the score variable as compared to the precision with which agents can actively manipulate this variable.

6 In preparation for a new election, the new council size must be known well ahead of time as certain preparations directly depend on it. For example, each party will name a number of candidates that is (typically) exactly as many as there are council seats.

additional committees that can oversee these responsibilities. Those kinds of effects, however, are not included in the definition of the treatment effect, as treatment, *per se*, has not yet started. The researcher might be willing to redefine treatment, however, specific care has to be given to exactly what the object of interest is.

Apart from problems in interpretation, these endogenous decisions might also pose a threat to the validity of the identification, particularly in small samples. Assume that the simultaneous endogenous decision is in fact independent from the treatment. As with any postdetermined variable the researcher can only hope to not pick a strangely unbalanced sample in which the observations just right and just left are different by random selection. However, as opposed to other variables the timing of those endogenous institutional choices coincides exactly with the determination of treatment. This makes it much more likely that an unfavorable sample is picked. In Bavaria, for example, there is a trend to have more full-time mayors and to locate additional responsibilities at the local level. Naturally, these decisions are made at exactly the same time as council size increases: just before the new election cycle.

4.3   Institutional setting

The German federal system comprises of four tiers. Apart from the federal, state and county level, some key decisions are taken by local municipalities. This local authority decides, among other issues, on local roads, theaters, cultural events, local business development, as well as school buildings and administers social welfare programs, kindergarten spending, etc. Furthermore, they often own and control key parts of the local economy such as waste disposal, public transport, as well as the energy and water supply. As the municipalities are the lowest tier of the federal system, most laws regulating their decision mechanisms, freedoms, and duties are exogenous to them: in Bavaria alone there are hundreds of state laws and by-laws that refer to municipalities.[7] As the state laws apply to all communities, the state legislature often uses population thresholds to adjust the rules to different requirements of smaller and larger communities.

We worked through the most relevant parts of the applicable state legislation to detect rules that use population thresholds. We found 14 (excluding the changes in council size) rules that cover nine of the ten thresholds determining the council size (see table 4.1 for an overview of the thresholds relevant to the council size and corresponding further rules).[8]

---

7   All laws and by-laws are available online at a website provided by the government of Bavaria: http://www.gesetze-bayern.de/jportal/portal/page/bsbayprod.psml (retrieved in March 2011).

8   Given the amount of laws and bylaws that regulate municipal decision making, it is still possible that there are further undetected thresholds.

Table 4.1: Changes at council size population thresholds

	Population thresholds at # of inhabitants (in tsd)									
	1	2	3	5	10	20	30	50	100	200
Panel 1: Thresholds used in Egger and Koethenbuerger (2010)										
Council size	x	x	x	x	x	x	x	x	x	x
Wage of elected civil servants					x		x	x	x	
Panel 2: Further thresholds defining local institutions										
Wage of full-time mayors		x	x	x	x		x	x	x	
Wage of part-time mayors	x		x	x						
Full-time council members					x					
Petition for referendum					x	x	x	x	x	
Referendum quota								x	x	
City districts									x	
Open council					x				x	
Accounting committee				x						
Mayor status				x	x					
Panel 3: Further thresholds defining budgeting rules										
County free city								x		
Status of larger city							x			
Vehicle Tax				x						
Fiscal equalization				x	x			x	x	

Notes: We have included only those rules and thresholds that correspond to the thresholds relevant for the council size. For a more detailed description the changes at each of those population thresholds see tables 4.6 and 4.7. *Source*: Own research.

We found rules that define both local institutions and affect budget size. With regards to budgeting, we found five rules (see table 4.6 in the appendix for a detailed description).[9] For example, communities with more than 5,000 inhabitants receive 7.6 percent of the vehicle tax collected in their territory, while smaller communities do not receive anything – at the same threshold the council increases from 16 to 20 members. Another rule states that a city with more than 50,000 inhabitants may apply to become a county free city. If choosing to do so, the city takes over all the duties previously pro-

---

9 Following the state development program (*Landesentwicklungsprogramm Bayern*, December 22, 2009 version) communities may also be grouped into one of five levels that indicate regional relevance for public services. While there are population thresholds among the criteria, these thresholds do not refer to the community itself but rather to the total population of the respective community plus the population of the communities it serves.

vided by the county and receives additional transfers accordingly. We conclude that larger cities receive more transfers and provide more services than smaller cities and that the thresholds typically coincide with the community council size thresholds.

Regarding local institutions, there are even more rules that depend on population thresholds (we found nine, see table 4.7 in the appendix for details). These prescriptions range from relatively minor directives (e.g. that the council in cities with more that 5,000 inhabitants must include an accounting committee) to setting key rules of the local game. The latter include stipulations for the remuneration of the mayor[10] and a detailed regulation concerning local referendums. The requirements to bring a proposed referendum to the ballot are much higher in small communities (where 10 percent have to sign the petition) than in very large cities (where only three percent need to sign) with multiple steps in the signature requirement in between. The same general logic applies to the participation quota in the referendum itself.[11]

We conclude that while the number of seats in the council is an important feature of local institutions, there are several other important local institutions that also change at the same population thresholds. This leads to double or multiple simultaneous treatment at any given threshold. The same applies when population thresholds also change the financial endowment of the community (see paragraph above).

Apart from setting population thresholds with budgetary and institutional relevance, the state laws also provide the communities with many choices in those dimensions. For example, the communities may decide to take over tasks from the county, which brings along new responsibilities, funds and administrative work. Tasks that communities may take over from higher government levels include: maintaining certain types of roads (compare *Finanzausgleichsgesetz*, Article 13a, version of 2010/06/03), construction supervision (compare Article 53, *Bayerische Bauordnung*, version of 2010/02/25), and waste disposal (compare Articles 5, 7 *Bayerisches Abfallwirtschaftsgesetz*, version of 2010/03/24). While some of the tasks that communities acquire from higher levels of government only induce small changes in revenue (e.g. construction supervision), others trigger large increases in revenues and spending (e.g. waste disposal).

Moreover, the municipality must regularly make decisions about institutional questions such as: Should we have a full-time mayor?, How many full-time working council members do we want? As mayors are elected at the same time that the council is elected and because additional responsibilities are also more likely to be taken over

---

10 This is likely to be of significant importance for their performance and may hence affect government spending. Compare e.g. Besley (2004), Gagliarducci and Nannicini (2009), Messner and Polborn (2004), Ferraz and Finan (2009)

11 e.g. Romer, Rosenthal, and Munley (1992) and Holcombe and Kenny (2008) show that referendum requirements affect spending.

at the beginning of the electoral cycle it is probable that such decisions also coincide with increases in council size. The econometric implications of the resulting possible simultaneous endogenous decision making are discussed in section 4.2.

4.4 Results

Our empirical analysis generally builds on the strategy and data presented by Egger and Koethenbuerger (2010).[12] Similar to their work, we use data on 2,056 municipalities from the German state of Bavaria over the 1983 to 2004 period. To investigate our specific points of interest, we complement their data base with information on the revenue side of the municipality budget and the status of the town mayor (part-time or full-time).[13] The result section is split into three parts: (1) the importance of simultaneously determined finances, (2) the need to control for endogenous (but simultaneous) decisions of the municipality, and (3) the potential manipulation by local authorities of population numbers around thresholds.

4.4.1 Importance of simultaneous exogenous co-treatment

In the above section, we illustrate that legislative population thresholds in Bavaria not only affect council size but also a number of other important institutional features. Among those features are legislative rules that affect the budgeting of communities. Naturally, those direct fiscal consequences for the community are crucial in the identification of the effect of legislative size and governmental spending.

To understand the structure of municipality budgets in more detail, we illustrate some of the basic figures in table 4.8 (see appendix). The average municipality budget in Bavaria (for all 2056 municipalities in the period 1983–2004) reaches 1909 Euro per capita in total expenditures.[14] On the expenditure side, we highlight the shares of three major budget components that are (partly) in the discretion of the municipality: expenditures on personnel, on materials, as well as investments.[15]

Below, we present important categories from the revenue side. Under the full discretion of the local authority are three tax rates[16]: (1) property tax A on agricultural land, (2) property tax B on all non-agricultural property and (3) a trade tax on local businesses. In column (2) we highlight the share that each category has in the overall

---

12 We obtained the data and Stata-dofiles from the authors through the journal website.

13 This additional data is publicly available and can be obtained free of charge from the Bavarian statistical service.

14 The same figure has to appear on the revenue side, as all expenditures have to be refinanced either by tax income, grants or increases in new debt.

15 Other important expenditures that are not included are expenditures for debt repayments and expenditures for mandated social services. These are usually not directly in the control of the municipality.

16 Only the tax rates are at the discretion of the municipalities – the rules defining the tax base are set by higher government levels.

budget. We find that local taxes account for 20.6 percent of the total revenue with the major part of that income generated by the trade tax. Local property taxes contribute only about 4.4 percent to local finances.

Equally important are grants from other tiers of government and fees for communal services. We document that about 12.7 percent of revenues come from grants and 9.4 percent are raised through fees on local services.[17] It is important to note that the communities have only very limited decision power when it comes to influencing grants. Of course, they can lobby to receive grants and they have some discretion in setting fees, however, for the most part grants underlie legislative rules and many fees are regulated by the state.[18]

Table 4.2: Replication of the results by Egger and Koethenbuerger (2010)

	Outcomes (15 percent window)				
	Log Total Expenditures	Log Debt	Log Prop Tax Rate A	Log Prop Tax Rate B	Log Trade Tax Rate
	(1)	(2)	(3)	(4)	(5)
Treatment	0.109**	0.137*	0.055***	0.058***	0.009**
	(0.052)	(0.074)	(0.009)	(0.008)	(0.004)
N	22631	22162	22631	22631	22631
R2	0.00	0.00	0.00	0.00	0.00

Notes: Significance levels: * $p < 0.10$, ** $p < 0.05$, *** $p < 0.01$. We use the program provided by Egger and Koethenbuerger (2010) to replicate their main results (see their tables 3 and 6). Standard errors in parentheses are robust. The dependent variable are indicated above. Treatment is defined by being right to the population thresholds. All regressions include a third order polynomial in population that is flexible on both sides of the threshold. The estimation is done within the 15 percent window of population around the thresholds. *Source*: Own calculations based on the program provided by Egger and Koethenbuerger (2010).

Table 4.2 replicates the results reported by Egger and Koethenbuerger (2010).[19] Egger and Koethenbuerger estimate a version of eq. 4.2 for the thresholds at which population size changes and document the effect on total expenditures to be an immense 10.9 percent increase (see column 1, table 4.2) or 4.2 percent for every additional seat.[20] Given the average total expenditure (per capita) of 1909 Euro, the effect is hence argued to increase expenditures by the order of about 200 Euro (per capita and year). The

---

17 Those fees are levied on services such as water supply, sewage and waste management, kindergartens, etc.

18 The remaining part of the revenue comes from higher levels authorities and are raised, in part, through income tax and VAT. The community gets a fixed share of these revenues and has no control over the tax rate. Moreover, revenues can also be generated through new debt.

19 We use the same dofiles and data and get the exact some results from their table 3 and table 6.

20 The average increase in the number of seats at the thresholds is 2.56.

size of this effect is to be evaluated even larger considering that only part of the local expenditures is effectively under local control.

Looking at the revenue side of the effect, Egger and Koethenbuerger (2010) report the estimates on debt, both types of property tax and the local trade tax (see columns 2–5 in table 4.2). They find sizable and significant effects primarily for the two property tax rates A and B of 5.5 percent and 5.8 percent increases respectively. They argue that municipalities mainly rely on those sources of revenue to finance the additional expenditures (see Egger and Koethenbuerger (2010, p. 211)). However, given that the property taxes only account for 4.4 percent of total revenue, an increase by about 5.8 percent in the those taxes is likely to increase revenue by only 5 Euro (per capita and year).[21]

Table 4.3: The results of council size on state grants and municipality fees

	Outcome (15 percent window)		
	Log General Grants	Log Invest Grants	Log Muni Fees
	(1)	(2)	(3)
Treatment	0.089*	0.273***	0.236***
	(0.047)	(0.085)	(0.070)
N	21513	21383	21511
R2	0.00	0.00	0.00

Notes: Significance levels: * $p < 0.10$, ** $p < 0.05$, *** $p < 0.01$. We use the program provided by Egger and Koethenbuerger (2010) to estimate the regressions using their setup, however, with the outcome variables that we have added to the data. Standard errors in parentheses are robust. The dependent variable are indicated above. Treatment is defined by being right to the population thresholds. All regressions include a third order polynomial in population that is flexible on both sides of the threshold. *Source*: Own calculations partly based on the program provided by Egger and Koethenbuerger (2010).

Given the exploration on the institutional changes at population thresholds, we suspect that the additional spending is largely driven by automated changes in the rules that affect grants as well as the services communities provide (and hence fees collected). In table 4.3 we apply the design to estimate the increase in grants and fees at the thresholds. We show that there are substantial, significant increases both in grants (27.3 percent in additional investment grants) and communal fees (23.6 percent additional revenue). In total, the increases in grants and fees account for about 81 Euro per capita. Hence, we can explain a substantial part of the expenditure increase (although

---

21 The effect that they report on the local trade tax is very small with less than 1 percent increase, which implies that this source of revenue does not play an important part in financing the expenditure increase. The point estimate on the debt is in fact quite large and could explain a substantial part of the expenditure increase. However, it is insignificant at the 5 percent level.

not the entire effect) by automated changes in revenues provided by higher levels of government to larger communities.

We document that the identification of the council size effect may suffer from co-treatment effects that are simultaneously determined by the same population thresholds. Without the detailed institutional knowledge and more specific data on all aspects of the revenue sources[22] it is impossible to distinguish between the "true" effect of legislative size and other changes at the same thresholds.

4.4.2 Simultaneous endogenous decision making

Causal analysis is further complicated by the fact that municipalities must make important decisions on the structure of the local institutions and the services provided by the community. It is in the nature of political cycles that the timing of those endogenous choices coincides with adjustments in council size. As explained above those decisions can have substantial consequences for municipal fiscal situations. We investigate one important feature of local institutions, namely whether the mayor is working part-time or full-time.

In figure 4.2 in the appendix we highlight the share of full-time mayors over the population distribution. The vertical lines indicate the population thresholds used in the council size analysis. Significant differences in the share of full-time majors can be observed around the 2000 and 3000 inhabitants thresholds.[23] To further investigate the differences, we present the distribution of full-time majors just around those two marks in figure 4.3 in the appendix. As indicated by the local kernel regression fitted onto the data, we observe substantial differences right of the cut-off points.

Moreover, we show that the differences in mayor status also prevail in the entire sample. Using the same estimation setup, we use the analysis to predict the mayor status (see table 4.4). If mayor status is independent of council size, the estimates should be insignificant from zero. Our results indicate that there is a sizable and significant effect of the population thresholds on the probability of choosing a full-time mayor.[24]

The above findings indicate that mayor status differs significantly between the observations just to the left and just to the right of the thresholds. The important question

---

22 To rule out all automated changes in revenues / expenditures one would have to get detailed data on very specific grants that are given from the state or federal level to the communities.

23 As described above, there are two legal thresholds at 5,000 and 10,000 inhabitants that prescribe consequences for the mayor status. However, those rules are non-binding and only suggestions. We find that the probability of choosing a full-time mayor does not seem to be altered systematically at those thresholds. Rather, the important changes are at thresholds below 5,000.

24 We present the results within the 4 window sizes used by Egger and Koethenbuerger (2010). A window size of 15 implies that only municipalities within 15 percent of the population threshold are used in the analysis.

Table 4.4: The results of council size on predetermined mayor status

Window size	Probability of having a full-time mayor			
	15 Percent	20 Percent	25 Percent	30 Percent
	(1)	(2)	(3)	(4)
Treatment	0.068***	0.058**	0.051**	0.064***
	(0.026)	(0.023)	(0.020)	(0.019)
N	22611	29783	37177	44295
R2	0.00	0.00	0.00	0.00

Notes: Significance levels: * $p < 0.10$, ** $p < 0.05$, *** $p < 0.01$. In this regression, we estimate the effect of council size on the mayor status defined as a dummy variable which takes the value 1 if the mayor is full-time employed. Standard errors in parentheses are robust. Treatment is defined by being right to the population thresholds. All regressions include a third order polynomial in population that is flexible on both sides of the threshold. In general, the setup is similar to the regressions run by Egger and Koethenbuerger (2010). *Source*: Own calculations partly based on the program provided by Egger and Koethenbuerger (2010).

is how that affects the estimates of the council size effect. In table 4.5 we repeat the estimation including a dummy for each observation that takes the value one when the municipality employs a full-time mayor during that year. For comparison, we highlight the results from Egger and Koethenbuerger (2010) in panel 1 of table 4.5. In the panels below we show the results controlling for mayor status (panel 2) and additionally controlling for year fixed effects (panel 3).

Including a control for mayor status, we find that the point estimates reported in Egger and Koethenbuerger (2010) drop significantly and are no longer statistically significant in the preferred specifications. The specification using a 15 percent window is shown to exhibit no more effects of the council size on governmental spending.[25] If the mayor status is a predetermined variable, this result would immediately suggest that the RDD is invalid. However, as argued above, the timing is specific. The mayor status is determined after the new council size is fixed, yet before this new council takes office. One could argue that it is in anticipation of the new council members that the old council decides to employ a full-time mayor and that this in turn increased spending. This would mean to change the interpretation of the effect drastically. However, we believe that the choice of the mayor's status is in fact unrelated to the future

---

25 In table 4.9 in the appendix, we show that this is also true for the effect of council size on the disaggregate spending categories (referring to table 5 in Egger and Koethenbuerger (2010)). However, when we include the mayor dummy in the analysis on revenue sources, we can not reject their estimates for the local tax rates. In table 4.10 in the appendix, we show that the effects on property taxes and trade tax remain stable when we include the mayor dummy. As these categories are true choice variables of the community, they might reflect a different dynamic than the categories steered by choices of responsibilities and grants from other tiers.

Table 4.5: Main results – council size effect with controlling for mayor status

	Log Total Expenditures			
Window size	15 Percent	20 Percent	25 Percent	30 Percent
	(1)	(2)	(3)	(4)
	Panel 1 : Replication of Egger and Koethenbuerger (2010)			
Treatment	0.109**	0.121***	0.149***	0.202***
	(0.052)	(0.045)	(0.041)	(0.037)
N	22631	29803	37197	44324
R2	0.00	0.00	0.00	0.00
	Panel 2 : Controlling for mayor status			
Treatment	0.024	0.049	0.087***	0.124***
	(0.040)	(0.034)	(0.031)	(0.028)
Mayor status	1.240***	1.233***	1.227***	1.217***
	(0.010)	(0.009)	(0.008)	(0.007)
N	22611	29783	37177	44295
R2	0.42	0.42	0.41	0.41
	Panel 3 : Controlling for mayor status and year effects			
Treatment	−0.006	0.019	0.044	0.063***
	(0.034)	(0.030)	(0.027)	(0.024)
Mayor status	1.157***	1.146***	1.129***	1.118***
	(0.009)	(0.008)	(0.007)	(0.006)
N	22404	29483	36766	43809
R2	0.47	0.47	0.47	0.46

Notes: Significance levels: * $p < 0.10$, ** $p < 0.05$, *** $p < 0.01$. Standard errors in parentheses are robust. The dependent variable is the log of total expenditures. Panel 1 replicates the results in Egger and Koethenbueger (2010) (see their table 3). In panel 2, we control for the mayor status in the estimation by including a dummy variable that takes the value 1 if the mayor is full-time employed. Panel 3, additionally also controls for year fixed effects. In those last estimations we also excluded bigger communities that had the status of a county free city. Treatment is defined by being right to the population thresholds. All regressions include a third order polynomial in population that is flexible on both sides of the threshold.
Source: Own calculations partly based on the program provided by Egger and Koethenbuerger (2010).

council size. Under this assumption, results imply that the RDD fails to identify the causal effect of an increase in council size.

Interestingly, we observe a large estimate for the mayor status dummy, implying a 124 percent increase in total spending when the mayor is full-time. We do not intend to interpret this to be a causal effect. Rather, we believe that is it very likely that this estimate reflects the importance of the complete choice set of the community at the time of elections. It is precisely when the council decides to take over more responsibilities from other tiers (like child care, water supply, etc.) that they also choose to have a full-time mayor that administers the local administration.

4.4.3 Manipulation of the population numbers around the thresholds

We show above that simultaneous co-treatment as well as simultaneous endogenous choices are posing a threat to the validity of the causal inference. As argued in the section on the empirical methodology, the important identifying assumption is the argument that municipalities can not sort around the population thresholds (continuity assumption). This is of specific concern here as the population figure is generally observable at all times and action can be taken to manipulate the precise figures before the deadlines in question. Municipalities could act to manipulate the statistical numbers directly within the administration or (more likely) they could start programs designed to attract new residents.[26] Given that the thresholds involve a multitude of consequences both for the political institutions and the fiscal budgeting of the municipality, the concern of manipulation needs to be taken seriously.

Egger and Koethenbuerger (2010) indicate the total number of observations just left (10914 obs) and just right (11690 obs) within the window of the limited sample.[27] However, it is standard praxis in applications of RDD to show a histogram of the frequencies just around the thresholds. In figure 4.1, we present such a histogram for the data used throughout this analysis (within the 15 percent window).

The graph indicates that the frequencies of observations just right and left of the thresholds differ systematically. There is a definite jump in the number of observations if one compares the two groups just below the threshold (about 700 obs each) compared to the one group just above (about 900 obs). The difference is further indicated by the gap in the local kernel regression fitted onto the data.[28] In figure 4.4 in the appendix, we investigate the frequency histogram for each of the thresholds individually. With the exception of the 2,000 threshold, the frequency tend to be always higher just to the right of the threshold. Of considerable difference are the jumps in the graphs for the 1,000, 3,000, 5,000 and 50,000 thresholds.[29]

This observation has direct consequences to the validity of the estimation design. If communities have the capability to manipulate their population figure at the margin,

---

26 Municipalities could, for example, open new community areas for housing projects, guarantee kindergarten spots to newcomers or give direct financial incentives to move to the town.

27 Their results are presented in their table 3.

28 We also ran flexible polynomial regressions on the binned data to obtain standard errors on the observed difference. As shown in the histogram, the data are quite variable between the bins. Nevertheless, the jump is significant at the 10 percent significance level when we run linear and quadratic specifications and at the 5 percent level using a third order polynomial that is flexible on either side.

29 We also tested differences of important predetermined variables such as total expenditures the year before the election and mayor status during the last election period. However, we found no significant differences there, which implies that sorting is not along those dimensions.

Figure 4.1: RDD validity – frequency check

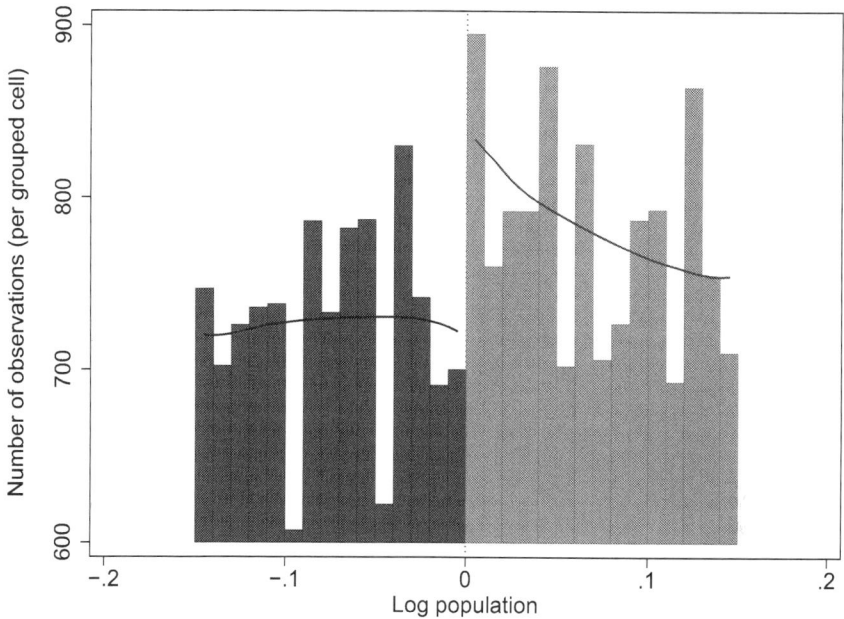

Notes: The figure shows the frequencies of observations in the analysis in grouped bins within the 15 % window (using 30 bins with a size of one percent each). The thresholds in the analysis have been normalized to zero. The line fitted onto the data is based on a local kernel regression using Epanechnikov weights. A regression analysis using those bin averages and a flexible polynomial specification in the log of population shows that the difference at the threshold is both sizable and significant at least at the 10 percent level (at 5 percent level when one uses a third order polynomial specification). *Source:* Own calculations partly based on the program provided by Egger and Koethenbuerger (2010).

the continuity assumption for the RDD does not necessarily hold and the estimates are potentially biased due to selection effects. It might be the fast growing communities that seek to take on more responsibilities which manage to end up just to the right of the thresholds.

4.5   Conclusions

In this paper, we identify and discuss three main challenges requiring careful attention when using population thresholds in regression discontinuity designs. First, the population threshold may define changes in multiple rules and not only the treatment considered. Second, when changes in population trigger the observed treatment it is likely that endogenous institutional choices occur simultaneously. Third, political entities may seek to manipulate the official number of inhabitants knowing that it affects institutions at certain thresholds.

Revisiting Egger and Koethenbuerger (2010), we find evidence that our three concerns are of practical relevance. (1) The population thresholds used by the authors not only trigger changes in council size but also affect many other budgetary and institutional rules. Bigger communities have more responsibilities, receive more transfers and differ in institutions. We show that a large share of the spending increase at population thresholds relevant for the seat count stems from increases in grants from higher government levels. (2) We observe that when city councils grow in seats, the communities often decide endogenously to have their mayor work full instead of part time. When we include the information on the status of the mayor the spending effects of additional seats found by Egger and Koethenbuerger (2010) become insignificant. (3) We find evidence for manipulation of the population count, again indicating that the reported estimates are likely to be invalid. We conclude that the causal effect of council size on government expenditures in Germany is still an open question.

From our results we find that it is crucially important to thoroughly verify the identifying assumptions of the RDD when using population thresholds. Taking into account the complexity of institutions and exogenous rules, notably at the local level, we recommend that researchers carefully document the legislative setting throughout the period of observation. In particular, they should discuss in detail whether population thresholds are used for other institutions (including the applicable laws and thresholds) and what other endogenous decisions might be taken simultaneously. The responsibility lies entirely on the researcher as the precise institutional setting is hard to assess for any outsider and near to impossible to judge from the pure data analysis. Further, the underlying continuity assumption needs to be discussed with great detail and all available tests have to be carried out such as to illustrate that the assumption is indeed supported by the data.

Appendix

Figure 4.2: Share of full-time mayors over the population distribution (in 1984)

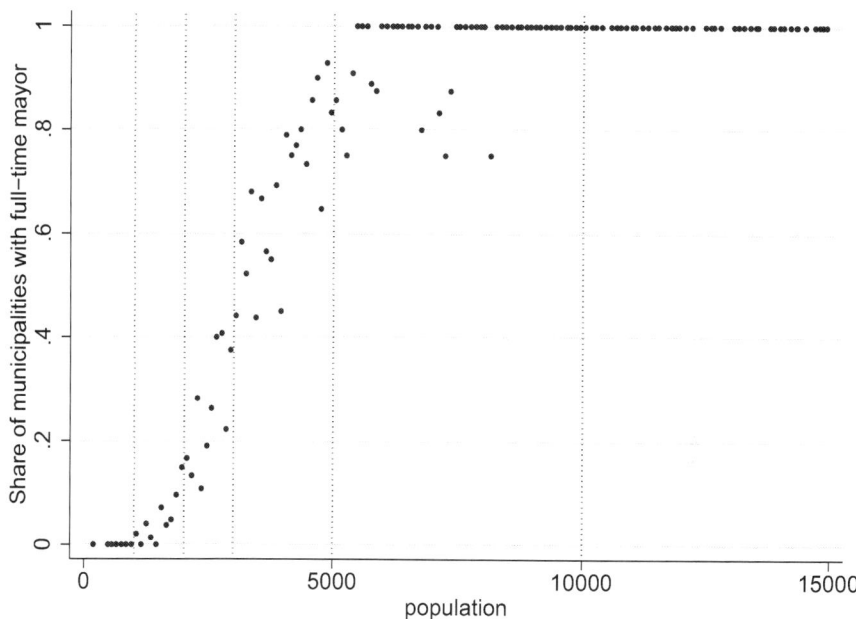

Notes: This figure illustrates the share of full-time mayors over the distribution of the population below 15000 inhabitants (there are no changes above). Each point represents the share within a bin (bandwidth equals 100 inhabitants) including all municipalities of that size. The vertical lines illustrate where the thresholds at with the council size changes are. *Source:* Own calculations.

Figure 4.3: Distribution of full-time mayors around thresholds

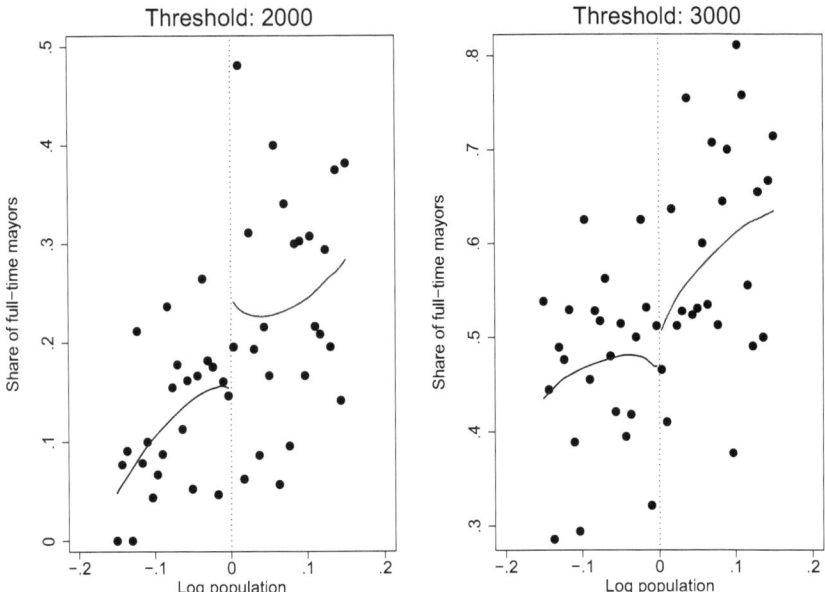

Notes: The figure investigates the share of full-time mayors just around the thresholds of 2000 and 3000 inhabitants. Similar to Egger and Koethenbuerger (2010), we present the results within the 15 % window (using 46 bins representing about 2/3 of one percent). The lines fitted onto the data is based on a local kernel regression using Epanechnikov weights. *Source:* Own calculations partly based on the program provided by Egger and Koethenbuerger (2010).

Figure 4.4: RDD validity – frequency check

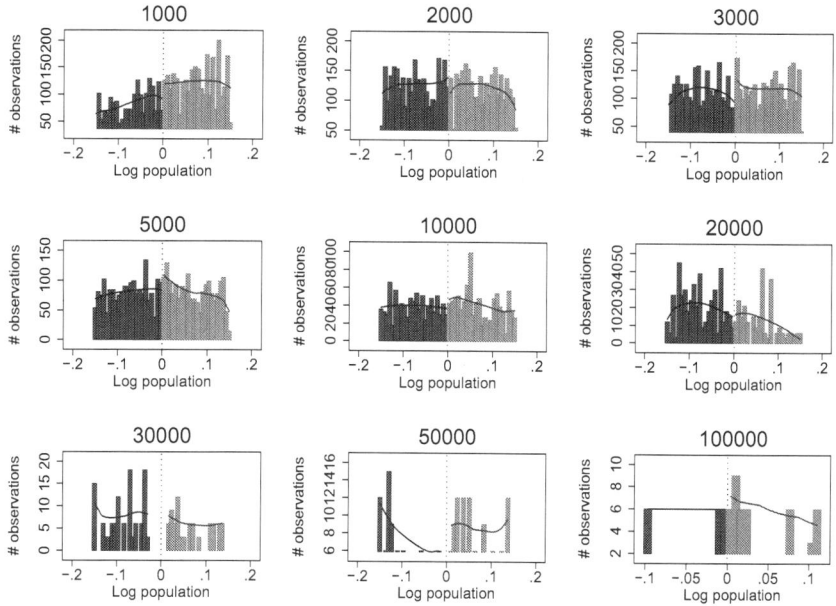

Notes: The figure shows the frequencies of observations at all thresholds below 200,000 in grouped bins within the 15 % window (using 30 bins with a size of one percent each). The lines fitted onto the data is based on a local kernel regression using Epanechnikov weights. *Source:* Own calculations partly based on the program provided by Egger and Koethenbuerger (2010).

Table 4.6: Defining the budget: population thresholds in Bavarian law

Rule	Population thresholds	Legal source	Description
County free city	50,000	e.g. FAG, Art. 2, 9, 12	Cities with more than 50,000 inhabitants can apply to become a county free city ('Kreisfreie Stadt'). That means that the city legally leaves the county it belonged to before and takes over all tasks that were executed by the county until then. These tasks include such important and costly assignments as social welfare, vocational schools, and car registration. The transfer of tasks also includes a transfer of the budget associated with these tasks. The additional funds that the council free city enjoys stem both from additional state transfers and a county levy that the city now no longer needs to pay.
Larger city	30,000	GO, Art. 5a	Communities with more than 30,000 inhabitants can apply for the larger city status ('Große Kreisstadt'). Once awarded the larger city status the community takes over some of the duties that are usually carried out by the county to which the community belongs. The additional tasks include construction supervision and road traffic authority. Some of these tasks also create additional revenue for the cities (e.g. fees of the construction supervision authority).
Vehicle Tax	5,000	FAG, Art. 13a	Communities with more than 5,000 inhabitants receive 7.6 percent of the vehicle tax collected on their territory, the rest of the tax revenue remains with the state government. Smaller communities do not receive a share of the vehicle tax. Whenever communities – regardless of their size – take over the responsibilities for certain types of roads they receive an even larger share of the vehicle tax.
Water management	90,000; 143,750; 300,000; 600,000	FAG, Art. 9	County free cities are in charge of managing all issues related to water in their city. To help them cover the associated cost county free cities receive a per capita allowance of 80 cents per inhabitant but not more than 115,000 EUR which is equivalent to a population threshold of 143,750. Beyond they also receive a supplemental lump sum allowance that depends on their size. This lump-sum is 25,000 EUR for cities below 90,000 inhabitants, 35,000 EUR for cities with more than 90,000 and up to 300,000 inhabitants, 50,000 EUR for cities with more than 300,000 and up to 600,000 inhabitants and 100,000 EUR for all cities with more than 600,000 inhabitants.
Fiscal equal-ization	5,000; 10,000; 25,000; 50,000; 100,000; 250,000; 500,000	FAG, Art. 4	Next to own revenue the communities in Bavaria rely on transfers from the state government to finance their expenditures. One of the most important transfers is the so called 'key allocation' (Schluesselzuweisung). The larger the community is the more it receives in key transfers per capita. Communities with more than 5,000 inhabitants receive a per capita bonus for every additional inhabitant. The increase is 8 percent per inhabitants once the community reaches 5,000 inhabitants and is then a linear function on the population with several points a which the slope changes. For example at exactly 50,000 inhabitants the bonus is 35 percent compared to a community with less than 5,000 inhabitants. The population thresholds mentioned in this tables do not change the level of the key transfers discontinuously, however, the slope of the key transfer schedule (as a function of population size) changes. This change in the slope might in turn induce discontinuous changes in the optimizing strategy of the economic agent.

Legal sources: FAG – Finanzausgleichsgesetz fuer Bayern (version: June 2, 2010), GO – Gemeindeordnung für den Freistaat Bayern (version: August 17, 2009). *Source:* Own research.

Table 4.7: Defining local institutions: population thresholds in Bavarian law

Rule	Population thresholds	Legal source	Description
Full time council members	10,000	GO Art. 40	In communities with more than 10,000 inhabitants the council can elect additional full time council members that take over management functions in the local administration.
Wage elected civil servants [a]	2,000; 3,000; 5,000; 10,000; 15,000; 30,000; 50,000; 100,000.	BKBV, Art. 1; KWBG, supp. 1	The full-time mayor, the full-time deputy mayor(s), and the full time council members have the status of elected civil servants. Their remuneration depends on the size of the community. At each of the threshold indicated their salaries increase by one or two steps in the civil servants salary scale. For example in ordinary communities with more than 15,000 and up to 30,000 inhabitants the mayor is at the level B2 or B3 while in communities with more than 30,000 inhabitants she is at the level B3 or B4. An increase in one step in this system (from B3 to B4) implies about six percent wage increase (or EUR 400 per month) in Bavaria in 2010. Furthermore, elected civil servants receive a monthly expense allowance that depends on the population if the city is either a community free city or has the large city status. Then the allowance thresholds are 50,000, and 100,000 inhabitants. For example the mayor receives between 305.68 and 833.76 EUR in such communities with less than 50,000 inhabitants and between 437.72 and 965.79 EUR in communities with more than 50,000 but less than 100,000 inhabitants.
Cost allowance part time mayors	1,000; 3,000; 5,000	GO, supp. 1	Part time mayors receive a cost allowance that depends on the population size. The law sets overlapping allowance ranges for the different community size classes. For examples mayors in communities with up to 1,000 inhabitants receive a monthly allowance between 430.48 and 1,907.88 EUR while in communities with more than 1,000 and that amount increases to between 1,830.10 and 3,307.51 EUR in the size class above.
Petition for referendum	10,000; 20,000; 30,000; 50,000; 100,000; 500,000	GO, Art. 18a	The inhabitants in a community can request a referendum. To be considered, the organizers of the request need to gather signatures from the inhabitants. What share of the inhabitants they need to sign depends on the size of the community. Ten percent have to sign if the community has up to 10,000 inhabitants, 9 percent up to 20,000, 8 percent up to 30,000, 7 percent up to 50,000, 5 percent up to 100,000 and 3 percent have to sign if the community has more than 500,000 inhabitants.
Referendum quota	50,000; 100,000	GO, Art. 18a	Once a petition for referendum has reached the necessary number of signatures the voters are called to the ballot. Then the referendum needs to fulfill two conditions to pass. First, it has to get more then fifty percent of the votes. Second, these votes must represent at least 20 percent of the eligible electorate in communities with up to 50,000 inhabitants. In communities with up to 100,000 inhabitants the supporting votes need to represent at least 15 percent of the electorate and in communities with more than 100,000 inhabitants this share has to be at least 10 percent.
City districts	100,000	GO, Art. 60	Communities with more than 100,000 inhabitants are subdivided into several city districts. These city districts take over part of the administration of the city. The city council can decide to hand over decision powers to the districts. In this case they also have a district councils whose members are elected.
Open council	10,000; 100,000	GO, Art. 18a	In an open council ('Buergerversammlung') the constituents meet to discuss topics of local relevance. The meetings are chaired by the local administration. The open council can pass recommendations that then have to be discussed in the community council. In communities with less than 10,000 inhabitants five percent of the voters have to request the open council meeting, in communities with more than 10,000 inhabitants only two and a half percent need to request the open council. In cities with more than 100,000 inhabitants open council can also be held within a city district.
Accounting committee	5,000	GO, Art. 103	In communities with more than 5,000 inhabitants the council has to establish an accounting committee composed of council members to conduct an examination of accounts.
Mayor status	5,000; 10,000	GO, Art. 34	Communities with more than 10,000 inhabitants must have full-time mayors. Communities with more than 5,000 but not more than 10,000 inhabitants have a full time mayor by default. However, they can choose to have a part-time mayor instead if the council decides this not later than 67 days before the mayor election. Communities with 5,000 inhabitants or less are governed by part-time mayors by default. However, they can also choose to have a full-time mayor if the council decides so not later than 67 days before the mayor election.

Legal sources: BKBV – Bayerische Kommunalbesoldungs-erordnung (version: May 29, 2009), FAG – Finanzausgleichsgesetz fuer Bayern (version: June 2, 2010), GO – Gemeindeordnung für den Freistaat Bayern (version: August 17, 2009), KWBG – Gesetz ueber kommunale Wahlbeamte (version: August 17, 2009) *Source:* Own research.

a: Egger and Koethenbuerger (2010) state that the remuneration of the full time council members depends on the population thresholds but do not mention that this also applies to mayors and deputy mayors. As full time council members can only be elected in communities with more than 10,000 inhabitants they conduct a robustness that only includes communities with less than 10,000 inhabitants to make sure that remuneration steps for full time council do not play a role for their identification.

Table 4.8: Communal budgeting – shares of expenditure and revenues

	Mean	Share in %
Expenditures (Euro per capita)		
Total	1909.5	100.0
on Personnel	369.6	19.4
on Materials	251.2	13.2
in Investment	368.3	19.3
Revenues (Euro per capita)		
Total	1909.5	100.0
from Property Tax A	6.3	0.3
from Property Tax B	77.9	4.1
from Trade Tax	310.1	16.2
from General Grants	146.4	7.7
from Investment Grants	96.3	5.0
from Fees	178.6	9.4
Average debt (Euro per capita)	788.4	

Notes: This table illustrates basic figures of an average municipality budget. Column 2 presents the population weighted average number of Euro per capita in each category over all 2056 municipalities during the period of observation (1984–2004). Column 2 highlights the share that the individual item has on total expenditures or revenues respectively. The categories named are not exclusive, rather, we refer to all categories used in the analysis. *Source*: Own calculations.

Table 4.9: The results on expenditure categories controlling for mayor status

	Expenditure Categories (Window size 15 percent)		
	Invest Expend	Material Expend	Personnel Expend
	(1)	(2)	(3)
	Panel 1 : Replication of Egger and Koethenbuerger (2010)		
Treatment	0.103*	0.143**	0.169***
	(0.061)	(0.059)	(0.059)
N	22623	22626	22631
R2	0.001	0.001	0.001
	Panel 2 : Controlling for mayor status and year effects		
Treatment	−0.047	0.026	0.052
	(0.048)	(0.039)	(0.038)
Mayor status	1.157***	1.373***	1.367***
	(0.012)	(0.010)	(0.010)
N	22396	22399	22404
R2	0.310	0.488	0.505

Notes: Significance levels: * $p < 0.10$, ** $p < 0.05$, *** $p < 0.01$. Standard errors in parentheses are robust. The dependent variables are indicated above. Panel 1 replicates the results in Egger and Koethenbueger (2010) (see their table 5). In panel 2, we control for the mayor status in the estimation by including a dummy variable that takes the value 1 if the mayor is full-time employed. Additionally, we also control for year fixed effects and we excluded bigger communities that had the status of a county free city. Treatment is defined by being right to the population thresholds. All regressions include a third order polynomial in population that is flexible on both sides of the threshold. *Source*: Own calculations partly based on the program provided by Egger and Koethenbuerger (2010).

Table 4.10: The results on revenues controlling for mayor status

	Revenues in Logs (Window size 15 percent)					
	Debt	Prop Tax A	Prop Tax B	Trade Tax	Gen. Grants	Invest Grants
	(1)	(2)	(3)	(4)	(5)	(6)
Treatment	0.031	0.066***	0.066***	0.009**	0.136*	0.106**
	(0.060)	(0.009)	(0.008)	(0.004)	(0.077)	(0.049)
N	21935	22404	22404	22404	21186	21314
R2	0.256	0.050	0.052	0.019	0.181	0.454

Notes: Significance levels: * $p < 0.10$, ** $p < 0.05$, *** $p < 0.01$. The dependent variables are indicated above. In this regression, we estimate the effect of council size on the mayor status defined as a dummy variable which takes the value 1 if the mayor is full-time employed. Standard errors in parentheses are robust. Treatment is defined by being right to the population thresholds. All regressions include a third order polynomial in population that is flexible on both sides of the threshold. In general, the setup is similar to the regressions run by Egger and Koethenbuerger (2010). *Source*: Own calculations partly based on the program provided by Egger and Koethenbuerger (2010).

Chapter 5: Do creditors discipline local governments?

Evidence from German municipalities[1]

Abstract: Using a new, unique, data set comprising all 8,750 West-German municipalities, this paper shows that credit markets ignore common fiscal indicators when setting interest rates for municipal debt in Germany. The analysis relies on an instrumental variable approach exploiting detailed information on debt, budget, revenue and background variables for each municipality between 1998 and 2006. This paper is the first study investigating public debt consisting of loans, and not bonds, as well as the first work for the special case of German municipalities, where most creditors are publically owned banks and bailouts occur regularly.

5.1   Introduction

Calculating and explaining yields of securities is a core topic in banking and finance. Naturally, this literature applies to sovereign debt, which also sees lots of attention by public economists studying, for example, the effects of budget rules and debt ratios on the refinancing costs of the public sector. Recently, refinancing issues of several European countries and ensuing interest rate hikes and the downgrade of US Federal debt brought the topic to the political agenda.

This paper investigates the question at the lowest tier of government by researching the differences in the interest rates that German municipalities pay on their debt. In particular, I test the effects of several indicators of the soundness of municipal finances on refinancing costs. These indicators cover a wide range of possible explicatories of the interest rate and include per capita debt, debt increase, two debt to budget measures, the share of cash credits and debt repay support in total debt.

Based on an instrumental variable identification strategy, I find that the creditors of German municipalities do not charge interest rate premia to municipalities with poor financial soundness indicators. The results also show some rules that debtees follow when deciding on interest rates of municipalities – the rates for municipalities with more medium and long term debt are higher than those for municipalities with more short-term debt.

The data set comprises of data from all West-German municipalities (excluding city-states) for the years 1998 to 2006. The debt data set is new, analyzed for the first time

---

1   I would like to thank Charles B. Blankart, Ronny Freier, Viktor Steiner and seminar participants at the Freie Universität Berlin for helpful comments and suggestions.

and allows allows for the first analysis of the credit market of German municipalities so far. One feature of the credit market for German municipalities is that it almost exclusively relies on loans (as opposed to bonds), which makes this analysis also the first to look at a municipal liabilities market characterized by loans.

The empirical analysis relies on identification through a GMM panel instrumental variable approach, which is necessary to control for endogeneity of interest rate and debt.

The remaining part of the paper is structured as follows: Section 5.2 gives an overview of the literature on the determinants of interest rates and previous work for Germany, section 5.3 presents the specific rules and institutional conditions for German municipalities, section 5.4 presents the data and descriptive statistics, section 5.5 discusses the empirical strategy, section 5.6 evaluates the empirical results and finally section 5.7 concludes.

5.2 Literature review

This paper adds to the literature on yields in banking, finance, and public economics that discusses three big factors that determine the interest rate: (1) Liquidity risk; (2) default risk; and (3) general conditions (return on the risk free asset, inflation, term structure).

(1) Liquidity risk is the risk to find a buyer when one wants to sell an asset. In particular, it is the risk to be able to sell the asset quickly and without negative impact on the price. This is an important determinant of the interest rates as multiple studies show (e.g. Covitz and Downing 2007; Chen, Lesmond, and Wei 2007).

(2) Default risk is the the probability that an issuer cannot disburse interest or principal. Typically, a situation is already considered as default when a payment is late (compare Moody's 2011). There is a large body of literature establishing that default risk is a key determinant of the interest rate (compare e.g. Duffee 1999; Merton 1974). Some even argue that it is the most important determinant (e.g. Longstaff, Mithal, and Neis 2005).

(3) General conditions also play a key role for the interest rate. The risk free interest rate at a given moment in time is the starting point for any security evaluation. Furthermore, the prevailing term structure influences a security's return (compare e.g. Merton 1974; Rodriguez 1988). Beyond, the general economic condition and future prospects play a role, as does default history in the case of jurisdictions (Hastie 1972; Bayoumi, Goldstein, and Woglom 1995)).

In economics the discussion on the yields of (local) government bonds focuses on default risk. From this discourse one can identify two main drivers of default risk

150

affecting the interest rate. On the one hand there is indebtedness which is – simplified – the ratio of debt to GDP, on the other hand there is the institutional setting. The latter includes fiscal rules, institutions affecting expenses and revenues (mainly rules of the decision making process such as direct democracy) and rules affecting bailout probability (which are mainly the rules regarding the relationship between different tiers of government).

The first driver of default risk, indebtedness, can be measured by several ratios: debt relative to the tax base, debt to GDP, debt to revenue, interest payments to budget and so on. For example Hastie (1972) estimates that cities with higher overall debt/true property value ratios pay higher interest rates, and Bayoumi, Goldstein, and Woglom (1995) find that a one percentage point increase in debt debt to state GDP raises the interest rate about 23 basis points. Feld, Kalb, Moessinger, and Osterloh (2011) investigate spreads of Swiss cantonal bonds to federal bonds and find that a one percentage point increase in debt to GDP increases the yield by 0.9 basis points. Capeci (1994) looks at municipal borrowing costs of municipalities in New Jersey. The author finds that both the size of the existing outstanding debt and the current year debt increase impact the interest rates of new bond issues. One standard deviation debt increase leads to an increase in the interest rate of 0.66 percentage points. Ejsing, Lemke, and Margaritov (2011) estimate the effect of fiscal deficits (measured by deficit to GDP) on sovereign bond interest rate spreads for several countries in the Euro-area. The authors find that higher deficits lead to higher spreads towards German government bonds - an effect that has increased since the beginning of the financial crisis (in fall 2008).

The second driver of default risk, the general institutional setting, also plays a key role for default risk. Fiscal rules are important institutions and are analyzed e.g. by Poterba and Rueben (1997), who find that balanced budget rules and debt restrictions lead to lower interest rates on bonds issued by US states. Furthermore, states with expenditure limits pay lower rates while states with revenue limitations pay higher rates. Feld et al. (2011) analyze the market for Swiss cantonal bonds and find that fiscal rules (such as automatic tax increases should a balanced budget not be met) reduce the spread to federal government bonds.[2]

Beyond fiscal rules, rules determining the inter-liability of governments, often denoted as bail out rules, are highly deterministic for the probability of default. Gehrmann (2011) develops a model arguing that small municipalities are unlikely to be bailed out in a federal state as their political relevance is low compared to bigger municipalities. The largest municipalities may, however, not be bailed out either as the ensuing high rescue outlays would be too costly politically. It follows, *ceteris paribus,* that both small and very large municipalities should pay higher interest rates than medium

---

2   There is a large literature on fiscal rules and their effects on interest rates, see Feld, Kalb, Moessinger, and Osterloh (2011, ch. 2.3) for an overview.

sized municipalities. One way to check how much bailout expectations matter is to investigate possible exogenous changes to these expectations. There are two papers (Fasten 2006; Feld et al. 2011) that use a ruling by the Swiss federal court from 2003 as exogenous variation. The court ruled that the canton of Valais did not have to bail out the bankrupt municipality of Leukerbad[3] – a verdict that changed bailout expectations. Fasten (2006) investigates the yields of municipal bonds as he expects that their interest rates will increase after the ruling as municipalities are less likely to be bailed out than before. In the analysis he does, however, not find evidence that municipal bond yields reacted to the ruling. Feld et al. (2011) look at the cantonal bonds using the same reasoning. They expect that the spreads of cantonal bonds fall after the ruling as the risk of having to bail out municipalities decreases. Empirically they find that the risk premia of cantons (compared to federal bonds) fell by 25 basis points after the ruling and that the link between a canton's risk premium and the financial situation of its municipalities ceased to exist. Kidwell and Trzcinka (1982, 1983) investigate another event, the 1975 New York city financial crisis, that finally ended with the federal government providing loans to the city. The authors find that this crisis did only have a very short and small effect on the municipal bond market and did not change the medium and long term risk perceptions in the market.

Also more general institutions, such as rules of the decision making process, are proven to affect the refinancing costs. For example, Kuettel and Kugler (2002) investigate the market for Swiss cantonal bonds and find that cantons in which the people can more easily limit government spending through referenda pay lower interest rates, while states where the electorate can participate more through direct democracy (excluding fiscal referenda) pay higher interest rates. Furthermore, these authors do not find that financial soundness indicators (such as debt/taxes, debt /income, interest/income, budget balance, taxes/income) significantly determine the interest rate.

Looking at Germany the literature on the determinants of sovereign debt interest rates and default risk is not very extensive. Schulz and Wolff (2009) look at the spreads between bonds issued by the German states and those issued by the federal government. They find that while general risk aversion is a key driver of the spread, debt per capita of the states hardly changes the risk premia. A dummy indicating a ruling of the German federal court to not bail out Berlin in 2006 did not significantly affect the spreads. Heppke-Falk and Wolff (2008) perform a similar analysis for risk premia of state bonds compared to federal bonds. These authors find that per capita debt actually increases the interest rate spread. For each EUR 1,000 in per capita debt, the interest rate spread increases by 4.6 basis points. Furthermore, they investigate the effect of the interest payments to revenue ratio as the German constitutional court argued in its 1992 ruling that a high value indicates financial distress and can justify a bailout by the federal government. Empirically the authors now find that an increase in this

---

3   For a description of the Leukerbad case see also Blankart (2007).

ratio by one percentage points decreases the risk premium by 2.5 basis points. This – at first surprising – effect shall be interpreted as the market's reaction to an increased bailout-probability. Schuknecht, von Hagen, and Wolswijk (2009) find that that the monetary union changed the rules of the game for German states – while before they did not have to pay a premium for higher fiscal deficits they had to up the ante after the completion of the union, which may be explained by changed bail-out perceptions.

I conclude that so far there is clear evidence that institutions (fiscal rules, bailout rules, and rules of the decision making process) matter for yields on sovereign debt and that financial soundness indicators are also relevant even though there are cases where they are not significant. For my work it is of particular interest that yields depend on financial soundness indicators for German states, as the study by Heppke-Falk and Wolff (2008) points out. With the German municipalities operating in an overall similar framework and financial market this implies the hypothesis that these indicators will matter for German municipalities too.

5.3 Institutional background

German municipalities are the lowest tier in German federalism. Below the national level there are 16 states, of which 13 are non-city states. These 13 states are subdivided into roughly 450 counties and 12,500 municipalities. Larger cities fulfill both duties of municipalities and counties. With respect to local expenditures, it is important that a large share of municipal and county tasks are mandated by either the state or the federal governments, although there are some areas where municipalities have full discretion (e.g. culture). Further, their financial resources depend heavily on transfers, yet there are several taxes that municipalities can determine, most importantly the business tax and the property taxes. When it comes to debt, there are two mechanisms can municipalities can use. The standard are liabilities for investment or investment assistance. For legal reasons this debt option cannot be used for financing other purposes. Debt incurred by this vehicle must be approved by the supervision of the municipalities by the state, which looks at debt levels and the municipal budget among others. The second debt tool of municipalities are the so called cash credits (or liquidity safeguarding credits) that shall help municipalities to cover short term liquidity need. This tool does not require approval by the municipality supervision authorities[4]. For this reason, this tool is popular with municipalities needing for cash (compare table 5.1 and Staedtetag

---

4   For a legal description on these two tools and the according rules compare e.g.: *Kreditwirtschaft der kommunalen Körperschaften einschließlich ihrer Sonder- und Treuhandvermögen.* RdErl. d. MI Niedersachsen v. 22.10.2008 – 33.1-10245/1, available at http://www.recht-niedersachsen.de/20300/33,1, 10245,1-htm, retrieved June 27, 2011.

2011). However, under the new double bookkeeping that is being gradually introduced in the German states, there are increasing limits to cash credits.[5]

Taking into account that cash credits are easily available to municipalities, it is no surprise that some municipalities accrue more and more debt, eventually landing in a budgetary crisis. In this situation municipalities can profit from two key legal norms. First – and most general – the German constitutional text guarantees in its article 28 the autonomy of municipalities, including "financial self-responsibility". Second, Germany insolvency law (article 12) says that insolvency proceeding cannot be be started against entities that are subject to public law if state law says so (and state law does say so)[6]. While from the norms it remains unclear what would actually happen if a municipality could not service its debt and other obligations any more, states have always decided to bail out municipalities in financial distress. Seitz (2000) presents that all non-city states had funds to bail out close-to-bankrupt municipalities in 1998. For the support funds to be disbursed, municipalities had to enter a consolidation path. More recently, in 2011, seven states had general bailout funds[7] (Staedtetag 2011). For example the state of Lower Saxony established a fund to finance "future treaties" with several municipalities under financial distress. Via this tool the city of Hildesheim will receive EUR 140 mn (representing 46% of its total debt of EUR 307 mn)[8]. Further, Baden-Württemberg, which does not have a general bail out fund, helped the municipality of Aulendorf in 2010 by taking over a total of 63 percent of the municipality's debt (40 out of 63 million EUR)[9].[10] Overall, it is likely that markets incorporate these bailouts in their expectations. Following Blankart (2007), one might expect that markets will not charge premia to more indebted municipalities – a hypothesis that stands in contrast to the empirical results from Heppke-Falk and Wolff (2008), who find that interest rates of German states, which are also expected to be bailed out by the federal government if problems become too severe, depend on financial soundness indicators.

When analyzing financing conditions of municipalities, it is also important to investigate who loans German municipalities money. Taking into account that municipalities

---

5 Compare e.g. http://www.haushaltssteuerung.de/ weblog-kassenkredit-schuldenbremsen-in-der-kommunalen-doppik.html (retrieved September 27, 2011) for an overview of the recent limitations.

6 See for example for: Baden-Wuerttemberg – Article 45 *Gesetz zur Ausführung des Gerichtsverfassungsgesetzes und von Verfahrensgesetzen der ordentlichen Gerichtsbarkeit*, Lower Saxony – Article 136, 2 *Niedersächsische Gemeindeordnung*, North Rhine-Westphalia – Art 128, 2 *Gemeindeordnung für das Land Nordrhein-Westfalen*

7 Hesse, Saxony-Anhalt, North-Rhine Westphalia, Lower Saxony, Mecklenburg-West Pomerania

8 According to local newspaper *Hildesheimer Zeitung* from 29. December 2010.

9 According to the local newspaper, *Stuttgarter Zeitung,* from 9. December 2009.

10 There is one case where a municipality sued the county to take over some of its debt. The arguing of the municipality of Niederoderwitz in the state of Saxony was that the supervising entity (the county) had not prevented the municipality from taking a disadvantageous financing decision for a sports facility. Niederoderwitz ultimately prevailed in a ruling by the Federal Court of Justice (Blankart 2007).

are bailed out whenever the debt burden becomes too high and that insolvency procedures cannot be opened, one would expect that municipalities would have no problems refinancing themselves on the normal bank market. As it turns out, however, they incur most of their debt with public banks. According to DSGV (2011) the large majority of municipal debt is financed by public banks in 2010 (about 45.3% are held by the municipality owned savings banks and state banks and another 23.2% held by other public banks, such as the *Kreditanstalt für Wiederaufbau*). Furthermore, municipalities rarely issues bonds (Staedtetag 2011). One interpretation is that private banks and the bond market are typically not willing to offer credit as cheaply as the public banks do. This might hint at different perceptions of the riskiness of municipal debt[11].

Considering that municipalities mainly borrow from public banks and that bailouts occur on a regular basis, there are strong incentives to borrow more than is sustainable in the long run, which leads to the hypothesis that debt will have minimal, if any, influence on interest rates.[12]

5.4 Data and descriptive statistics

I use a new data set that includes information all 8,750 West-German municipalities (about 8,750 in total). The data was provided by the statistical offices in each state. While parts of the data set are used in other studies (those data on revenues and taxes e.g. Ade (2011)[13]), the data on the composition of the municipal debt is new and analyzed here for the first time. I excluded the three city-states (Bremen, Hamburg, and Berlin), as city-states do not have municipal levels comparable to the non-city states. East German municipalities are excluded from the analysis because during the observation period there were waves of amalgamation that confound the pure effect of financial indicators that are investigated in this paper.[14]

The data is from 1998 to 2006 and presents aggregated yearly values for each municipality. Hence, the debt data does not contain information on individual loans or bonds but rather data that summarizes all outstanding debt. The same holds for interest payments. The interest rate a municipality pays on its debt is not explicitly contained in the data but is calculated as total interest payments divided by total outstanding debt. In particular I use the interest payments of period *t+1* divided by outstanding debt at

---

11 Only in October 2011 a public bank in North-Rhine Westphalia seems to have drastically changed its risk perceptions of municipalities and decided against providing loans to the municipalities under the greatest financial distress any more (see the *Mindener Tageblatt* from October 19, 2010).

12 Motivated from the learnings of the Leukerbad case, Blankart (2011) proposes two steps to overcome the problem of inefficient municipal credit markets that could also work for Germany. First a strict bailout regime should be established; and, second, more transparency through municipality evaluation by rating agencies would resolve the asymmetrical information problem between creditor and debtor.

13 This paper is identical with chapter 1 of this dissertation.

14 However the effects of amalgamation on debt and interest rate and the respective incentives for the municipalities that come with mergers are a promising area for further research.

the end of period t as this procedure is prone to less measurement error than the alternative of dividing interest in t by debt in t.[15] The chosen procedure leads to a loss of one year in the data I can use for estimation.

The rate represents an average that comprises both loans that were incurred in previous years as well as the loans taken out during the year under observation. The data also contains information identifying when outstanding debt will mature, whether in $t+1$, $t+2$, $t+3$, $t+4$ or later than $t+4$.

Those observations with zero debt are not included from the analysis as it is not possible to calculate an interest rate. Further municipalities were excluded for data availability/outlier reasons (see Appendix for a detailed description). In regressions using debt increases I cannot use the year 1998 as it does not have a previous year for which a debt increase could be calculated. Summary statistics of the key regression variables are in Table 5.1.

The average interest rate of all observations is 5.3 percent; over the years interest rates slightly fall from 5.55 percent in 1998 to 4.71 in 2005. There is relatively large variation in the interest rates paid by the municipalities (see table 5.1) .

In the empirical analysis, this paper tests the effects of four key financial soundness indicators[16] The first of those is debt per capita, which is EUR 604 on average. Municipalities increase this burden on average by EUR 14 per year (the second indicator). However, in the majority of observations, municipalities actually reduce their per capita debt (the median is EUR -12 per year). The third and fourth indicator relate interest and debt to the budget. Interest payments represent about 2.41 percent of local budget on average, while total debt is about 46.1 percent of the total budget.

The state laws in Germany provides for two types of municipal debt. On the one hand there is regular debt, which is only allowed for investments and must be approved by supervision authorities. On the other hand there are *Kassenkredite*, cash credits, which are meant to guarantee short term liquidity just like overdraft loans do for private households. During the observation period, cash credits could be incurred without

---

15 Dividing the interest payments of period $t+1$ by outstanding debt at the end of period t is the best way to calculate the interest rate if interest payments are annual and the term of any loan is at least one year. However, the calculated interest rate may be imprecise if (part of the) interest payment on loans occur multiple times a year and/or loans have a total term of less than one year. The alternative of relating the interest payments of a year to the debt stock of the same year is prone to produce even more measurement error – just imagine the case of a municipality that reduces its debt at the end of November by 50 %. This municipality reports the interest accrued in the eleven months for the debt it repays at the end of November and the interest of the debt it holds over the whole year in the statistic. On the other hand the municipality will report the end of year debt level. Hence, the calculated rate will be almost twice as high as the actual rate.

16 An explanation of how the indicators were chosen is given in section 5.6.

involvement of the municipal supervision. This paper uses the share of cash credits of total debt as signal indicator for financial distress. The idea is that only those municipalities that cannot get authorization by the supervising authorities will incur large amount of cash credits. In the data the share of cash credits of total debt is 3.10 percent on average while in more than 50 percent of the observations the municipalities did not have any outstanding cash credits at the end of the year. Another feature of local financing in Germany, which the paper uses as signal indicator, is debt repayment help provided to the municipalities (*Schuldendienstbeihilfen*). This help is granted to municipalities in order to support repay debt incurred for specific projects and is not a bailout. The idea behind including this measure is that a municipality need not be in severe financial problems when one looks at the financial soundness indicators while at the same time the state government believes that a municipality will have a hard time paying back its obligations in the future and thus provides debt repay support. These aids represent, on average, 2.42 percent of outstanding debt and the majority of municipalities does not receive any.

The municipalities take on debt with rather long maturities: out of debt outstanding (excluding cash credits) about two-thirds mature in more than four years, and each year about 10.5 percent of the debt total debt outstanding at the end of the year will have been incurred during that year (either replacing maturing debt or new debt)[17].

5.5   Empirical strategy

The analysis relies on a panel approach using data from West German municipalities. The basic model takes the following form for municipality i in year t:

$$rate_{it} = \alpha_i + \delta_t + \sum_k \beta_k x_{kit} + e_{it} \qquad (5.1)$$

where $rate_{it}$ is the average interest rate of the municipality, α_i are municipality dummies, δ_t are year dummies, β_k are the parameters of interest and x_{kit} are explanatory variables where k indexes the explanatory variables. In an extended model I also include selected lagged explanatory variables denoted h_{lit} (where l indexes the lagged explanatory variables) to cover for the effect that only a part of the interest rate in t actually depends on new loans from t. The equation then becomes:

$$rate_{it} = \alpha_i + \delta_t + \sum_k \beta_k x_{kit} + \sum_l \gamma_l h_{lit} + e_{it} \qquad (5.2)$$

When analyzing panel data researchers hope to obtain unbiased estimates by using a fixed effects approach that captures unobserved individual specific effects and unobserved time effects. However, in the models laid out above, the key variables of interest

---

17   This includes only general debt but no short term cash credits.

Table 5.1: Descriptive statistics

Variable	Unit	Obs.	Mean	Median	Std. Dev.	Min.	Max.
interest rate	percent	55,487	5.30	5.08	1.851	1.19	19.75
total debt	thsd EUR	55,487	8,568	1,272	65,185	1	3,397,133
debt per capita	thsd EUR	55,487	0.604	0.470	0.547	0.0002	14.139
debt increase per capita	thsd EUR	48,475	0.014	−0.012	0.162	−11.825	3.914
debt to budget ratio	percent	55,487	46.09	38.56	44.30	0.01	1,910.83
interest to budget ratio	percent	55,487	2.41	2.00	2.32	−1.44	91.13
cash credits to debt ratio	percent	55,487	3.10	0	10.88	0	99.96
debt help to debt ratio	percent	55,487	2.42	0	8.51	−35.95	99.35
population	absolute	55,487	9,088	2,847	32,993	8	1,259,677
population density	inh./sq.km	55,487	226.31	124.99	302.79	3.05	4058.23
area	sq. km	55,487	36.18	22.4	40.26	0.45	465.16
net migration share	percent	55,487	0.351	0.284	4.94	−37.04	72.73
population < 15 (share)	percent	55,487	17.35	17.30	2.43	0	52.00
population > 64 (share)	percent	55,487	22.02	22.36	4.94	1.14	47.96
refinanced / total debt	percent	55,487	10.49	0	25.01	0	3,600
maturities < 1 yr share	percent	55,487	10.08	6.62	12.99	0	100
maturities 1–2 yrs share	percent	55,487	8.50	6.38	8.71	0	100
maturities 2–3 yrs share	percent	55,487	7.81	6.25	7.07	0	100
maturities 3–4 yrs share	percent	55,487	7.24	6.06	5.92	0	100
maturities >4 yrs share	percent	55,487	66.65	72.87	22.78	0	100

in x_{kt} are most likely endogenous to the interest rate $rate_{it}$. For example, it is likely that a municipality with a low interest rate might take on more debt because it can get credit inexpensively. Following the same reasoning, a municipality with a higher interest rate might consider incurring less debt as it is relatively expensive. Hence, not only does the interest rate react to the debt level but also the debt level reacts to the interest rate.[18]

To cure this endogeneity issue, I implement an instrumental variable strategy. As there are no suitable contemporaneous instruments available I use past values of the endogenous variables as instruments. To estimate the relationship given in eq. 5.1 and eq. 5.2 I use either an Arrelano-Bond twostep difference GMM estimators or a twostep system GMM estimator depending on specification tests (see Cameron and Trivedi 2010, pp. 295–302; Arellano and Bond 1991). Whenever possible I prefer the system estimator as it is known that the difference estimator has a downward bias (particularly if the true value is high, see Blundell and Bond (1998)) and because the system estimator is more efficient (Cameron and Trivedi 2010, p. 301). Overall, I use a GMM estimator here instead of a standard panel-IV estimator to achieve maximum

---

18 Furthermore, this may leads to a downward bias when estimating the β_k for variables such as debt per capita and debt increase per capita. That means that estimate of β_k for these variables would be too low in a standard panel model.

efficiency (and even most of the GMM estimates produce insignificant results though the point estimate have an economically significant size).

In the sensitivity analysis I apply spline regressions to check for possible heterogeneous effects along the distribution of the key explanatory variables (see subsection 5.6.2 for details).

5.6   Results

5.6.1   Main analysis

In this section I present the results of the empirical analysis. I first discuss the individual results for several financial soundness (tables 5.2 and 5.3) and signal indicators (table 5.4). Each of these tables contains three specifications that do not differ over the tables (except for the variable of interest). Then I turn turn to a joint analysis of all indicators. I finally present a sensitivity analysis.

Financial soundness indicators are shown in the literature to be deterministic for the yield of sovereign debt (compare section 5.2). While one of the most broadly used indicators, debt to GDP, cannot be calculated for the data in this paper, since there is no municipality level data for GDP, there is a multitude of other important indicators that can be calculated. Of those, debt per capita is the most general indicator that grasps the overall severity of the debt burden. It is important as many transfers and tax receipts (e.g. the share of the VAT) are directly linked to the population size. With a high value in the debt per capita indicator, a municipality will have a hard time servicing and repaying its obligations.

Table 5.2 displays the fixed effects and instrumental variable estimates for the effect of per capita debt on the interest rate. In column (1) are the results of a time and municipality fixed effects regression that report a negative and significant impact of per capita debt on the interest rate. The coefficient of -2.01 means that for every additional 1,000 EUR in per capita debt, the interest rate falls by about two percentage points or 201 basis points. The regression also includes further covariates that might directly affect the interest rate. Municipalities with a higher population density, positive net migration and a relatively high share of population over 65 pay lower rates. Also, the term structure of the outstanding debt plays a significant role for the interest rate. The estimates indicate that municipalities that have a higher share of debt maturing in more than 12 months pay higher rates (the variable indicating the share of debt maturing in less than twelve months was excluded from the regression for collinearity). In column (2) the equation is extended by lags of the debt per capita variable. This is because only a small share of the loans outstanding at the end of year t date from that year. Hence, loan agreements from former year also influence the interest rate in t. The estimate for debt per capita is still negative and significant and is now -2.98. The point estimates for the lagged debt measures are all positive and significant and range between 0.19 and 0.27.

The estimates in column 1 and 2 alone indicate an overall negative effect of per capita debt on the interest rate. However, as discussed in section 5.5 these estimates are likely to be biased downwards: on the one hand, one expects municipalities with higher per capita debt to pay higher interest rates as a sign of market discipline, on the other hand municipalities with a lower interest rate might be inclined to borrow more as it is less expensive for them. This endogeneity may lead to a downward bias in the estimate of the parameter for debt per capita as municipalities adjust their behavior to the interest rate. To address this problem I instrument per capita debt with its lagged values. The respective results are reported in column (3). The point estimate for per capita debt is now slightly positive yet insignificant. The estimators for the lagged values of debt per capita are also all insignificant and three of them are negative now (while all were positive in the fixed effects case).[19] A test of a of serial autocorrelation in the first differenced errors does not suggest that the model is misspecified. Also a Sargan test of the overidentifying restrictions does not reject the hypothesis that these restrictions are valid[20]. The values reported in the table are based on the Windmejer estimator (Windmeijer 2005) for the standard errors. Summing up, the analysis of the effect of per capita debt on the interest rate does not provide evidence that the capital markets require an interest rate premium from higher indebted municipalities.

Even though there is no positive connection between debt per capita and the yield on local government debt, there might be other channels that banks evaluate when deciding on interest rates. Table 5.3 presents three further reasonable soundness indicators that banks might use. The debt increase per capita (which more or less is the budget deficit per capita) might be important as it provides information on the financial path that a municipality is on. A high value indicates that a municipality is spending much more than it receives in taxes and transfers. Even with low total debt a municipality with a high debt increase might be considered a problem while a municipality with a high total debt that is however on a consolidation path might be less of an issue.

The results of per capita debt increases on the interest rate are in panel 1 of table 5.3. The background variables and the lags of the dependent variables in specification (3) are omitted from this and the following tables as they are broadly in line with those estimates in table 5.2. In the two fixed effects specifications (1) and (2) the point estimates for the debt increase are negative and significant as are the lagged debt increases in col-

---

19 The GMM estimator used here and in the following tables is a difference GMM estimator that is shown to be downward biased, particularly when the true value is high (Blundell and Bond 1998). A system GMM estimator could not be used as there was no reasonable specification that passed the Sargan test.

20 The Sargan test is computed based on a regression with the conventional variance estimator for GMM as it is not available for the robust Windmeijer estimator.

umn $(2)^{21}$. The difference GMM instrumental variable estimation does not change the signs and rough magnitudes – the point estimates all have negative signs too but are not significant[22]. I conclude that there is no evidence that financial markets increase interest rates when municipalities take on additional debt per capita.

One may now ask whether the debt increase per capita measure is really something that banks look at. It might be that the debt to budget ratio and the interest to budget ratio are more important as they focus on the strain that the debt burden puts on the business of the municipality. A high debt to budget ratio, similarly to the debt per capita measure, shows that it will be difficult to repay debt, while the interest to budget ratio shows how much the municipality is limited in its budgeting process by interest payments already today.

Panel two and three of table 5.3 present the evidence regarding these two measures. And again, there is no evidence that these indicators are important. While the variables seem to be negatively related to the interest rate in the base case regression in column (1), earlier lags of the measures have a positive impact while more recent lags have a negative in column (2). And none of the realizations of the variables is significant in the IV regression that controls for the endogeneity problem.

There are two more measures that are more signals than financial soundness indicators, which banks might consider. The first emerges from the composition of the tools that municipalities use to refinance themselves. As discussed in section 5.3, municipalities can either seek approval for their new loans from their supervising administration or they can take on money bypassing the supervision if they declare the money as short term liquidity credit (cash credit). If municipalities do not get approval they must choose the second option. Taking the share of short term credit as a signal of financial distress, one might expect that banks charge higher rates to such municipalities. A second sign that banks might observe when looking at municipalities is the share that debt repay support represents in total debt. Typically less well off municipalities receive such payments. Table 5.4 presents the results for these two indicators. The estimates for the cash credits to total debt ratio (in panel 2) overall do not support the hypothesis that this ratio matters. In panel 1 are the results for the debt support share of total debt. This is the only case where the contemporaneous estimator is positive and significant in the fixed effects panels. The lags of the ratio are all insignificant and small yet positive (except for the third lag). The IV estimate reports a larger positive effects for the contemporaneous estimator although it is not significant. The lags of the ratio in column 2 are also not significant and negative in three cases. From these

---

21 There are only three lags of debt increase per capita as there is one year less data available than for variables presented in the other panels.

22 Sargan and autocorrelation tests do not indicate that the model is misspecified (the same applies to all following regressions).

results I find that there is no robust evidence that the markets used the two ratios as signals for local default risk.

So far, from the results one may conclude that banks ignore the discussed financial soundness and the two signal indicators when making credit decisions – but other soundness indicators not analyzed could still play a role. That is why additional measures expressing the financial situation of a municipality were tested in robustness checks[23]. There was no indication that there is a robust relationship between a poor financial situation and higher interest rates.

As a last check, all explanatory variables are tested jointly in table 5.5. In column (1) are the base case results of a fixed effects regression that includes the explanatory variables without lags. In column (2) are the results of a fixed effects regression that also includes lags of the explanatory variables. As discussed above, the lags should be included in order to cover for the effect that only a small part of the current debt stock was incurred in t. Here I use three lags (as opposed to four lags in most specifications above) as I can use one period less because I include the per capita debt increase in the model. Column (3) reports the results using a difference GMM instrumental variable estimator and column (4) depicts the estimation output generated by a system GMM instrumental variable estimator. In the instrumental variable estimations I instrument the endogenous explanatory variables (i.e. the contemporaneous endogenous variables and their lags) with their past realizations. Both autocorrelation and Sargan tests do not indicate problems with the specifications in (3) and (4)[24].

Overall the message from table 5.5 is the same as from the individual regressions: there is no robust evidence that banks charge higher rates to municipalities that are in a poor financial situation. While there are some indicators for which the table now reports positive effects on the interest rate in specification (1) (debt increase per capita, interest to budget ratio and debt help to debt ratio), these effects vanish or even turn negative in specification (2). Further the IV estimations do not support the view of market discipline. Nonetheless, in the system GMM estimations in column (4) there is an indication (at the five percent level) that an increase in the contemporaneous debt to budget ratio by one percentage point increases the interest rate by about 4 basis points. However, the lagged values coefficients are all negative (with only the second lag significant at the ten percent level), thus casting serious doubts on an overall positive effect.

---

23 These indicators include debt to tax revenue (business tax, income tax), debt to tax base (business tax), debt to primary revenues (revenues excluding new debt), share of debt increase to total debt. The results are available upon request.

24 Again, background variables are omitted from the table.

5.6.2 Sensitivity

When examining about the relationship between indebtedness and interest rates, one might argue that there should only be a weak connection for low levels of debt but a strong one for higher levels of debt. The idea behind is twofold: on the one hand a municipality with a "low" debt burden can be considered financially stable and "low" can include a whole range of e.g. debt per capita ratios. On the other hand a severe increase in debt might change the perception – once a municipality's debt burden is not perceived as "low," additional debt might affect the interest rate. If this reasoning were true, my whole sample estimates might hide a positive effect for municipalities with high values of the financial soundness indicators. To check whether this is a valid argument I run spline regressions that estimate several coefficients of the variable of interest. Each coefficient refers to a certain "spline" or interval in the explanatory variable (for a brief introduction to spline regression see Greene (2003) and for an application Gruber and Saez (2002)). I define 10 splines each containing a ten percent percentile of the distribution of the variable of interest. In the case of the effect of per capita debt on the interest rate that means that I estimate several coefficients for the ten ranges of per capita debt. The knots for these splines are in EUR: 104, 188, 278, 367, 470, 589, 729, 922, and 1,249. The first spline coefficient "spline 1 control" in table 5.6 thus refers to the values below EUR 104 and the last spline coefficient "spline 10 control" to the values above EUR 1,249.

Table 5.6 presents the results of time and municipality fixed effects spline regression for the financial soundness indicators discussed above. Looking at the estimates and the significance levels of all indicators (except debt repay help to debt) one finds that the values for the higher percentile spline are typically negative and significant (as they are for the lower percentile splines). Based on this, there is no evidence that my main estimates in tables 5.2 to 5.5 could potentially cover positive relationships in the higher percentiles. The results of debt repay help to debt in column (5) suggest, however, that there is a positive relationship for the highest two percentiles while the values for the third-highest percentile is negative.[25] This, however, does not come as a surprise as the non IV-estimates in column (2) and (3)5.4 are also positive and significant. Whether the is a robust positive effect must however be doubted as the IV estimates in table 5.4 are overall insignificant.

5.7 Conclusion

The goal of this paper is to explore whether creditors discipline local governments for taking on more debt. I conclude that – based on common financial soundness and two signal indicators – there is no evidence that the creditors of German municipalities charge higher rates to municipalities that are in a worse financial situation. This

---

25 There are no estimates for percentiles two to seven as all observation in these percentiles have a value of zero in the debt repay help to debt ratio. In the first percentile are observations with a negative ratio.

may sound surprising at first as the literature suggests that default risk – which is assumed to increase with worsening indicators – is a major driver of the interest rate. However, there are two institutional features that might incapacitate the link between indebtedness and default risk in the case of German municipalities. First, the debtees of German municipalities are mainly public banks (some of them are even owned by the municipalities themselves) and private banks are rarely used by the municipalities. One may speculate that the latter have a different risk perception that requires higher rates for some municipalities. Second of all, there are frequent bail-outs of municipalities by States. It may well be that the market expects these bailouts and hence refrains from charging higher rates to municipalities with poor financial soundness indicators. An important avenue for further research might thus be to analyze the incentives at work in the market for municipal debt and to investigate how the moral hazard problem generated by repeated bailouts affects municipal financial responsibility.

Appendix

Detailed description of changes to the data set

The data set used was compiled from several data bases produced by the state statistical offices as discussed in section 5.4. There are observations where needed data is missing or where calculated ratios show implausible values. These observations were deleted from the data set. In the next paragraph follows a detailed description of the deletions made.

I deleted observations for which the population count for ages above 65 and under 15 is not available (323 observations) and municipalities for which no maturity structure is available (1573 observations) and observations for which no budget data is available to compute the debt to budget ratio (four observations). I also excluded observations that indicate that the interest payments are more than 100 percent of the budget (14 observations), observations that indicate the share of the population above 64 or below 15 is above 100 percent (eight / one observations). I also exclude those observations where the debt repay help reported in the data is more than 100 percent of debt (117 observations). One observation was excluded because the share of maturities under one year was negative, another observation was deleted because the share of maturities higher than four years was more than 100 percent. Furthermore, I excluded observations for which the calculated interest rate is either above the 99 percent percentile or below the 1 percent percentile. The reason is that the interest rates in the data are calculated based on year end debt stocks and over the year interest payments. As discussed in section 5.4 this may lead to outliers in the data which do not represent the actual rate paid by the municipality.

Time to maturity shares used in the analysis are approximated by the time to maturity shares of credit market debt as the maturity structure is not available for total debt.

Credit market debt constitutes about 94 percent of total debt in the sample why I believe that it is fair use credit market time to maturity shares. Calculating an interest rate for credit market debt consistently is unfortunately not possible as the classification of interest payments changed over the observation horizon.

Tables

Table 5.2: Effect of debt per capita on interest rates

	(1)	(2)	(3)
debt per capita	−2.0081***	−2.9849***	0.2284
	(0.0730)	(0.1193)	(4.7854)
L1 debt per capita		0.1900***	−2.9738
		(0.0685)	(3.2052)
L2 debt per capita		0.2185***	0.8764
		(0.0703)	(3.0525)
L3 debt per capita		0.2565***	−0.3616
		(0.0649)	(0.3306)
L4 debt per capita		0.2737***	−0.1292
		(0.0674)	(0.4695)
population	−0.0000	−0.0001	−0.0001
	(0.0000)	(0.0001)	(0.0001)
pop. density	−0.0033***	−0.0024	−0.0000
	(0.0013)	(0.0017)	(0.0023)
area	−0.0038	−0.0579*	0.0347
	(0.0199)	(0.0331)	(0.0619)
migration share	−0.0158***	−0.0165**	0.0057
	(0.0049)	(0.0075)	(0.0251)
pop. > 64 share	−0.0104***	0.0491**	0.0453
	(0.0036)	(0.0216)	(0.0350)
pop. < 15 share	0.0130	0.0498**	0.0451
	(0.0132)	(0.0221)	(0.0320)
maturities 1–2 yrs share	0.0118***	0.0114***	0.0128**
	(0.0017)	(0.0028)	(0.0056)
maturities 2–3 yrs share	0.0090***	0.0114***	0.0158**
	(0.0018)	(0.0027)	(0.0079)
maturities 3–4 yrs share	0.0110***	0.0096***	0.0143*
	(0.0019)	(0.0031)	(0.0079)
maturities > 4 yrs share	0.0051***	−0.0019	−0.0081**
	(0.0011)	(0.0021)	(0.0038)
L1 interest rate			0.0871
			(0.1642)
L2 interest rate			0.0702
			(0.1187)
N	55,487	25,247	18,519
r2	0.1434	0.1805	

* $p<0.10$, ** $p<0.05$, *** $p<0.01$, robust standard errors in parenthesis Estimates (1) and (2) are panel fixed effects estimates with time and municipality fixed effects. Estimates (3) rely on a difference GMM (also with time and municipality fixed effects). Sargan and overidentifying restrictions tests do not indicate problems with the specification.

Table 5.3: Effect of per capita debt increase and the debt and interest to budget ratios on interest rates

	(1)	(2)	(3)
	Panel 1: debt increase per capita		
debt incr. per cap.	−1.1225***	−2.3897***	−2.8813
	(0.1274)	(0.0981)	(18.5649)
L1 debt incr. per cap.		−1.8943***	−2.6159
		(0.0947)	(3.7653)
L2 debt incr. per cap.		−1.3641***	−1.8030
		(0.0917)	(5.8475)
L3 debt incr. per cap.		−0.6505***	−1.9176
		(0.1413)	(5.8586)
	Panel 2: debt to budget ratio		
debt to budget ratio	−0.0051***	−0.0037***	−0.0140
	(0.0007)	(0.0006)	(0.0155)
L1 debt to budget ratio		−0.0022***	−0.0167
		(0.0004)	(0.0139)
L2 debt to budget ratio		−0.0017***	−0.0192
		(0.0003)	(0.0197)
L3 debt to budget ratio		0.0039***	0.0024
		(0.0006)	(0.0076)
L4 debt to budget ratio		0.0026***	−0.0051
		(0.0007)	(0.0071)
	Panel 3: interest to budget ratio		
interest to budget ratio	−0.0312***	−0.0316***	−0.0387
	(0.0056)	(0.0059)	(0.1429)
L1 interest to budget ratio		−0.0201***	0.0783
		(0.0055)	(0.1523)
L2 interest to budget ratio		−0.0169***	0.2068
		(0.0049)	(0.3757)
L3 interest to budget ratio		0.0376***	−0.0365
		(0.0121)	(0.1110)
L4 interest to budget ratio		0.0257**	0.0281
		(0.0125)	(0.1027)
N	55487	25247	18519

* p<0.10, ** p<0.05, *** p<0.01, robust standard errors in parenthesis
Estimates (1) and (2) are panel fixed effects estimates with time and municipality fixed effects. Estimates (3) rely on a difference GMM (also with time and municipality fixed effects). Sargan and overidentifying restrictions tests do not indicate problems with the specification. Background control variables and lags of explanatory variables are omitted from table for readability. N for Panel 1 48475 / 25735 / 18850

Table 5.4: Effect of debt repay help and and cash credit ratio on interest rates

	(1)	(2)	(3)
	Panel 1: debt repay help to debt ratio		
debt help to debt ratio	0.0202***	0.0288***	0.0363
	(0.0024)	(0.0067)	(0.1630)
L1 debt help to debt ratio		0.0031	0.1649
		(0.0035)	(0.2458)
L2 debt help to debt ratio		0.0037	−0.1574
		(0.0036)	(0.2079)
L3 debt help to debt ratio		−0.0006	0.0473
		(0.0036)	(0.0625)
L4 debt help to debt ratio		0.0018	−0.0254
		(0.0032)	(0.0861)
	Panel 2: cash credits to total debt ratio		
cash credits to total debt ratio	−0.0435***	−0.0432***	−0.0691
	(0.0017)	(0.0019)	(0.0600)
L1 cash credits to total debt ratio		0.0005	0.0264
		(0.0017)	(0.0430)
L2 cash credits to total debt ratio		0.0026*	0.0725
		(0.0014)	(0.0529)
L3 cash credits to total debt ratio		0.0029*	−0.0055
		(0.0015)	(0.0164)
L4 cash credits to total debt ratio		−0.0018	−0.0150
		(0.0019)	(0.0229)
N	55487	25247	18519
r2	0.1157	0.1234	

* $p<0.10$, ** $p<0.05$, *** $p<0.01$, robust standard errors in parenthesis
Estimates (1) and (2) are panel fixed effects estimates with time and municipality fixed effects. Estimates (3) rely on a difference GMM (also with time and municipality fixed effects). Sargan and overidentifying restrictions tests do not indicate problems with the specification. Background control variables and lags of explanatory variables omitted from table

Table 5.5: Joint effects on interest rates

	(1)	(2)	(3)	(4)
debt per capita	−1.7004***	−1.1022	−11.2940	2.0368
	(0.0950)	(1.0560)	(20.0140)	(10.9051)
L1 debt per capita		−0.4852	−24.7428	−22.7764
		(0.9746)	(31.3355)	(21.1195)
L2 debt per capita		1.0512	−1.9976	−21.1396
		(1.1032)	(30.6020)	(20.7428)
L3 debt per capita		−0.4036	40.6855	42.3813
		(1.1679)	(39.3492)	(28.9842)
debt incr. per cap.	0.2388**	−0.3237	7.9828	−4.6952
	(0.0955)	(1.0272)	(20.1183)	(10.9849)
L1 debt incr. per cap.		0.2543	34.6952	19.0492
		(0.9967)	(29.7777)	(13.2182)
L2 debt incr. per cap.		−0.3042	37.5950	41.5038
		(1.2619)	(39.1465)	(28.4290)
L3 debt incr. per cap.		0.3228	−0.4960	−0.2338
		(0.9321)	(1.9665)	(0.8466)
debt to budget ratio	−0.0088***	−0.0023	0.0330	0.0408**
	(0.0021)	(0.0018)	(0.0454)	(0.0199)
L1 debt to budget ratio		−0.0012	−0.0069	−0.0178
		(0.0017)	(0.0263)	(0.0182)
L2 debt to budget ratio		−0.0016	−0.0040	−0.0216*
		(0.0017)	(0.0322)	(0.0119)
L3 debt to budget ratio		−0.0006	0.0167	−0.0000
		(0.0019)	(0.0379)	(0.0163)
interest to budget ratio	0.1429***	−0.1558***	−0.7909	−0.8649**
	(0.0371)	(0.0315)	(0.7604)	(0.3489)
L1 interest to budget ratio		−0.1710***	−0.0715	0.2343
		(0.0302)	(0.4123)	(0.3187)
L2 interest to budget ratio		−0.1639***	−0.2837	0.2357
		(0.0292)	(0.3934)	(0.2029)
L3 interest to budget ratio		−0.0719**	0.0083	0.1986
		(0.0361)	(0.3741)	(0.1838)
debt help to debt ratio	0.0131***	0.0105	0.0691	0.0767
	(0.0029)	(0.0087)	(0.1187)	(0.0649)
L1 debt help to debt ratio		−0.0037	−0.1133	−0.0823
		(0.0038)	(0.1088)	(0.0660)
L2 debt help to debt ratio		0.0090**	−0.0329	0.0058

(continued)

	(1)	(2)	(3)	(4)
		(0.0039)	(0.0711)	(0.0436)
L3 debt help to debt ratio		0.0059	0.1196	−0.0022
		(0.0044)	(0.1278)	(0.0503)
cash credits to total debt ratio	−0.0290***	−0.0377***	−0.0807	−0.0329
	(0.0019)	(0.0028)	(0.0630)	(0.0353)
L1 cash credits to total debt ratio		0.0054**	0.0655	0.0291
		(0.0024)	(0.0620)	(0.0397)
L2 cash credits to total debt ratio		0.0036**	0.0187	0.0381
		(0.0018)	(0.0896)	(0.0436)
L3 cash credits to total debt ratio		0.0012	−0.1018	−0.0402
		(0.0021)	(0.0654)	(0.0265)
share of debt either refinanced or new	−0.0032**	−0.0203***	−0.0446	−0.0313
	(0.0012)	(0.0026)	(0.0321)	(0.0205)
L1 share of debt either refinanced or new		−0.0162***	−0.0318	−0.0112
		(0.0018)	(0.0287)	(0.0201)
L2 share of debt either refinanced or new		−0.0114***	0.0278	0.0085
		(0.0016)	(0.0300)	(0.0144)
L3 share of debt either refinanced or new		−0.0061***	0.0192	0.0055
L1 interest rate			0.5953**	0.5877***
			(0.2805)	(0.1178)
L2 interest rate			0.3419*	0.1865
			(0.1827)	(0.1299)
N	48475	18850	18850	25735
r2	0.1837	0.2227		

* p<0.10, ** p<0.05, *** p<0.01, robust standard errors in parenthesis
Estimates (1) and (2) are panel fixed effects estimates with time and municipality fixed effects. Estimates in (3) rely on a difference GMM and (4) on a system GMM estimator (both with time and municipality fixed effects).
Sargan and overidentifying restrictions tests do not indicate problems with the specification. Background control variables omitted from table

Table 5.6: Spline regressions

	(1)	(2)	(3)	(4)	(5)	(6)
			spline variable			
	debt per capita	debt incr. per capita	debt to budget r.	interest to budget r.	debt help to debt r.	cash cr. to total debt r.
spline 1 control	-15.1082***	-0.3180**	-0.1703***	-0.4331*	-0.0229	
	(2.0191)	(0.1414)	(0.0203)	(0.2558)	(0.0151)	
spline 2 control	-9.6190***	0.8819	-0.0942***	-0.8893***		
	(1.0968)	(1.2917)	(0.0112)	(0.1968)		
spline 3 control	-7.3949***	5.4402*	-0.0807***	-0.4276***		
	(0.7710)	(3.2390)	(0.0079)	(0.1503)		
spline 4 control	-3.7389**	7.4330	-0.0421***	-0.1352		
	(0.5596)	(5.2403)	(0.0057)	(0.1201)		
spline 5 control	-3.4971***	10.5563	-0.0438***	-0.1775		
	(0.4267)	(8.7133)	(0.0049)	(0.1083)		
spline 6 control	-3.2148***	39.5551***	-0.0250***	-0.2250**		
	(0.3404)	(10.4281)	(0.0040)	(0.0906)		
spline 7 control	-2.2278***	-31.3547***	-0.0246***	-0.1334**		
	(0.2460)	(3.1528)	(0.0031)	(0.0678)		
spline 8 control	-1.7771***	-1.1528	-0.0148***	-0.1295***	-0.3695***	
	(0.1915)	(0.8050)	(0.0023)	(0.0483)	(0.1204)	
spline 9 control	-1.7363***	-3.1520***	-0.0211***	-0.0512	0.0267**	-0.0540***
	(0.1399)	(0.4001)	(0.0016)	(0.0346)	(0.0132)	(0.0049)
spline 10 control	-0.7644***	-1.0545***	0.0002	0.0001	0.0220***	-0.0414***
	(0.0708)	(0.1079)	(0.0002)	(0.0050)	(0.0028)	(0.0023)
N	55,487	48,475	55,487	55,487	55,487	55,487
r2	0.1853	0.1141	0.1762	0.0880	0.0819	0.1158

* $p<0.10$, ** $p<0.05$, *** $p<0.01$, robust standard errors in parenthesis: Each spline represents a ten percent percentile of the spline variable. E.g. in column (2) -0.3180 is the point estimate for the lowest ten percent of debt increase. All estimates are panel fixed effects estimates with time and municipality fixed effects. Background control variables and lags of explanatory variables are omitted from table for readability.

Bibliography

ABRAMOWITZ, A. I. (1975): "Name Familiarity, Reputation, and the Incumbency Effect in a Congressional Election," *The Western Political Quarterly*, 28(4), 668–684.

ACEMOGLU, D. (2005): "Constitutions, Politics, and Economics: A Review Essay on Persson and Tabellini's The Economic Effects of Constitutions," *Journal of Economic Literature*, 43, 1025–1048.

ADE, F. (2011): *Constitutions matter - evidence from a natural experiment at the community level.* Paper presented at EEA-ESEM 2011.

ADE, F., AND R. FREIER (2011): "Divided Government versus Incumbency Externality Effect: Quasi-Experimental Evidence on Multiple Voting Decisions," *DIW Berlin Discussion Paper*, 1121.

ALESINA, A., AND H. ROSENTHAL (1995): *Partisan politics, divided government, and the economy.* Cambridge University Press.

———— (1996): "A Theory of Divided Government," *Econometrica*, 64(6), 1311–1341.

ANGRIST, J. D., AND J.-S. PISCHKE (2009): *Mostly Harmless Economietrics: An Empiricist's Companion.* Princeton University Press.

ANSOLABEHERE, S., S. HIRANO, J. M. SNYDER, AND M. UEDA (2001): "Party and Incumbency Cues in Voting: Are They Substitutes?," *Quarterly Journal of Political Science*, 1(2), 119–137.

ANSOLABEHERE, S., E. C. SNOWBERG, AND J. M. SNYDER (2006): "Television and the Incumbency Advantage in U.S. Elections," *Legislative Studies Quarterly*, 31(4), 469–490.

ANSOLABEHERE, S., AND J. M. SNYDER (2004): "Using Term Limits to Estimate Incumbency Advantages When Officeholders Retire Strategically," *Legislative Office Quarterly*, XXIX, 487–515.

ANSOLABEHERE, S., J. M. SNYDER, AND C. STEWART (2000a): "Old Voters, New Voters, and the Personal Vote: Using Redistricting to Measure the Incumbency Advantage," *American Journal of Political Science*, 44(1), 17–34.

———— (2000b): "Old Voters, New Voters, and the Personal Vote: Using Redistricting to Measure the Incumbency Advantage," *American Journal of Political Science*, 44(1), 17–34.

ARELLANO, M., AND S. BOND (1991): "Some test of specification for panel data: Monte Carlo evidence and an application to employment equations," *Review of Economic Studies*, 58, 277–297.

BAQIR, R. (2002): "Districting and Government Overspending," *The Journal of Political Economy*, 110(6), 1318–1354.

BAYOUMI, T., M. GOLDSTEIN, AND G. WOGLOM (1995): "Do Credit Markets Discipline Sovereign Borrowers? Evidence from U.S. States," *Journal of Money, Credit and Banking*, 4, 1, 1046–1059.

BESLEY, T. (2004): "Joseph Schumpeter Lecture: Paying Politicians: Theory and Evidence," *Journal of the European Economic Association*, 2(2-3), 193–215.

BESLEY, T., AND A. CASE (2003): "Political Institutions and Policy Choices: Evidence from the United States," *Journal of Economic Literature*, 41, 1, 7–73.

BICKERS, K. N., AND R. M. STEIN (1996): "The Electoral Dynamics of the Federal Pork Barrel," *American Journal of Political Science*, 40(4), pp. 1300–1326.

BLANKART, C. B. (2007): *Föderalismus in Deutschland und Europa*. Nomos Verlagsgesellschaft.

——— (2011): "An Economic Theory of Switzerland," *CESifo DICE Report*, 3/2011, 74–82.

BLANKART, C. B., AND G. B. KOESTER (2006): "Political Economics versus Public Choice: Two views of political economy in competition," *Kyklos*, 59, 171–200.

BLANKART, C. B., AND D. C. MUELLER (2004): "The Advantages of Pure Forms of Parliamentary Democracy over Mixed Forms," *Public Choice*, 121, 431–453.

BLUME, L. (2009): *Regionale Institutionen und Wachstum? Sozialkapital, Kommunalverfassungen und interkommunale Kooperation aus regional und instiutionenoekonomischer Perspektive*. Metropolis-Verlag.

BLUME, L., T. DOERING, AND S. VOIGT (2008): "Fiskalische Effekte der Kommunalverfassungsreformen der 1990er Jahre in Deutschland.," *Jahrbuecher fur Nationaloekonomie und Statistik*, 228, 4, 317–344.

BLUME, L., J. MUELLER, AND S. VOIGT (2009): "The economic effects of constitutions: replicating and extending Persson and Tabellini," *Public Choice*, 139, 1-2, 197–225.

BLUNDELL, R., AND S. BOND (1998): "Initial conditions and moment restrictions in dynamic panel data models," *Journal of Econometrics*, 87, 115–143.

BORCHMANN, M., AND E. VESPER (1976): *Reformprobleme im Kommunalverfassungsrecht*. Verlag W. Kohlhammer.

BORCK, R., M. CALIENDO, AND V. STEINER (2007): "Fiscal Competition and the Composition of Public Spending: Theory and Evidence," *FinanzArchiv*, 63, 2, 264–277.

BRENNAN, G., AND J. M. BUCHANAN (1984): "Voter Choice: Evaluating Political Alternatives," *American Behavioral Scientist*, 28, 185–201.

BRENNAN, G., AND A. HAMLIN (1998): *The New Palgrave Dictionary of Economics and the Law*, chap. Constitutional Economics, pp. 401–409. MacMillan.

BROLLO, F., T. NANNICINI, R. PEROTTI, AND G. TABELLINI (2009): "Federal Transfers, Corruption, and Political Selection: Evidence from Brazil," *University of Bocconi Working Paper*.

BUCHANAN, J. M. (1989): *Explorations into Constitutional Economics*. A&M University Press.

———— (1990): "The domain of constitutional economics," *Constitutional Political Economy*, 1, 1, 1–18.

BUETTNER, T. (2000): "Determinants of tax rates in capital income taxation: a theoretical model and evidence from Germany," *FinanzArchiv*, 56, 363–388.

———— (2005): "The incentive effect of fiscal equalization transfers on tax policy," *Journal of Public Economics*, 90, 477–497.

BUNDESBANK (2007): "Zur Entwicklung der Gemeindefinanzen seit dem Jahr 2000," *Deutsche Bundesbank Monatsbericht*, 2007, 7.

BUSS, A. (2002): *Das Machtgefuege in der heutigen Kommunalverfassung. Zur Machtverteilung zwischen Vertretungskoerperschaft und Hauptverwaltungsorgan bei Urwahl der Buergermeister.* Nomos Verlagsgesellschaft.

CAIN, B., J. FEREJOHN, AND M. FIORINA (1984): "The constituency service basis of the personal vote for U.S. representatives and British members of parliament," *American Political Science Review*, 78(1), 110–125.

CAMERON, C. A., AND P. K. TRIVEDI (2010): *Microeconometrics Using Stata.* Stata Press, revised edn.

CAMPBELL, J. E., AND J. A. SUMNERS (1990): "Presidential Coattails in Senate Elections," *The American Political Science Review*, 84(2), 513–524.

CAPECI, J. (1994): "Local fiscal policies, default risk, and municipal borrowing costs," *Journal of Public Economics*, 52, 73–89.

CAUGHEY, D. M., AND J. S. SEKHON (2010): "Regression-Discontinuity Designs and Popular Elections: Implications of Pro-Incumbent Bias in Close US House Races," Travers Department of Political Science, UC Berkeley.

CHAMON, M., J. M. P. DE MELLO, AND S. FIRPO (2009): "Electoral Rules, Political Competition and Fiscal Spending: Regression Discontinuity Evidence from Brazilian Municipalities," *Escola de Economia de Sao Paulo Discussion Paper*, 208.

CHEN, L., D. A. LESMOND, AND J. WEI (2007): "Corporate Yield Spreads and Bond Liquidity," *Journal of Finance*, 62, 1, 119–149.

COASE, R. (1998): "The New Institutional Economics," *American Economic Review*, 88, 2, 72–74.

COVER, A. D. (1977): "One Good Term Deserves Another: The Advantage of Incumbency in Congressional Elections," *American Journal of Political Science*, 21(3), 523–541.

COVITZ, D., AND C. DOWNING (2007): "Liquidity or Credit Risk? The Determinants of Very-Short-Term Corporate Yield Spreads," *Journal of Finance*, 62, 5, 2302–2328.

COX, G. W., AND J. N. KATZ (1996): "Why Did the Incumbency Advantage in U.S. House Elections Grow?," *American Journal of Political Science*, 40(2), pp. 478–497.

———— (2002): *Elbrigde Gerry's Salamander: The Electoral Consequences of the Reappointment Revolution.* Cambridge University Press.

DIERMEIER, D., AND T. J. FEDDERSEN (1998): "Cohesion in Legislatures and the Vote of Confidence Procedure," *American Political Science Review*, 92, 3, 611–621.

DRESSLER, U. (2003): *Kommunalpolitik in den deutschen Laendern*, chap. Kommunalpolitik in Hessen, pp. 131–152. Westdeutscher Verlag.

DRESSLER, U., AND U. ADRIAN (2005): *Hessische Kommunalverfassung*. Hessische Landeszentrale fuer politische Bildung, 17 edn.

DSGV (2011): "Fakten, Analysen, Positionen Nr. 42," *www.dsgv.de/_download_ gallery/FAP/FAP_42_Kommune.pdf, retrieved September 20, 2011*.

DUFFEE, G. R. (1999): "Estimating the Price of Default Risk," *The Review of Financial Studies*, 12, 1, 197–226.

EGGER, P., AND M. KOETHENBUERGER (2010): "Government Spending and Legislative Organization: Quasi-experimental Evidence from Germany," *American Economic Journal: Applied Economics*, 2(4), 200–212.

EGGER, P., M. KOETHENBUERGER, AND M. SMART (2008): "Disproportionate Influence? Special-interest politics und proportional and majoritrian electoral systems," *mimeo*.

———— (2010a): "Do fiscal transfers alleviate business tax competition? Evidence from Germany," *Journal of Public Economics*, 94, 235–246.

———— (2010b): "Electoral Rules and Incentive Effects of Fiscal Transfers: Evidence from Germany," *mimeo*.

EGGERS, A. C., AND J. HAINMUELLER (2009): "MPs for Sale? Returns to Office in Postwar British Politics," *American Political Science Review*, 103 (4), 513–533.

EJSING, J., W. LEMKE, AND E. MARGARITOV (2011): *Sovereign bond spreads and fiscal fundamentals - a real time, mixed frequency approach*. Paper presented at EEA-ESEM 2011.

ERIKSON, R. S. (1988): "The Puzzle of Midterm Loss," *The Journal of Politics*, 50(04), 1011–1029.

FASTEN, E. (2006): *Market Mechanisms to Restrict Irresponsible Politicians - Lessons from Switzerland*. Paper presented at EPCS 2006.

FELD, L. P., A. KALB, M.-D. MOESSINGER, AND S. OSTERLOH (2011): "Sovereign Bond Market Reactions to Fiscal Rules and Bailout Clauses - The Swiss Experience," *mimeo*.

FEREJOHN, J. A., AND R. L. CALVERT (1984): "Presidential Coattails in Historical Perspective," *American Journal of Political Science*, 28(1), 127–146.

FERRAZ, C., AND F. FINAN (2009): "Motivating Politicians: The Impacts of Monetary Incentives on Quality and Performance," *NBER Working Paper*, w14906.

FERREIRA, F., AND J. GYOURKO (2009): "Do Political Parties Matter? Evidence from U.S. Cities," *The Quarterly Journal of Economics*, 124(1), 399–422.

FIORINA, M. P. (1976): "The Voting Decision: Instrumental and Expressive Aspects," *Journal of Politics*, 38, 390–415.

FOLKE, O. (2010): "Parties, Power and Patronage," Ph.D. thesis, Stockholm University.

FOLKE, O., AND J. M. SNYDER (2010): "Gubernatorial Midterm Slumps," *Columbia University Working Paper*.

FREIER, R. (2011): "Incumbency as the major advantage - The scopes and determinants of the electoral advantage for incumbent mayors," *DIW Discussion Paper*, 1147.

FREIER, R., AND C. ODENDAHL (2011): "Do Parties Matter? Estimating the effect of political representation in multi-party systems," *Unpublished manuscript*.

FUNK, P., AND C. GATHMANN (2008): "Does Direct Democracy Reduce the Size of Government? New Evidence from Historical Data, 1890-2000," *University Pompeu Fabra Working Paper*, 1123.

——— (2009): "How Do Electoral Systems Affect Fiscal Policy? Evidence from State and Local Governments, 1890 to 2005," *Available at SSRN: http://ssrn.com/abstract=1260446*.

GAGLIARDUCCI, S., AND T. NANNICINI (2009): "Do Better Paid Politicians Perform Better? Disentangling Incentives from Selection," *IZA Discussion Paper*, 4400.

GEHRMANN, B. (2011): *Soft Budget Constraints in German Fiscal Federalism: Lessons for Fiscal Governance*. Nomos Verlagsgesellschaft.

GELMAN, A., AND G. KING (1990): "Estimating Incumbency Advantage without Bias," *American Journal of Political Science*, 34(4), 1142–1164.

GERRING, J., S. C. THACKER, AND C. MORENO (2009): "Are Parliamentary Systems Better?," *Comparative Political Studies*, 42, 327–359.

GEYS, B., F. HEINEMANN, AND A. KALB (2009): "Voter Involvement, Fiscal Autonomy and Public Sector Efficiency: Evidence from German Municipalities," *WZB Discussion Paper*, SP II 2009-02.

GILLIGAN, T. W., AND J. G. MATSUSAKA (2001): "Fiscal Policy, Legislature Size, and Political Parties: Evidence from State and Local Governments in the First Half of the 20th Century," *National Tax Journal*, 54, 1, 57–82.

GORDON, S. C., AND G. A. HUBER (2007): "The Effect of Electoral Competitiveness on Incumbent Behavior," *Quarterly Journal of Political Science*, 2(2), 107–138.

GREENE, W. H. (2003): *Econometric Analysis*. Prentice Hall, 5th edition edn.

GRIMMER, J., E. HERSH, B. FEINSTEIN, AND D. CARPENTER (2011): "Are Close Elections Random?," *Working Paper*.

GRUBER, J., AND E. SAEZ (2002): "The elasticity of taxable income: evidence and implications," *Journal of Public Economics*, 84, 1–32.

HAHN, J., P. TODD, AND W. VAN DER KLAAUW (2001): "Identification and Estimation of Treatment Effects with a Regression-Discontinuity Design," *Econometrica*, 69, 201–209.

HAINMUELLER, J., AND H. L. KERN (2005): "Incumbency Effects in German and British Elections: A Quasi-Experimental Approach," *mimeo*.

——— (2008): "Incumbency as a source of spillover effects in mixed electoral systems: Evidence from a regression-discontinuity design," *Electoral Studies*, 27, 213–227.

HASTIE, L. K. (1972): "Determinants of Municipal Bond Yields," *The Journal of Financial and Quantitative Analysis*, 7, 3, 1729–1748.

HELLER, W. B. (2001): "Making Policy Stick: Why the Government Gets What It Wants in Multiparty Parliaments," *American Journal of Political Science*, 45, 4, 780–798.

HEPPKE-FALK, K. H., AND G. B. WOLFF (2008): "Moral Hazard and Bail-Out in Fiscal Federations: Evidence for the German Laender," *Kyklos*, 61, 3, 452–446.

HINNERICH, B. T., AND P. PETTERSSON-LIDBOM (2010): "Democracy, Redistribution, and Political Participation: Evidence from Sweden 1919-1950," *Stockholm University Working Paper*.

HOGAN, R. E. (2005): "Gubernatorial Coattail Effects in State Legislative Elections," *Political Research Quarterly*, 58(4), 587–597.

HOLCOMBE, R., AND L. KENNY (2008): "Does restricting choice in referenda enable governments to spend more?," *Public Choice*, 136, 87–101.

HUBER, J. D. (1996): "The Vote of Confidence in Parliamentary Democracies," *American Political Science Review*, 90, 2, 269–282.

IMBENS, G., AND T. LEMIEUX (2008): "Regression Discontinuity Designs: A Guide to Practice," *Journal of Econometrics*, 142, 615–635.

IPSEN, J. (2007): *Handbuch der Kommunalen Wissenschaft und Praxis - Band 1 Grundlagen der Kommunalverfassung*, chap. Die Entwicklung der Kommunalverfassung in Deutschland, pp. 565–660. Springer.

JACOBSON, G. C. (1987): "The Marginals Never Vanished: Incumbency and Competition in Elections to the U.S. House of Representatives, 1952-82," *American Journal of Political Science*, 31(1), 126–141.

KERN, H. L., AND J. HAINMUELLER (2006): "Electoral balancing, divided government and midterm loss in German elections," *The Journal of Legislative Studies*, 12, 127–149.

KIDWELL, D. S., AND C. A. TRZCINKA (1982): "Municipal Bond Pricing and the New York City Fiscal Crisis," *Journal of Finance*, 37, 5, 1239–1246.

——— (1983): "The Impact of the New York City Fiscal Crisis on the Interest Cost of New Issue Municipal Bonds," *The Journal of Financial and Quantitative Analysis*, 18, 3, 381–399.

KING, G., AND A. GELMAN (1991): "Systemic Consequences of Incumbency Advantage in U.S. House Elections," *American Journal of Political Science*, 35(1), 110–138.

KIRCHGAESSNER, G. (1992): "Towards a theory of low-cost decisions," *European Journal of Political Economy*, 8, 305–320.

KIRCHGAESSNER, G., AND W. W. POMMEREHNE (1993): "Low-cost decisions as a challenge to public choice," *Public Choice*, 77, 107–115.

KNACK, S. (1994.): "Does rain help the Republicans? Theory and evidence on turnout and the vote," *Public Choice*, 79 (1-2), 187–209.

KNUTSEN, C. H. (2009): "The economic growth effect of constitutions revisited," *mimeo*.

KOST, A., AND H.-G. WEHLING (2003): *Kommunalpolitik in den deutschen Laendern.* Westdeutscher Verlag.

KREHBIEL, K., AND J. R. WRIGHT (1983): "The Incumbency Effect in Congressional Elections: A Test of Two Explanations," *American Journal of Political Science*, 27(1), 140–157.

KUETTEL, D., AND P. KUGLER (2002): "Explaining Yield Spreads of Swiss Canton Bonds: an Empirical Investigation," *Financial Markets and Portfolio Management*, 16, 2, 208–218.

LEE, D. S. (2008): "Randomized experiments from non-random selection in U.S. House elections," *Journal of Econometrics*, 142, 675 – 697.

LEE, D. S., AND T. LEMIEUX (2009): "Regression Discontinuity Designs in Economics," *NBER Working Paper*, 14723.

LEE, D. S., E. MORETTI, AND M. BUTLER (2004): "Do Voters Affect or Elect Policies? Evidence from the U.S. House," *Quarterly Journal of Economics*, 119(3), 807–859.

LEVITT, S. D., AND C. D. WOLFRAM (1997): "Decomposing the Sources of Incumbency Advantage in the U. S. House," *Legislative Studies Quarterly*, 22(1), 45–60.

LIENERT, I. (2005): "Who Controls the Budget: The Legislature or the Executive," *IMF Working Paper*, WP/05/115.

LINDEN, L. L. (2004): "Are Incumbents Really Advantaged? The Preference for Non-Incumbents in Indian National Elections," *MIT working paper*.

LITSCHIG, S., AND K. MORRISON (2010): "Government Spending and Re-election: Quasi-Experimental Evidence from Brazilian Municipalities," *University of Pompeu Fabra Working Paper.*

LONGSTAFF, F. A., S. MITHAL, AND E. NEIS (2005): "Corporate Yield Spreads: Default Risk or Liquidity? New Evidence from the Credit Default Swap Market," *Journal of Finance*, 60, 5, 2213–2253.

MAYHEW, D. R. (1974): "Congressional Elections: The Case of the Vanishing Marginals," *Polity*, 6(3), 295–317.

MCCRARY, J. (2008): "Manipulation of the running variable in the regression discontinuity design: A density test," *Journal of Econometrics*, 142(2), 698 – 714.

MERTON, R. C. (1974): "On the Pricing of Corporate Debt: The Risk Structure of Interest Rates," *Journal of Finance*, 29, 2, 449–470.

MESSNER, M., AND M. K. POLBORN (2004): "Paying politicians," *Journal of Public Economics*, 88(12), 2423 – 2445.

MEYER, B. D. (1995): "Natural and Quasi-Experiments in Economics," *Journal of Business & Economic Statistics*, 13, 2, 151–161.

MEYERSSON, E. (2009): "Islamic Parties and the Emancipation of the Poor and Pious. Evidence from Turkey," *mimeo*, IIES, Stockholm University.

MIGUEL, E., AND F. ZAHIDI (2004): "Do Politicians Reward their Supporters? Regression Discontinuity Evidence from Ghana," *UCB working paper.*

MONDAK, J. J. (1990): "Determinants of coattail voting," *Political Behavior*, 12, 265–288.

MONDAK, J. J., AND C. MCCURLEY (1994): "Cognitive Efficiency and the Congressional Vote: The Psychology of Coattail Voting," *Political Research Quarterly*, 47(1), 151–175.

MOODY'S (2011): "Corporate Default Risk Service," *http://v2.moodys.com/cust/content/Content.ashx?source=StaticContent/Free%20Pages/Products%20and%20Services/Downloadable%20Files/Corp_DRS_FAQ.pdf accessed on August 19, 2011.*

MUELLER, D. (2007): "Torsten Persson and Guido Tabellini, The Economic Effects of Constitutions," *Constitutional Political Economy*, 18(1), 63–68.

MUELLER, D. C. (2003): *Public Choice III*. Cambridge University Press.

NORRIS, P., AND F. FEIGERT (1989): "Government and third-party performance in midterm by-elections: The Canadian, British and Australian experience," *Electoral Studies*, 8(2), 117 – 130.

OSTER, R. (2003): *Kommunalpolitik in den deutschen Laendern*, chap. Kommunalpolitik in Rheinland-Pfalz, pp. 221–237. Westdeutscher Verlag.

PERSSON, T., G. ROLAND, AND G. TABELLINI (2000): "Comparative Politics and Public Finance," *Journal of Political Economy*, 108, 6, 1121–1161.

PERSSON, T., AND G. TABELLINI (2002): *The economic effects of constitutions*. MIT Press.

PETTERSSON-LIDBOM, P. (2006): "Does the Size of the Legislature Affect the Size of Government? Evidence from Two Natural Experiments," *Stockholm University Working Paper*.

——— (2008): "Do Parties Matter for Economic Outcomes? A Regression-Discontinuity Approach," *Journal of the European Economic Association*, 6(5), 1037–1056.

POTERBA, J. M., AND K. S. RUEBEN (1997): "State Financial Institutions and the U.S. Muncipal Bond Market," *NBER Working Paper*, 6237.

PRIEBE, C. F. (1997): *Die vorzeitige Beendigung des aktiven Beamtenstatus bei politischen Beamten und Wahlbeamten*. Duncker & Humblot.

REPP, H. (1989): "Der Buergermeister nach der hessischen Gemeindeordnung," Ph.D. thesis, Justus-Liebig-University Giessen.

ROCKEY, J. (2010): "Reconsidering the Fiscal Effects of Constitutions," *University of Leicester Working Paper*, 10/16.

RODRIGUEZ, R. J. (1988): "Default Risk, Yield Spreads, and Time to Maturity," *The Journal of Financial and Quantitative Analysis*, 23, 1, 11–117.

ROMER, T., H. ROSENTHAL, AND V. G. MUNLEY (1992): "Economic incentives and political institutions: Spending and voting in school budget referenda," *Journal of Public Economics*, 49(1), 1 – 33.

ROUBINI, N., AND J. D. SACHS (1989): "Political and economic determinants of budget deficits in he industrial democracies," *European Economic Review*, 33, 903–938.

ROWLEY, C. K. (1997): "The Relevance of Public Choice for Constitutional Political Economy," *Public Choice*, 90, 1/4, 1–10.

SCHALTEGGER, C. A., AND L. P. FELD (2009): "Do large cabinets favor large governments? Evidence on the fiscal commons problem for Swiss Cantons," *Journal of Public Economics*, 93(1-2), 35 – 47.

SCHEFOLD, D., AND M. NEUMANN (1996): *Entwicklungstendenzen in der Kommunalverfassung in Deutschland: Demokratisierung und Dezentralisierung*. Birkhaeuser Verlag.

SCHRAMEYER, M. (2006): *Das Verhaeltnis von Buergermeister und Gemeindevertretung. Aufgaben, Machtverhaeltnisse, Rechtsstellung*. Erich Schmidt Verlag.

SCHUKNECHT, L., J. VON HAGEN, AND G. WOLSWIJK (2009): "Government Risk premiums in the bond market: EMU and Canada," *European Journal of Political Economy*, 25, 371–381.

SCHULZ, A., AND G. B. WOLFF (2009): "The German Sub-national Government Bond Market: Structure, Determinants of Yield Spreads and Berlin's Forgone Bail-out," *Journal of Economics and Statistics (Jahrbuecher fuer Nationaloekonomie und Statistik)*, 229, 1, 61–83.

SEITZ, H. (2000): "Subnational Government Bailouts in Germany," *Inter-American Development Bank Research Network Working Paper*, R-396.

SNYDER, J. M., O. FOLKE, AND S. HIRANO (2011): "A Simple Explanation for Bias at the 50-50 Threshold in RDD Studies Based on Close Elections1Are Close Elections Random?," *Working Paper*.

SNYDER, J. M., AND S. HIRANO (2009): "Using Multi-Member Districts to Decompose the Incumbency Advantage," *American Journal of Political Science*, 53(2), 292–306.

STAEDTETAG, D. (2011): "Der Gemeindefinanzbericht 2011 im Detail," *Der Staedtetag*, 64, 5, 11–81.

STATACORP (2009): "Stata: Release 11," Statistical Software, StataCorp LP.

STEIN, R. M., AND K. N. BICKERS (1997): *Perpetuating the pork barrel: Policy subsystems and American democracy*. Cambridge University Press.

TITIUNIK, R. (2009): "Incumbency Advantage in Brazil: Evidence from Municipal Mayor Elections," *University of Michigan Working Paper*.

TOLLISON, R. D. (2007): "Old wind, new wine," *Public Choice*, 1323-5, 3–5.

UPPAL, Y. (2005): "The (Dis)advantaged Incumbents: Estimating Incumbency Effects in Indian State Elections," in *Symposiom: Democracy and Its Development*, no. Paper G05-06. Center for the Study of Democracy.

VOIGT, S. (1997): "Positive constitutional economics: A survey," *Public Choice*, 90, 11–53.

——— (2011): "Positive Constitutional Economics - A Survey of Recent Developments," *Public Choice*, 146, 205–256.

WEHLING, H.-G. (2003): *Kommunalpolitik in den deutschen Laendern*, chap. Kommunalpolitik in Baden-Wuerttemberg, pp. 23–40. Westdeutscher Verlag.

WILLIAMSON, O. E. (2000): "The New Institutional Economics: Taking Stock, Looking ahead," *Journal of Economic Literature*, 38, 3, 595–613.

WINDMEIJER, F. (2005): "A finite sample correction for the variance of linear efficient two-step GMM estimators," *Journal of Econometrics*, 126, 25–51.